Eng'd by J.A.J. Wilcox, Boston.

James Walker

Reason, Faith, and Duty.

SERMONS

PREACHED CHIEFLY IN THE COLLEGE CHAPEL

BY

JAMES WALKER, D.D., LL.D.,

LATE PRESIDENT OF HARVARD COLLEGE.

BOSTON:
ROBERTS BROTHERS.
1877.

BX
9843
.W18
R4

Copyright, 1876,
BY ROBERTS BROTHERS.

CAMBRIDGE:
PRESS OF JOHN WILSON AND SON.

The revered author of these Discourses should not be held responsible for their publication. Long since, he gave to the flames far the greater part of his unpublished Sermons. After repeatedly refusing the friend, to whom he had given the scanty remnant, the privilege of publishing a portion of them, he allowed his scruples to be in a measure overcome, at the time of their last interview.

Should any surviving friend of President Walker ask whether he himself valued one of these Sermons above another, we might reply, The only one, hitherto unpublished, which he designated, is that "Upon the Sin of being Led Astray."

INTRODUCTION.

SHOULD there be found any one to ask, "Who was James Walker?" there are many to answer, "He was the man who first made me believe that religion is a real thing: in my college days, the strength of his logic, and the majesty of his earnestness, took my mind and heart captive."

Others, whose memories go back further, will reply, "More than all men else, he was 'a son of consolation' when my house was left unto me desolate." And they will add, "He built up a strong parish from slender beginnings; his church in Charlestown stood like a lighthouse to warn the young, from far and near, of their perils; wherever he preached, he was listened to as if men saw in his every look and word the unmistakable credentials of a 'great ambassador.' In the homes of the people he was simple as a child, yet profound as a philosopher; at one moment overflowing with pungent humor, his countenance the next moment eloquent with pathetic seriousness."

He was a man unrivalled in sententious conversation, one who, in later life, drew toward him the mingled homage and respect of the learned men around him in other chairs of the College which he honored successively as Professor and President; the man on whose counsel the student pre-eminently relied, when his mind was vexed with those problems which concern themselves with the conduct of life, or the choice of a profession. And he lived to grow old; he went gently to his rest with the benedictions of pupils following him from their widely scattered homes, with the gratitude of the broken households who yet survived to revere the Pastor who had served them more than thirty years before.

Never devoid of catholicity of spirit, the vehemence of the youthful theologian became more and more mellowed by a wide course of reading, and through the experience of life, until at last we saw in him an impersonation of the apostolic "meekness of wisdom," the like of which, in this world, we can scarce believe that our eyes shall rest upon again.

Is it too much to hope, that without the magic of that voice which filled all the chambers of the soul which it pierced, without that pleading look which compelled the prodigal to "come to himself," without the kingly silence in which the preacher seemed to stand enthroned, without the retinue of thirsting eyes which we saw fastened upon him, — these words of his, saved from the ashes to which he had almost doomed them, may fan the embers of our better natures into a flame of heartier consecration?

* JAMES WALKER was born in Burlington (near Woburn), Mass., Aug. 16, 1794. He was fitted for Harvard College (which he entered in 1810) under Mr. Caleb Butler, Preceptor of the Groton Academy.

He delivered the second English oration at his graduation, in 1814. Among the classmates gathered before him, when he appeared as their class-orator that year, were the late Rev. Dr. Greenwood, and the historian, Prescott. Upon leaving college, he spent a year at Exeter, N. H., as an assistant teacher in connection with the memorable Dr. Benjamin Abbot, Principal of "Phillips Exeter Academy."

The two subsequent years he passed in the pursuit of his Theological studies at Cambridge, graduating in the class which first left the Divinity School, in 1817.

* In the preparation of this biographical notice, we have been very much aided by a discriminating and beautiful sketch of President Walker, prepared by Professor Joseph Lovering, his life-long friend, for the "American Academy of Arts and Sciences."

After declining an invitation to settle in Lexington, Mass., he was ordained as the Pastor of the Harvard Church in Charlestown, Mass., Feb. 11, 1818. During the twenty-one years of this ministry (which was a ministry to the social and educational interests of the town, as well as to his own parish), he was challenged again and again to come forth as a leader, upon conspicuous occasions. In 1832, he addressed "the citizens of Charlestown upon the one hundredth anniversary of Washington's birth-day." His ringing voice, bidding men "be of good cheer," carried courage to many a faint-hearted church and its youthful minister, upon the day of ordination. The pages of the "Christian Examiner" bear witness to his zeal in "every good word and work." Besides many contributions at other periods to its pages, he was its sole editor between the years 1831 and 1839. But a change of employment was at hand.

He retired from his auspicious ministry in Charlestown, July 14, 1839, that he might become "Alford Professor of Natural Theology, Moral Philosophy, and Civil Polity" in Harvard College. The public foresaw his illustrious career at Cambridge (for his name had been suggested in some quarters as a candidate for President as early as the date of the lamented President Kirkland's resignation in 1828). But we cannot wonder that his devoted parish clung to him to the very last, and interposed every possible solicitation to compel him to decline this invitation to the Alford Professorship. Nor were they wholly alone in their regrets. In the many homes in which Mr. Walker was enthusiastically welcomed, when he made "an exchange of pulpits," there must have been those among old and young, whose hearts sadly testified that this summons, "Friend, go up higher," betokened their being left, far more than before, beyond the range of his voice or the clasp of his hand. After leaving the impress of his character upon many successive classes who were brought into more familiar relations with him than often happens at college, at the expiration of fourteen years (in 1853) he was transferred from the Professor's chair to the office of President; which latter post he filled with signal ability during the ensuing seven years, until, in 1860, his impaired health counselled his resignation. But this event did not remove him from all concern in the interests of the College which he had loved so intensely all his life; the College towards which he had long since taught the eyes of Charlestown boys to look wistfully. To its councils he had been called thirty-five years previous as Overseer; of its Corporation he had been a member for nineteen years, before he became its President. And now, after a brief respite, we find him once more, for ten years, a member of the Board of Overseers.

He survived his retirement from the Presidency more than fourteen years. He had so meekly borne the honors with which men had crowned him, that these later years of comparative retirement were not rendered insipid from lack of excitement, but were, as he alleged, among his happiest; save only that a portion of them were overshadowed by the death of the wife, who for nearly forty years had been the companion of his studies, and the eager dispenser of his hospitality. Mrs. Catherine Walker (daughter of Dr. George Bartlett of Charlestown, Mass.,) died June 13, 1868, aged 70.

On his eightieth birth-day, Aug. 16, 1874, through the happy instigation of his life-long friend, Rev. Dr. Samuel Osgood, of New York, a beautiful cup and salver were presented to him by friends who had known and loved him in Charlestown, Cambridge, and elsewhere. A few weeks previous, he had the rare felicity of welcoming at his dinner table, upon Commencement Day, seven of his surviving classmates.

Dr. Walker edited "Reid's Essay on the Intellectual Powers, abridged, with notes from Sir William Hamilton," and Dugald Stewart's "Philosophy of the Active and Moral Powers of Man."

In 1840, and for three consecutive years, he delivered courses of lectures, before the Lowell Institute, upon Natural Religion, which excited a very deep and wide-spread interest.

In 1863, a memoir of Hon. Daniel Appleton White, of Salem, Mass., was printed, which Dr. Walker had prepared at the request of the Massachusetts Historical Society; and in 1867, he prepared a memoir, for the same society, of President Quincy.

The fervor of his patriotism was attested alike at the beginning and at the close of our gigantic civil war. In 1861, he published a kindling discourse, delivered in King's Chapel, Boston, upon "The Spirit proper to the Times." The oration which he delivered, in 1863, before the Alumni of Harvard College, remains in its massive simplicity an inspiring memorial of his patriotic counsels.

A former series of sermons was published by him after his retirement from the College Presidency.*

He died Dec. 23, 1874. His remains rest in Forest Hills Cemetery, West Roxbury.

W. O. W.

KEENE, N. H.,
October, 1876.

The compiler takes great pleasure in acknowledging the assistance of Rev. HENRY W. FOOTE, of Boston, in the preparation of this volume for the press.

---

* Dr. Walker testified his attachment to Harvard University in the gift, by his will (with liberal increase), of the timely and generous benefaction which his friends had sent him upon his resigning the office of President. This bequest amounted to fifteen thousand dollars. In addition, he gave the College, in the same instrument, his entire library. He bequeathed one thousand dollars each to the American Unitarian Association, and to the "Society for the Relief of Aged and Indigent Clergymen."

CONTENTS.

I. PAGE

Religion not a Science, but a Want 1

II.

Man's Competency to know God 18

III.

The Philosophy of Man's Spiritual Nature in Regard to the Foundations of Faith . . . 37

IV.

Providence 62

V.

Spiritual Death 88

VI.

Means of Strengthening an Infirm Faith . . 105

VII.

Nominal Christians 125

VIII.

The Daily Cross 137

IX.

On Keeping the Promises we Make to Ourselves 156

X. PAGE
Jesus Christ made Perfect through Sufferings 172

XI.
He Knew what was in Man 185

XII.
Spiritual Discernment 202

XIII.
Public Opinion 222

XIV.
Am I not in Sport? 241

XV.
Honesty 257

XVI.
The Dangers of College Life 272

XVII.
White Lies 288

XVIII.
How to make the Sun Stand Still 306

XIX.
On the Sin of being Led Astray 321

XX.
The Young Man's Dream of Life 335

XXI. PAGE

Moral Distinctions not Sufficiently Regarded in Social Intercourse 358

XXII.

St. Thomas, or the Doubting Disciple 373

XXIII.

The Sermon on the Mount 392

XXIV.

The Power of Christ's Resurrection 409

XXV.

Our Duty in Respect to Other Men's Consciences 424

XXVI.

Perfection the Christian's Aim 440

SERMONS.

I.

RELIGION NOT A SCIENCE, BUT A WANT.

"*As the hart panteth after the water-brooks, so panteth my soul after thee, O God! My soul thirsteth for God, for the living God: when shall I come and appear before God?*" — PSALM xvii. 1, 2.

THE beautiful and plaintive psalm from which my text is taken appears to be the composition of a Hebrew captive and exile, moaning over his hard fate in being doomed to live in a strange land and among an idolatrous people. Continually derided by those around him for still trusting in Jehovah, by whom he had been to all appearance forsaken; shocked and disgusted by the impure and cruel rites he was witnessing from day to day, — his heart yearned to be back among his countrymen, and take part once more in the only worship which was worship to him, which met and satisfied an irrepressible longing of his spiritual nature. "As the hart panteth after the water-brooks, so panteth my soul after thee, O God! My soul thirsteth for

God, for the living God: when shall I come and appear before God?"

I am aware of no words in Scripture, nor indeed in any other book, which so strongly express *the soul's need of religion.* They will therefore introduce very properly what I am going to say on that subject. I cannot help thinking that many perplexities in matters of faith would be cleared up, and many so-called religious controversies be set at rest, if men would accustom themselves to look upon religion not as a science, but as a want.

First of all, let me explain as clearly as I can what is meant when religion is spoken of as being not a science, but a want.

You know how it is with man's relations to society; — society is not a science, but a want. Of course, we can make society a matter of science; that is to say, we can speculate about the origin of society, and about what constitutes a true society, and come to the same or to different conclusions, or to no conclusion, on the subject. But these speculations do not make society any more, or any less, a want of our nature. The want is founded in needs and cravings which pertain to our nature itself, and exist antecedently to all speculation, and independently of it.

So it is with religion. Some, perhaps, will object that there is no analogy between the two laws here supposed; or, at any rate, that the analogy fails in an essential point. They may say our want of society can be traced back to an instinct implanted in our nature, — the instinct of sympathy; just as our want of knowledge can be traced back to another instinct implanted in our nature, — the instinct of curiosity: but there is no such special instinct to which we can trace back our want of religion, — the soul's thirst for the living God. To this, however, I would reply: when we refer to special instincts in man we must not make them to be separate entities, the aggregate of which constitutes human nature. Human nature is a single entity; and these instincts, as that term is here used, are but the spontaneous and controlling tendencies which this nature manifests in the process of its development: and one of these spontaneous and controlling tendencies is to religion, — to religion of some sort or other.

Again, you know how it is with morality; — morality is not a science, but a want. Of course, we can make morality a matter of science; that is to say, we can speculate about its foundation and motive and end, and the result will be a system of ethics. But men do not become moral beings by the study of ethics, any more than they become rational beings by the study of logic. Men are moral beings because they have a moral nature;

that is, a conscience, an innate, inextinguishable sense of right, which makes morality to be a want.

In the same sense, and for the same reason, religion is not a science, but a want. I do not mean that there is no such thing as a science of religion; but this I say, — the scheme of religion is not religion, any more than the science of friendship is friendship. We speculate about God and immortality, about faith and prayer, and the terms of the Divine acceptance, and come to various conclusions; and these various conclusions constitute our various theologies and creeds, — that is, our science of religion. But mankind were religious long before they had any thing to do with these religions and creeds. Men are religious beings because they have a religious nature; just as they are social beings because they have a social nature, and moral beings because they have a moral nature.

Religion, therefore, taking the term in its most general acceptation, is a human want; not so called because a want always felt, but because a foundation is laid in every soul for its being felt at times. It would be just as easy to find a people without a disposition to society, or a sense of moral distinctions, as to find one without any recognition whatever of Divinity, — without reverence, faith, worship, religious aspiration under some form or other, and in some degree or other.

Here, then, is a view of religion quite distinct from the question of the truth or falsity of any particular and definite form of it; quite distinct, also, from a consideration of its moral claims and uses; and yet of great practical moment.

In the first place it helps to clear up what would otherwise be a perplexing fact in history. I mean the existence and prevalence of rude, grotesque, and sometimes savage and cruel modes of faith and worship. A religion which is to supply a natural want will take more or less of its character from the character of the want itself as actually developed and felt at the time. It certainly must have been so with the various forms of paganism; for these were nothing but the growth of a particular state of society and the human mind, and must therefore be expected to betray the limitations, the defects, the vices of their source. And even where the religion originates in an express revelation, we must presume that the whole will be accommodated to the actual capacities and wants of the people and the age. Accordingly we have a succession of revelations, — the patriarchal, the Mosaic, and the Christian. It has been objected to the first two, that they are confessedly imperfect when compared with the last, and therefore cannot have come from a perfect being. But those who take this ground forget that the perfection of a religion consists in its perfect adaptation to its purpose; in other words, that the best religion for any people is not that which is best in itself, but that which will best satisfy their moral and religious wants, — in short, the best which they can bear. "I have yet many things to say unto you," our Lord is here speaking to the twelve, "but ye cannot bear them *now*."

Certainly, therefore, we have the best authority for holding that revelation itself is, and must be, accommodated more or less to the condition of those to whom it is addressed, — to their capacities and their wants. And this applies especially to a public religion; that is, to a religion intended for a whole people, and not merely for the enlightened few.

You will sometimes hear it said that religion is wholly an affair between the individual and his Maker; which is true in one sense, but not in another. Everybody knows that there must be a public as well as a private or personal religion; in other words, there must be a public religion in order that there may be a private or personal religion, — for the latter is nothing but the former individualized, with slight variations. The public religion must also take a positive form; that is to say, it must express itself by means of institutions of faith and worship, which are generally received; and to be generally received, they must be such as the age, the community, the sect are generally in a condition to understand and appreciate. To a certain extent, therefore, it is with the institutions of religion — by which I mean its outward forms and professions — just as it is with the institutions of government. It is to no purpose to say that the truest institutions of government are the best: they are the best if the people are prepared for them, and can bear them; if not, they are the worst. In reading ecclesiastical history, many are offended and disgusted at the superstitions which prevailed in the Church of the Middle Ages. But why this disposition to find fault with what was manifestly a wise ordering of things? A simple and more rational ministration of Christianity would not have taken hold of the imagination and the feelings of the people of that period; that is to say, it would not have satisfied the religious wants of the then existing condition of society; in one word, it would not have answered its purpose.

But is not this to reduce all rites and creeds to a level? — to make one religion as good and as true as another? I answer, No! The best and truest religion, in itself considered, is that which is best for the best people; but it does not follow that it would be best for all people. The stumbling block of the so-called radical reformers consists in ignoring the obvious fact, that minds must be educated up to a condition or capacity to receive the highest truths. The truth, these men will tell you, can never do any harm; which nobody denies, if by truth is meant truth *understood;* but truth *misunderstood*, as it will be if men are not prepared for it, is one of the subtlest and often one of the most mischievous of errors. It is still our interest and our duty to seek out and to disseminate the truest exposition of Christianity, — the truest in itself considered; but this can be done in no other way than by preparing ourselves and others to understand and appreciate it. Meanwhile, differences will and must exist. Not different gospels, as some are fond of saying: there is but one Gospel, as there is but one Nature; nothing hinders, however, the one Gospel any more than the one Nature from being variously interpreted. Nay, paradoxical as it may seem, these different interpretations, when adapted to the corresponding differences in men's minds, will so balance and complement each other as actually to promote the only unity and identity we can desire. I mean unity and identity of effect; that is, the satisfaction of the common religious want.

This, then, is the first lesson to be gathered from the doctrine that religion is not a science, but a want. Under a scientific point of view, it is plain there can be but one absolutely true faith; it argues however neither wisdom nor piety, but a pitiable self-conceit, in any individual or in any sect to think to have found it. Happily it is not necessary to do so. It suffices, if the humble follower of our Lord has found enough of this truth to make him an earnest, trusting, and devout man. Elevate him if you can into the region of higher and more spiritual wants; but, taken as he is, that religion is practically *the truth for him*, which will best answer the ends of religion in his case. Of course, on this principle we must expect diversity, — "diversities of gifts," "differences of administrations," "diversities of operations," — nevertheless, as the Apostle says, "it is the same God which worketh all in all." Observe, too, that the practical *evils* sometimes incident to this diversity do not come from the law of the diversity as here laid down. They come from not understanding, or from attempts to contravene, that law; in other words, they come either from urging reforms prematurely, — that is, before people are prepared for them, — or else from a struggle to retain and perpetuate institutions which the world has outgrown. Let us hope there is a tendency to agreement and unity in what is absolutely true. And that this tendency may become effective, let all the ways of progress be thrown open; let the thought of man

1*

be as free as the air. What will satisfy him to-day will not probably satisfy him to-morrow; still it is true to-day as well as to-morrow that that religion is the best for him, which, for the time being, will best satisfy his religious wants, — the cry of his soul "for God, for the living God."

Two other lessons are also to be gathered from the doctrine of this discourse, which are more directly practical: the first, respecting what we are to do for others; the second, respecting what we are to do for ourselves.

It is common for persons of cultivated and refined minds to express surprise and impatience at the superstitious notions and practices which still prevail. These superstitions, however, do but authenticate what has just been said in proof of man's religious nature. Such is the need, the craving, of the human mind for religion of some sort or other, that, rather than have none, it will accept it under the most grotesque and revolting forms. And, this being the case, it follows that the only effectual preventive or cure of superstition is to be found in the inculcation and prevalence of a purer worship. It is to no purpose to deride prevalent superstitions; it is to no purpose to rail against them; nay, it is to no purpose to refute them. The bulk of mankind will never be persuaded that their religion, however inadequate and corrupt, is not better than none. Some communication with the mysterious Infinite, some intercourse with the invisible world, they will and must have. If you are dissatisfied with the popular faith, inculcate a better, exhibit the fruits of a better, educate the people up to a capacity for a better; but do not hope to correct the evil of which you complain in any other way; do not think to put down superstition by setting up formalism, or scepticism, or infidelity.

We should also bear in mind that what is wanted is not a philosophy, but a religion. We may have all the argument on our side, and all the learning, and a full proportion of the integrity and honor; yet it will profit us nothing, if we are suspected of being deficient in faith and piety, if we have not an unction from the Holy One. The bulk of the community are not looking round for the truest or the most consistent form of worship, but for that which will best satisfy their religious wants. Hence that sect will be almost sure to be in the ascendant, which gives the most striking and unequivocal signs of seriousness and zeal; which loves the most, and prays the most, and does the most good. Enlightened views of Christianity derive an immense advantage on the intellectual side from the fact that they fall in with the great movements of the age, and with the highest and best thought on other subjects; but this advantage will be more than lost, if the profession of these views fails to be connected with that serious and devout habit of mind which is absolutely indispensable to render any religion popular. Let it, therefore, be universally understood, that the man or the woman who leads the public to associate with any set of religious opinions uncommon sanctity, does more to propagate those opinions than the most triumphant display of logic, or criticism, or eloquence.

Thus much we owe to others and to society. Knowing that there is a want in human nature which will lead either to religion or to superstition, we see at once that the only effectual prevention or cure of superstition is to be found in the prevalence of a pure and rational faith. This faith, therefore, the enlightened and educated classes are under a double motive and obligation to promote by word and deed, by profession and life: first, because it is the only legitimate means of satisfying men's religious wants; and, secondly, because it is the only effectual means of saving the whole community from debasing and ruinous superstitions.

And this is not all. In the last place, therefore, and under the light of the same general principle, let us consider what we are to do for ourselves.

I have said that religion, of some sort or other, is a universal and inextinguishable want; and this is true. But all men do not feel this want equally, and no one feels it equally at all times; and, what is more, many who feel their need of religion when they have occasion to use it, do not feel their need of it when they have opportunity to acquire it. There is nothing wonderful here; for it is just so with the most obvious and universal of our bodily wants, — the want of food. We all feel this want when hungry; but it is not every one who feels it or recognizes it at other times, so as to be put upon providing the necessary food beforehand. In the same way we all feel our need of religion when we have occasion to resort to it for support or solace, but not always when we have opportunity to acquire it; or we feel it but in a slight degree, — not sufficiently to induce earnest action. This is our great difficulty, the most serious obstacle to personal religion, as will readily appear on giving a moment's thought to the real springs of human action.

A man is not impelled to the pursuit of any good by his knowledge or opinion of its nature or relative value, but by his feeling of the want of it, and the uneasiness which this feeling creates. The spring of all human activity is in the uneasiness that accompanies desire. As it has been justly said, you may convince a man ever so much that plenty has its advantages over poverty; you may make him see and own that the handsome conveniences of life are better than pinching and squalid penury, — nevertheless, so long as he is content with the latter and finds no uneasiness in it, he will not move a finger to better his condition. In the same way a man may easily be brought to see and own, in a general view of things, that virtue is a more desirable object than wealth; still, if from any cause his want of wealth is the most keenly felt, he will bend all his energies to the attainment of that, and let the other go, at least for the present. And so with religion. Men may estimate it in their theories above all earthly possessions, and be perfectly sincere in those estimates; nevertheless, in point of fact, so long as they can content themselves without it as a habit of mind, or think they can dispense with it for the present, or imagine they already have enough of it, they will be sure to postpone its earnest and serious cultivation to any the most frivolous object which happens from any cause to be uppermost in their feeling of want. No matter how much they need religion, it is only in proportion as they actually *feel* this need that they will be put upon acquiring it. It is not enough that religion really is the best of things, and that every one needs it above all things; nay, it is not enough that we are made to see and own that religion is the best of things, and that every one needs it above all things. More than that, we must actually *feel* our want of it; it must become the object of *our predominant feeling of want*, creating in us an uneasiness which will not let us rest until it is attained. Why is it that the worldly-minded seek first and chiefly the gratification of their worldly ambition, even at the expense of what they know to be far higher and better? Simply and solely because in the existing state of their habits and tastes and prepossessions they long for the former, but do not long for the latter.

Here, then, we behold at a glance both the evil and the remedy. The evil is that we do not feel as we should our need of religion. I do not mean in particular exigencies, but as a habit of mind, as a quality of character; and the remedy is, to quicken or renew this feeling, to unfold and cultivate a sense of our moral and spiritual wants.

There are those, I believe, who think it sufficient evidence that they really do not want virtue and religion, because they do not feel this want. As if all the wants of our nature were upon its surface; as if it was not the effect of every step in human progress to awaken new and higher wants. The want of virtue and the want of religion are real wants of our nature, as much so as the want of knowledge or the want of bread. Nay, more, they are the highest wants of our nature; but before they are felt to be such, education, society, the individual, have something to do. All, I suppose, will agree that a well-conducted Christian education should aim to make the child sensible and alive, as soon as may be, to the highest wants of his highest nature. But who will say that this is attended to as it should be in education as commonly conducted at the present day? On the contrary, are not the prevailing influences, under which the rising generation are growing up, such as to give in most cases a premature development of their animal and earth-born wants, — the want of dress, and luxury, and praise, and money, — while the wants of the soul are not known; or, if known, are not felt; or, if felt, are not encouraged and sedulously cultivated?

What society and the world are not doing for us, we must do with the help of the Holy Spirit for ourselves. And, blessed be God! it is precisely here that the sublime prerogative of reason, or man's capacity of self-inspection, self-activity, and self-culture, are most gloriously revealed. The inferior animals can satisfy the wants of their nature as they arise; and this is all. It is given to man alone, by communion with his own spirit and with the Father of Spirits, by accepting the means of grace and living the life of the Son of God, by familiarity with noble sentiments and noble characters and noble deeds, to unfold the wants of his nature; to unfold them more and more, and to subordinate the lower to the higher, and all to the highest, that mysterious but inextinguishable longing after the Unseen and Eternal. "As the hart panteth after the water-brooks, so panteth my soul after thee, O God! My soul thirsteth for God, for the living God." And "Blessed are they which do hunger and thirst after righteousness, for they shall be filled."

1859.

II.

MAN'S COMPETENCY TO KNOW GOD.

"*Lo! these are parts of his ways; but how little a portion is heard of him? but the thunder of his power who can understand?*" — JOB xxvi. 14.

I APPROACH the subject on which I am now going to address you with unfeigned humility and distrust. Whenever finite minds aspire to know the Infinite Mind, they are admonished, at every step, of the limitation and inadequacy of their highest and best conceptions. After we have done all, we are constrained to say, in the words of the text, "Lo! these are parts of his ways; but how little a portion is heard of him? but the thunder of his power who can understand?"

These very words, however, while representing man's knowledge of God as necessarily partial and imperfect, make it nevertheless to be real and trustworthy as far as it goes. Accordingly they bring up and, to some extent, answer the two great questions, Are we competent to know God? And if so, to what extent?

These questions, I hardly need say, always have been and always will be at the foundation of all religion, natural or revealed. A new interest and importance is also given to them by the turn which infidel speculation has taken of late. The history of unbelief is easily traced. First came criticism, which led men to question every thing. This was the period of scepticism. Many who began with questioning the foundations of religion ended with denying them. This was the period of atheism. There, however, they found themselves pressed by new and unexpected difficulties. To deny is to affirm; it is to affirm a negative, making it necessary that the negative should be *proved*, which is always of all proofs the most embarrassing and unsatisfactory. The more thoughtful and consistent among them have therefore fallen back from this position and taken another. They do not deny the foundations of religion; they do not even so much as question them: they simply *ignore* them. It is the period of indifferentism.

The ground here taken against all positive religion is not only more consistent than any other, but also more specious and more formidable. It is no longer the pride of human reason; on the contrary, it would seem to be dictated by a modest distrust of human reason. It does not, like the atheism of the last century, undertake to account for the origin of things without a God; it stigmatizes all attempts to account for the origin of things *in any way* as a vain presumption. It does not dispose of the questions respecting the existence or the attributes of God by *answering* them, but by refusing to *entertain* them, as relating to matters which, whether true or not, transcend human intelligence.

And what makes it worse is that language equally strong, in respect to the incompetency of the human intellect, is sometimes met with in the writings of enlightened theologians and devout Christians. These men believe in the existence of God; but they would seem to do so under the express condition that this existence is wholly and absolutely incomprehensible. Are they aware that, by taking this ground, they are paving the way, however unconsciously, for that form of infidelity or irreligion from which, as I have shown, we now have the most to apprehend? Perhaps the language here objected to, especially when met with in devotional works, is used to express not so much a conviction as a feeling, — a feeling of dependence and self-abasement; or, more probably still, the words are to be regarded as words of course, like conventional phrases of civility in letters or conversation, — an outward form of respect. However this may be, one thing is clear if any thing is clear. If God, as God, cannot be brought in any way or in any degree under human cognizance, then what those who ignore all religion say, would follow: it would be folly, and worse than folly, to waste our time and thoughts on the subject. On this subject, however, I feel sure that Christians, if they would take the trouble to understand themselves and each other, would find that they do not differ so much as is generally supposed. Certainly we do not apply epithets to God without attaching to them any meaning whatever: we do not call him wise and good, perfect and infinite, without having *some* notion of what we mean by these terms. What could be more unreasonable than to expect a man to express, he knows not what, in words the meaning of which, in this connection, he does not know? And besides, supposing a man not to know what he had to express, I should like to be informed how it is possible for him to know, after he has done, whether he has expressed it or not. He can know it on the sole condition of being able to compare the expression with the idea, so as to see whether they agree or disagree; but how can he do this if he has no idea, not even an imperfect or indefinite idea?

I am aware of the distinctions sometimes resorted to in this case. To know that God *is*, we shall be told, is one thing; to know *what* he is, is another. We should begin by proving that God *is*, and then learn *what* he is, not from our own knowledge, but from revelation.

Before proceeding to expose the fallacy in this argument, I would emphatically disclaim all purpose to call in question the importance and necessity of the Christian Revelation, whether considered as a means of confirming or of enlarging our knowledge of God. Without meaning to deny that here and there an individual, like Socrates, for example, might attain to some just conceptions of the Deity by the light of Nature alone, I still think that no positive and public religion ever did exist, or ever will exist, unless purporting to be of divine origin and authority. It would argue an infinite conceit in the religious teachers of a community to expect that their private speculations on such a theme, varying and contradictory as they must needs be, would have much weight with the public or be listened to long. Whatever power or dignity the pulpit has, is owing mainly not to its learning or its eloquence, but to the generally acknowledged fact that it does not speak in its own name, but in that Name which is above every name, and before which every knee should bow.

What, however, has this to do with man's incompetency to know God? At the utmost it only shows, not that God cannot be known, but that he cannot be fully and adequately known without a special revelation, which revelation we have. I care not how much stress you lay on the importance and necessity of the Christian Revelation. Make the gospel to be every thing, and natural religion to be nothing; still I ask you to consider the inconsistency, the manifest inconsistency, of appealing to the gospel for proof that God cannot be known in any way, when, as we are expressly told again and again, the very purpose and object of the gospel is to make God known. "And they shall not *teach* every man his neighbor, and every man his brother, saying, Know the Lord; for all shall *know* me from the least to the greatest." "And this is life eternal, that they *might know* thee the only true God, and Jesus Christ whom thou hast sent."

But I go farther. I maintain not only that God is known through the gospel, but also that the gospel assumes or implies, in almost every line, that something at least was known of him *before;* that is, by man's unassisted reason. "For the invisible things of him from the creation of the world are clearly seen, being understood by the things that are made; even his eternal power and Godhead." And here, as hinted above, it is to no purpose to say we must begin by proving that God *is*, and afterwards learn *what* he is, not from our own knowledge, but from revelation. How can we prove that God is, without first understanding, at least to some extent, what he is? To prove that God exists, we must prove that a being exists possessing those qualities or attributes which make him to be God. But how can we do this while having no conception at all of what those qualities or attributes are? In all legitimate processes of reasoning, the only ground for reliance on the truth of the conclusion is that this conclusion is contained in the premises. But if we do not know, in any way or in any degree, what the conclusion means, what right have we to affirm, or even to conjecture, whether it is contained in the premises or not? So much, therefore, I hold to be incontrovertible: our knowledge must go as far as our proofs go. In other words, we cannot prove we know not what.

Nor is this all. Why do we *believe* in the truth of what is revealed in the Scriptures respecting God? On the evidence of miracles, it will be said. Make the most, however, of these miracles; in themselves considered they prove this only, that the revelation has the sanction of a Power which is able to suspend or overrule the laws of Nature.

To convert them, therefore, into a proof of the Christian revelation, we must first assume that God would not exert this power himself, or permit any other being to exert it, in order to sanction an imposture. Unless we assume all this *beforehand*, and unless we have a right to assume it, the argument from miracles, as all must allow, is not valid. Now, on what ground do we assume it? Evidently on this, that it is not consistent with God's moral attributes to permit a miracle to be wrought in attestation of what is not true. And this reasoning is good; but only on one condition, to wit, that we know what these attributes are: for if we do not, how can we know what is or is not consistent with them?

Moreover, we say as Christians, and say truly, that God has *revealed* what he is; but *how* has he revealed it? Immediate revelation is out of the question at the present day, except at any rate in very extraordinary cases. The Christian revelation was made more than eighteen centuries ago; it has been transmitted by means of human language, and exclusively, as Protestants contend, in a book. "The Bible, and the Bible only, is the religion of Protestants." Now what does the Bible reveal respecting the Divine attributes? Is it merely that God should be *called* wise and good, perfect and infinite? Is it a matter of *words* only?

Certainly not. It is not the words considered merely as spoken sounds or written characters, but the *sense* of the words, which constitutes the revelation. Obviously, therefore, it is only in so far as we have not only the words, but the sense of the words, that the revelation is a revelation *to us.*

This, then, is the conclusion to which I am brought. It may strike some, at first sight, as a commendable humility to allege the incomprehensibility of God; but if we push this doctrine to the extreme, if we take it to the letter, it will be at the peril of all religion, revealed as well as natural. As one of the old divines of the Church of England[1] has said: "To give no other account of the nature of God and his ways, than that they are unintelligible, is to encourage the atheist, and yield him the day; for that is the thing he does chiefly applaud himself in, that he is secure there is neither head nor foot in the mysteries of religion, and that the very notion of a God implies a contradiction to our faculties." This danger, then, was seen to exist two hundred years ago; how much more at the present day, when, as I have shown, it will have the effect to play directly into the hands of the latest form of infidelity! Indeed, it is not easy to see what

[1] Henry More.

material advantage, in a practical point of view, the theist would have over the atheist, or the Christian over the pagan, if neither the theist nor the Christian knows any thing of God, except that he exists, — nothing of his nature or character; nothing, that is, which he can reason either *to* or *from* in the way of conviction or instruction, of warning or comfort or hope.

Accordingly I cannot, I will not, believe that any thoughtful Christian, however he may sometimes express himself in his humility, or his perplexities, or for the honor of faith on this subject, really means to be understood as saying that God is incomprehensible in the sense of being wholly and absolutely unintelligible. I cannot, I will not, believe that under the accumulated lights of a better civilization, a more spiritual philosophy, and the Christian revelation, he would still have us go on and erect altars, as they did of old, with this inscription, " To THE UNKNOWN GOD."

But here another question arises of greater difficulty and delicacy. Granting man's competency to know God, how far does this competency extend? Granting that something can be known even of the divine attributes and perfections, how much can be known?

In the first place, we are able to conceive of those qualities and operations of the Divine mind, in which we are permitted in some humble measure to share. When we say that God is wise and just and benevolent, we know what we mean; we mean that he is wise and just and benevolent as men sometimes are, only in an infinitely higher degree. The mere circumstance that God's wisdom, justice, and benevolence are *infinite* does not alter the essential nature of these qualities; does not make them to be any thing more or less than wisdom, justice, and benevolence. You know how it is with space. The mere circumstance that space is infinite does not alter its essential nature; as space, it is still essentially the same thing as far as it goes, whether limited or unlimited. And so of the divine wisdom or knowledge; knowledge is still knowledge, whether finite or infinite. No doubt God has *modes* of knowing, and *objects* of knowledge, which we can neither understand nor conceive of; nevertheless, knowledge itself — that is, *to know*, simply considered and as far as it goes — must be essentially the same in all knowing beings. So likewise of God's moral perfections. I do not suppose that we can now *see* in all cases the justice and benevolence of the divine government; but this is owing to the limitation of our present views compared with the vastness and complexity of the scheme. We still hold that the scheme itself, in all its vastness and in all its details, alike in its means and in its ends, is in strict accordance with justice and benevolence, and with justice and benevolence as we understand them. We know what wisdom and justice and benevolence are in God, because we know what wisdom and justice and benevolence are in ourselves, — the latter answering to the former, not indeed in degree, but yet in essence and in kind, from the fact that God has created us, as the Bible says, in his own image.

I am aware that the ground here taken has been questioned even by Christians. Thus the author of "The Light of Nature Pursued" contends that "the faculties and operations of man differ *in kind*, as well as degree, from those of his Maker." According to this writer, instead of holding that man is really made after the likeness of God, it would be much nearer the truth to say "that the idea of God is taken from the likeness of man." We select the powers and endowments by which we ourselves are most distinguished, and after separating from them all we deem a weakness or imperfection, and heightening them to the utmost pitch that imagination can reach, we make the aggregate to be *our idea of God;* not because it corresponds to the reality, but because we can conceive of nothing better.

You will observe that writers of this class do

not regard the names they apply to God as expressing what he is; they use them merely as titles of respect and honor. But is this according to the Scriptures, or the obvious purpose and use of religion, or the general understanding of religious men? I think not. When we aver that God is wise and just and good, it is because we see, or think we see, evidence in his works and word that he really possesses those very qualities. And, besides, all religious trust proceeds on the assumption that God is wise and just and good, and in the sense in which men are so, only infinitely more entirely and perfectly. Make truth and justice to be one thing in God and another thing in man, not only in degree but also *in kind*, and after that, even though we have the gospel in our hands, how could we tell what to believe or what to expect; what to hope or what to fear?

There is also a still more radical defect in the doctrine under consideration. It does not recognize the divine element in the human soul. In other words, it does not recognize the identity of basis, if I may so express it, of all spiritual natures and all spiritual life; without which no foundation is laid for that oneness in the Father, that becoming "partakers of the divine nature," that life of God in the soul of man, of which the Scriptures continually speak, and on which they make all our heavenly aspirations to turn. Neither is it in the Scriptures alone that we have assurance of these divine affinities; they are testified to in the unutterable yearnings and longings of the spiritually minded men of all religions in all ages.

Thus far therefore, as it seems to me, we may safely go. We can know the moral and intellectual attributes of God, because they are reflected however faintly in ourselves, inasmuch as the human mind is made after the likeness of the Divine mind. But what shall we say of those incommunicable properties which belong to God alone as the infinite One? Can we know any thing of them? — and if so, how much?

God is revealed to us, in the universe and in the Scriptures, as an intelligent cause or force; and we know what this is, for every human mind is to a certain extent an intelligent cause or force. But in us the force, and the intelligence which directs it, are dependent on other things, and consequently are to this extent limited by other things. When however we suppose these limits away, as, in the case of a Being who has nothing to limit him, we must, then the force and the intelligence become infinite. To the reason, therefore, God stands revealed as infinite. Neither is this a merely negative revelation, helping us to know what God is not; namely, that he is not finite: for to know positively that God is, and at the same time that he is not finite, is to know positively that he is infinite. We also have a right to reason from this knowledge, and we do reason from it every day, in respect to many of the difficulties which trouble our faith. Even though it may not always enable us to explain away the difficulty, it will help to reconcile us to it; in other words the difficulty will cease to trouble us as an objection, when we consider that many things which are impossible with men must be possible with God.

Here then we see the reality and the importance, and at the same time the extent and the limits, of our knowledge of God as an Infinite Being. We find no difficulty in understanding that such a being exists; and, if he exists, we know that many things which are impossible with us must be possible with him: but *how* possible, we can neither know nor conceive.

Hence what are called the mysteries of religion, — the mysteries of creation, the mysteries of Providence, the mysteries of grace. It would be well if the Church had always known how to accept these mysteries without making them the occasion of strife and tyranny. I certainly cannot agree with those who contend that, "where the mystery begins, religion ends." But this I say, where the mystery begins, dogmatism should end, — dogmatism *for*, and dogmatism *against*. In order to turn a mystery into a dogma and impose it as a creed, you must first define it; but, as soon as you have defined a mystery, the mystery is gone. What remains is probably an unmeaning paradox, or it may be a ghastly contradiction.

It is well that we should know as much of God as is revealed in his works and word; and it is well that we should not pretend to know any more. When we pray, "O Lord, touch our hearts, that we may know the mysteries of the Kingdom of Heaven!" it is not that we may see through these mysteries so as to be able to understand them as we do ordinary occurrences, but only that we may know how to use them for spiritual edification. Mysteries are not for noisy debate, they are for devout meditation; they are not for the faith of the understanding, they are for the faith of the heart, — now to inspire and exalt, and now to overawe and subdue.

It is not enough considered that religious thought has two purposes; one of which is to *enlighten*, the other to *move and impress*. In the latter case, the very obscurity and indefiniteness of the thought often minister to its efficacy. Doubtless we are more enlightened by what is clearly seen; but it is equally certain that we are often more moved and impressed by what is seen only in part, by what is darkly suggested. Hence the secret of much of that mysterious and overpowering fascination which takes hold of most men amidst sublime scenes, and chains them to the spot. Neither is it in cultivated minds alone that this craving for the vague immense is revealed. Why does the savage pause in his midnight journey to gaze into the fathomless depths of the clear and tranquil heavens? What arrests his step on the sea-shore, and makes him look abroad on the boundless expanse of waters with a strange mingling of emotions which he cannot describe, and for which he has as yet no name? It is the instinctive sentiment of the infinite, struggling after an object with which to be satisfied and filled. That object is found in God alone, half understood and half not understood. As an old English writer has said with his accustomed quaintness: "Ever since our minds became so dim-sighted as not to pierce into that original and primitive blessedness which is above, our wills are too big for our understandings, and will believe their beloved prey is to be found where reason discovers it not. They will pursue it through all the vast wilderness of this world, and force our understandings to follow the chase with them; nor may we think to tame this violent appetite, or allay the heat of it, except we can look upwards to some Eternal and Almighty Goodness, which is alone able to master it."[1]

Let no one say, therefore, that our knowledge of God is less *real* or less *effective* because it is incomplete and imperfect. If we could comprehend the infinite as we comprehend the finite, theology might be a gainer, but religion would suffer. Religion, it cannot be repeated too often, is intended to supply not so much an intellectual as a moral and spiritual want. It addresses itself to our aspirations; not so much to the curiosity of men and the speculative understanding, as to the sentiments, and especially to that mystical but most characteristic sentiment in human nature, the desire in man to raise himself above himself.

Why then should we be unwilling to admit, as the final and crowning source of our knowledge of God, a practical, a direct, or if you will a mystical, insight into divine things?—a something in faith and worship, and in the thoughts which inform and inspire both, which the devout soul feels and knows, but which no logic can analyze and no language express? I speak not now of that false mysticism from which the world and the Church have suffered so much and so long; which disdains the wisdom it might gather from daily experience, and imagines impossible communications with the

[1] John Smith.

spiritual world. I mean a true mysticism, which is favorable if not necessary to the life and warmth of a sober and rational piety, — a mysticism which supposes a real communion of the soul with its Maker; which loves in order to know, instead of knowing in order to love; which knows the divine from sympathy with it, — a mysticism which holds no unintelligble language in speaking of things seen or unseen, which makes no boast of its inward experiences, nor construes them into an authority to dictate to others, — a mysticism, in fine, which understands that "faith without works is dead," which loves and serves the finite beings within its reach; and, when the question is of the Infinite, believes, adores, and is still.

1858.

III.

THE PHILOSOPHY OF MAN'S SPIRITUAL NATURE IN REGARD TO THE FOUNDATIONS OF FAITH.

"Now faith is the substance of things hoped for, the evidence of things not seen." — HEB. xi. 1.

FAITH is defined in Scripture as being "the substance of things hoped for, the evidence of things not seen." By it we can and do regard many things which lie beyond the sphere of our senses and actual experience as really existing, and are affected by them as realities. By it the spiritually minded of all religious persuasions, in proportion as they are spiritually minded, feel a confidence and practical assurance in the existence and reality of the spiritual world. It is this principle which constitutes man, unlike the inferior animals, a religious being; and it is by a right development of this principle that we become capable of seeing Him who is invisible, of being affected by those things which pertain to our inward and spiritual life as if addressed to the senses, and of holding free, intimate, and habitual communion with the Unseen, the Infinite, and the Eternal.

Now it is remarkable of the infidelity of the present day, that it strikes at the very existence of this principle considered as an element or property of the human soul. Not content with disputing in detail the evidences of natural and revealed religion, or driven perhaps from this ground, it thinks to cut the matter short by denying that man has any faculties for the apprehension of spiritual existences, or of any existences but such as are cognizable by the senses, and so far as they are cognizable by the senses. I have no fears that many amongst us, or that any who are accustomed to contemplate and study the workings of their moral and spiritual nature, will be seduced and carried away by this gross form of sensualism, which they must feel and know to be contradicted and entirely set aside by the facts of their own inward experience. Still it may be well in connection with the evidences of Christianity, to begin by setting forth, in the simplest and clearest language of which the subject is susceptible, the true philosophy of man's moral and spiritual nature in regard to the foundations of faith.

In the present discourse I shall endeavor to

establish, illustrate, and enforce, as much at length as my limits will permit, the three following propositions: —

First, that a little reflection will convince every one alive to noble thoughts and sentiments, that the *existence* of those spiritual faculties and capacities, which are assumed as the *foundation* of religion in the soul of man, is attested and put beyond controversy by the *revelations of consciousness.*

Secondly, that *religion in the soul*, consisting as it does of a manifestation and development of these spiritual faculties and capacities, is as much *a reality in itself, and enters as essentially into our idea of a perfect man*, as the corresponding manifestation and development of the reasoning faculties, a sense of justice, or the affections of sympathy and benevolence.

And, *thirdly*, that from the acknowledged existence and reality of spiritual impressions or perceptions we may and do assume *the existence and reality of the spiritual world;* just as, from the acknowledged existence and reality of sensible impressions or perceptions, we may and do assume the existence and realities of the sensible world.

These three propositions being established, it will follow that our conviction of the existence and reality of the spiritual world is resolvable into the same *fundamental law of belief* as that on which our conviction of the existence and reality of the sensible world depends.

I. My first proposition is, that a little reflection will convince every one alive to noble thoughts and sentiments, that the *existence* of those spiritual faculties and capacities, which are assumed as the *foundation* of religion in the soul of man, is attested and put beyond controversy by the *revelations of consciousness.*

Some writers contend for the existence of an unbroken chain of beings, starting from the lowest form of inorganic matter, and mounting upwards by regular and insensible gradations to the highest order of created intelligences. Others insist on a division of substances into material and immaterial, and make one of the principal arguments for the soul's spirituality and immortality to depend on the nature of its substance, and not on the nature of the laws and conditions imposed upon it. Happily, neither of these questions is necessarily implicated in the views I am about to offer, and both may therefore be dismissed at once from the discussion; the former as being a little too fanciful, and the latter as being a little too metaphysical, for the generality of minds. It is enough if persons will recognize the obvious fact, that in the ascending scale of being, as the vegetable manifests some properties which do not belong to crude and inert matter, and as the animal manifests some properties which do not belong to the mere vegetable, so man as man manifests some properties which do not belong to the mere animal. He is subject, it is true, to many of the laws and conditions of crude and inert matter, to many of the laws and conditions of vegetable life, and to many of the laws and conditions of animal life; but he also has part in a still higher life, — the life of the soul. He brings into the world the elements of a higher life, the life of the soul; the acknowledged phenomena of which can no more be resolved into the laws and conditions of mere sensation, than into those of vegetation or mere gravitation. This higher life, — consisting among other things of a development of conscience, the sentiment of veneration, and the idea of the perfect and the absolute, — constitutes the *foundation* of religion in the soul of man; the existence and reality of which is attested, as I hold, and is put beyond controversy, by the revelations of consciousness.

I do not suppose, of course, that the existence of the above-mentioned properties or affections of the soul is matter of sensation. I do not suppose that we can see, or hear, or feel, or taste, or smell a mental faculty, a moral sentiment, or an idea.

Their existence, supposing them to exist, *could* be revealed to us by consciousness alone; and by consciousness it *is* revealed to us: and the evidence of consciousness in a question of this nature is final and decisive. It is not a matter of sensation nor of logic, but of consciousness alone. We are conscious of their existence; and being so, whatever we may say or however we may argue to the contrary, we cannot, practically speaking, doubt it, even if we would, any more than we can doubt the testimony of the senses. Reflect for one moment. What evidence have you of the existence of your own mind, — of the power of thought, or even of the power or the fact of sensation itself, — but the evidence of consciousness? Nay, what evidence have you of your own individual being and personality, — that you are yourself, and not another; that you are a man, and not a horse or a tree; that you are awake and alive, and not asleep or dead, — but the evidence of consciousness? None whatever. You can say, "I am conscious of being what I am;" and that is all you can say. An archangel cannot say any thing more. It is not a matter of sensation or of argument, but of consciousness alone. If, therefore, you are conscious of possessing not only a sensual and an intellectual, but also a moral and spiritual nature, you have as good evidence for believing that this moral and spiritual nature really exists, and that you possess it, as you have for believing that you exist at all.

"True," the sensualist[1] may say, "this does prove the existence of something which we call our moral and spiritual nature; but it does not prove that this *something* belongs to our original constitution, that it has its root and foundation in the soul, that it cannot be resolved into a mere figment of the brain." And then, in the accustomed vein of this philosophy, he will be likely to urge: "Your conscience, — what is it? One thing in the child, and another thing in the man; one thing in this age or country, and another thing in that; here expressly forbidding what there it as expressly enjoins. And your sentiment of veneration, — what is it? To-day prostrate before sticks and stones, to-morrow adoring the host of heaven; among one people deifying a virtue, among another a man, among another an onion; now manifesting itself under the forms of the grossest superstition, and now breaking out into the excesses of the wildest fanaticism. And your idea of the Absolute and the Perfect, — what is it but an hallucination of the metaphysically mad; the finite vainly thinking to comprehend the infinite? Do not all

[1] The term is used in this discourse in its philosophical sense. — Ed.

these things therefore, though they exist or are thought to exist in the human mind, when a little more carefully examined, look very much like figments of the brain?"

How long is the plain, practical good sense of mankind to be abused by a sophistry like this, which owes all its apparent force and pertinency to a sort of logical sleight-of-hand, that, with a quickness making it imperceptible to slow minds, substitutes for the real question at issue another having nothing to do with the subject? So far as the present discussion is concerned, it matters not whether conscience, as already instructed and educated, always decides correctly, or never decides correctly. I am not contending, as everybody must perceive who is capable of understanding the argument, for the correctness or uniformity of the *decisions* of conscience, — a circumstance which must depend of course on the nature and degree of instruction and education it has received, — but for the *existence* of conscience itself, not as a figment of the brain, but as an element of our moral and spiritual nature. What I maintain is simply this: that every man is born with a moral faculty, or the elements of a moral faculty, which, on being developed, creates in him the idea of a right and a wrong in human conduct; which leads him to ask the question, "What is right?" or,

"What *ought* I to do?" which summons him before the tribunal of his own soul for judgment on the rectitude of his purposes; which grows up into an habitual sense of personal responsibility, and thus prepares him, as his views are enlarged, to comprehend the moral government of God, and to feel his own responsibility to God as a moral governor. My reasonings and inferences, therefore, are not affected one way or another by the actual state of this or that man's conscience, or by the fact that probably no two consciences can be found which exactly agree. A man's conscience we must presume, according to the influences under which he has acted, will be more or less excited and developed, and more or less enlightened and educated. Still, we hold it to be undeniable that every man has a conscience *to be* excited and developed, enlightened and educated; that in this sense conscience has its root and foundation in the soul; and that man herein differs essentially from the most sagacious of the inferior animals, and, unlike them, was originally constituted *susceptible* of religion.

And so, too, of the sentiment of veneration or devotion, considered as an original and fundamental propensity of the human mind, I care not so far as my present purpose is concerned under what forms it has manifested itself, or to what excesses or abuses it has led. These very excesses and abuses only serve to demonstrate the existence and strength of the principle itself, as they evince such a craving of our nature for religion that it will accept of any, even the crudest and most debasing, rather than have none. Could this be, if we were not made to be religious? No matter what may be the immediate or ostensible object of this sentiment, — a log, a stone, or a star; the god of the hills, or the god of the plains; "Jehovah, Jove, or Lord," — still it is veneration, still it is devotion. Neither can the principle itself, by any show of evidence or just analysis, be resolved into a mere figment of the brain or a mere creature of circumstances; for, in some form or other, it has manifested itself under all circumstances and in every stage of the mind's growth, as having its root and foundation in the soul. The sentiment may be, and often has been, misdirected and perverted; but there is the sentiment still, with nothing to hinder its being excited, developed, and directed aright: and the result is religion. There is the sentiment disposing man to look upward to a higher power, and inducing faith in the invisible; a quality in which the most sagacious of the inferior animals do not share in the smallest degree, and which proves, if final causes prove any thing, that man was made for worship and adoration.

One word more respecting our capacity to form an idea of the Absolute and the Perfect. The shallow and flippant jeer, that it is the finite vainly thinking to comprehend the infinite, comes from substituting the literal sense of the term *comprehend*, as applied to bodies, for its figurative sense as applied to minds; making the comprehension of an idea to resemble the grasping or embracing of a globe with the hands or the arms. Besides, we need not say that man can, strictly speaking, *comprehend* the Absolute and the Perfect, but only that he can *apprehend* them as really existing; and there is this difference between the literal import of apprehension and a full comprehension, that one can lay hold of what he would not think to be able at once to clasp. However this may be, it is certain that the idea of the infinite grows up in the human mind as it is cultivated and expanded, and becomes an essential condition of thought. As a proof of this, let any one try and see if he can separate the idea of infinity from his idea of space and duration; or, in other words, whether he can possibly conceive of mere space or mere duration as otherwise than infinitely extended. Moreover, the very idea of imperfection, as such, involves at least some faint glimmering of an idea of the perfect with which it is compared, and without which imperfection would be to us as perfection. In other words, if we had no idea of perfection we could have no idea of its absence, which is what we mean by imperfection. So likewise in contemplating things accidental and dependent, the idea of the Absolute grows up in the mind, — the idea of something that is *not* accidental and dependent, and on which every thing that is accidental and dependent leans and is sustained. In short, the mind of man is so constituted, that in the full development of its intellectual powers it can find no real satisfaction, no resolution of its doubts and difficulties, but in the idea of the Absolute and the Perfect. Take away this idea, and existence itself becomes an enigma, a meaningless and objectless phantasm. Give us back this idea, and it again becomes a consistent, intelligible, and magnificent whole. Man, unlike the most sagacious of the inferior animals, is so constituted that this reaching after the Absolute and the Perfect enters into and forms an essential element of his moral and spiritual nature, giving him not only a capacity but a predisposition for that faith which is "the substance of things hoped for, and the evidence of things not seen."

Therefore do we say, and say confidently, that a foundation for religion is laid in the soul of man, the existence whereof is attested and put beyond controversy by the revelations of consciousness.

This is my first proposition, and I have only to add in respect to it two brief suggestions. If, as we have seen, a foundation for religion is laid in the soul of man, can we bring ourselves to believe for one moment that it is laid there for nothing? And again, if, as we have seen, a foundation for a higher life than that of the senses is laid in the soul of man, must it not be accounted a sort of insanity in us, to say nothing of its sinfulness, to refuse or neglect to build upon it?

II. Here my second proposition comes in, which asserts that *religion in the soul*, consisting as it does of a manifestation and development of our spiritual faculties and capacities, is as much *a reality in itself, and enters as essentially into the idea of a perfect man*, as the corresponding manifestation and development of the reasoning powers, a sense of justice, or the affections of sympathy and benevolence.

Modern philosophy has revived an important distinction, much insisted on by the old writers, between what is *subjectively* true and real — that is to say, true and real so far as the mind itself is concerned — and what is *objectively* true and real, that is to say, true and real independently of the mind. Thus we affirm of things, the existence of which is reported by the senses, that they really exist both subjectively and objectively; that is to say, that the mind is really affected as if they existed, and that, independently of this affection of the mind, the things themselves exist. In other words, we have an idea of the thing really existing *in* the mind, and this is subjective truth and reality; and there is also an object answering to that idea really existing *out of* the mind, and this is objective truth and reality. One sense therefore there certainly is, in which the most inveterate sceptic must allow that religion has a real and true existence to the really and truly devout. Subjectively it is real and true, whether objectively it is real and true or not. All must admit that it is true and real so far as the mind itself is concerned, even though it cannot be shown to have existence independently of the mind. It is a habit or disposition of soul, and in any view of the matter the habit or disposition truly and really exists. It is a development of our nature, a development of character, and as such is as true and real as any other development of nature and character. Even if it feeds on illusions, it is not itself an illusion. Even if in its springing up it depends on nothing better than a fancy, a dream, its growth in the soul and the fruit of that growth are realities, — all-important, all-sustaining realities.

I dwell on this distinction, because it is one which the sensualists, from policy or perversity, would fain wink out of sight, making the question at issue to be, whether religion is or is not a mere illusion. This is not the question. Take any view of the matter, take the sensualist's view of the matter, and still it is undeniable that religion itself as it exists in the soul of the devout is a reality, as much so as any other habit or disposition of soul, as much so as taste, or conscience, or parental or filial affection; and its effects are as real.

Nor is this all. Religion in the soul enters essentially into our idea of a *perfect man*. Suppose a man perfect in his limbs, features, and bodily proportions, but entirely destitute of understanding; would he answer to anybody's idea of a perfect man? No. Give him then a perfect understanding, but still let him be entirely destitute of moral sensibility, — as dead to sentiment as before he was to thought, — would he answer to anybody's idea of a perfect man? No. And why not? Because we mean by a perfect man one in whom the whole nature of man is developed in its proper order, and just relations and proportions. Now, as has been demonstrated, a foundation for *religion* is laid in the human soul. In other words, we have spiritual faculties and capacities as well as intellectual and moral faculties and capacities; and the former constitute a part of our nature as truly as the latter; and this part of our nature must be developed. Otherwise the entire man is not put forth. Part of his nature, and of his higher nature too, it may be said, is yet to be born; and thus it is that a deep and true philosophy re-asserts and confirms the Christian doctrine of regeneration. We are born at first into the visible or sensible world; when we become alive to the invisible or spiritual world, we may be said to be born again: and it is not till after this second birth that we become all which, as men, we are capable of becoming. It is not, I repeat it, until after this second birth, consisting as I have said in a development of our spiritual faculties and capacities, that the entire man is revealed, or our idea of a perfect man realized or approached.

Every well constituted mind must be painfully conscious of this truth, though often without being aware of the cause of its uneasiness, in reading the lives or contemplating the fame of men of eminence, and sometimes perhaps of integrity and philanthropy, but destitute of religion. Doubtless a man may have some of the forms of greatness and goodness without having all; and nothing can be farther from my purpose or disposition than to derogate from any form of either, wherever found and however connected. Still, when we behold a manifestation of the lower forms of greatness and goodness without the higher, an impression is left on the mind similar to what is universally felt on seeing a foundation laid for a noble structure, and that structure carried up far enough with the richest materials to indicate the grand and comprehensive plan of the architect, which plan, however, from some cause has been interrupted and broken off midway.

Thus far have I reasoned, as you will perceive, from what consciousness attests and puts beyond controversy respecting the moral and spiritual nature of man. Waiving the question whether any thing exists *out of* the mind corresponding to our idea of religion *in* the mind, — waiving the question whether the objects of our faith have a true and real existence independently of the mind itself, — still the conclusion, as we have seen, is unavoidable, that this faith has its foundation in human nature; that its development is a true and real development of our nature; and that it is absolutely essential to our nature's entire and perfect development. Whether religion exists independently of the mind or not, we know that, to those who have it, it has a true and real existence *in the mind;* that it is a source of true and real strength, solace, and hope; and that men, as men, can truly and really do bear and enjoy with it what they could not do, bear, or enjoy without it. Even therefore if the discussion were to stop here, it would follow incontestably that to disown or neglect religion because of this or that real or supposed logical difficulty, would be to do violence at the same time to both those instinctive desires, from one or the other of which it is said a rational being as such must always act,—a desire of happiness and a desire of perfection.

III. But the discussion does not stop here. I maintain, and this is my third and last proposition, that, from the acknowledged existence, and reality of spiritual impressions or perceptions, we may and do assume *the existence and reality of the spiritual world;* just as, from the acknowledged existence and reality of sensible impressions or perceptions, we may and do assume the existence and reality of the sensible world.

Most of you, I presume, are apprised of the extravagance of scepticism into which men have been betrayed by insisting on a *kind* of evidence of which the nature of the case does not admit. Some have denied the existence of the spiritual world; others have denied the existence of the sensible world; and others again have denied the existence of both worlds, contending for that of impressions or perceptions alone. These last, if we are to believe in nothing but the facts of sensation, and what can be *logically* deduced from these facts, are unquestionably the only consistent reasoners.

For what logical connection is there between a fact of sensation, between an impression or perception, and the real existence of its object, or of the mind that is conscious of it? None whatever. I do not mean that a consistent reasoner will hesitate to admit the real existence of the objects of sensation. Practically speaking, he cannot help admitting their real existence if he would. Every man, woman, and child believes in his or her own existence, and in that of the outward universe or sensible world; but not because the existence of either is susceptible of proof by a process of reasoning. Not the semblance, not the shadow, of a sound logical argument can be adduced in proof of our own existence or that of the outward universe. We believe in the existence of both, it is true; but it is only because we are so constituted as to make it a matter of intuition. Let it be distinctly understood, therefore, that our conviction of the existence of the sensible world does not rest on a logical deduction from the facts of sensation, or of sensation and consciousness. It rests on the constitution of our nature. It is resolvable into a fundamental law of belief. It is held, not as a logical inference, but as a first principle. With the faculties we possess, and in the circumstances in which we are placed, the idea grows up in the mind, and we cannot expel it if we would.

Now the question arises, On what does a devout man's conviction of the existence and reality of the *spiritual world* depend? I answer, On the very same. He is conscious of spiritual impressions or perceptions, as he also is of sensible impressions or perceptions; but he does not think to demonstrate the existence and reality of the objects of either by a process of reasoning. He does not take the facts of his inward experience, and hold to the existence and reality of the spiritual world as a logical deduction from these facts, but as an intuitive suggestion grounded on these facts. He believes in the existence and reality of the spiritual world, just as he believes in his own existence and reality, and just as he believes in the existence and reality of the outward universe, — simply and solely because he is so constituted that with his impressions or perceptions he cannot help it. If he could, it would be to begin by assuming it to be possible that his faculties, though in a sound state and rightly circumstanced, may play him false; and if he could begin by assuming this as barely possible, there would be an end to all certainty. Demonstration itself, ocular or mathematical, would no longer be ground of certainty. It is said that sophistical reasoning has sometimes been resorted to in proof of the existence and reality of the spiritual world; and this perhaps is true: but the error has consisted in supposing that any reasoning is necessary. It is not necessary that a devout man's conviction of the existence and reality of the spiritual world should rest on more or on better evidence than his conviction of the existence and reality of the sensible world; it is enough that it rests on as much, and on the very same. It is enough that both are resolvable, as I have shown, into the same fundamental law of belief; and that, in philosophy as well as in fact, this law ought to exclude all doubt in the former case, as well as in the latter.

But how, it may be asked, according to the views here presented, can we account for the fact of such different and conflicting spiritual impressions or perceptions? If a spiritual world really exists, why do not all men apprehend it alike? Because, I hardly need reply, it is contemplated under such widely different aspects, and by persons whose spiritual faculties and capacities are variously developed, and above all because in spiritual things the best people are so prone to mix up and confound their inferences with their simple perceptions. There is nothing, therefore, in the real or apparent diversity of our spiritual impressions or perceptions which should shake our confidence in the principle, that, to a rightly constituted and fully developed soul, moral and spiritual truth will be revealed with a degree of intuitive clearness and certainty equal at least to that of the objects of sense. Besides, a like diversity in our views and theories prevails in respect to the material world; but nobody thinks, merely on the strength of this, seriously to raise a doubt whether the material world exists at all. And it is further urged, that the most spiritual men may sometimes be tempted to say of their religious experience, "Perhaps it may turn out to be an illusion;" yet it should be recollected that this is no more than what they may also, in moments of inquietude and despondency, be tempted to say of *all* their experience. They may say of all their experience, "Perhaps it may turn out to be an illusion." At this very moment, when I seem to myself to be writing a discourse on the Christian evidences, how do I know but that really I am in my bed dreaming about it? We may talk in this way, I know, about dreams, illusions, visions; but it is certain that to a well constituted and well ordered mind it never has occasioned any real doubt or difficulty, nor ever can, in regard to ordinary life; and for the same reason neither ought it to do so in regard to the life of the soul.

Once more. What, according to the doctrine advocated in these pages, shall we reply to those who may affirm that they never had any of our alleged spiritual impressions or perceptions? Precisely what we should to those who might say that they never had any of our alleged moral impressions or perceptions; any sense of justice, or honor, or disinterested benevolence, or natural affection. We should reply, — that we are very sorry for it. If, however, along with their scepticism they evince any love of the truth, any desire or willingness to have their doubts dispelled, any tenderness of conscience or of soul, we may reason with them, and not without some prospect of convincing them that their want of faith is to be ascribed to one or both of the two following causes: either to a vicious or defective development of their nature, or to their insisting on a kind of evidence, of which the subject, from its very nature, is not susceptible. Either, from some defect or vice of their peculiar moral constitution or training, they are not prepared to appreciate the only appropriate or possible evidence in the case; or, from ignorance of true philosophy, they require the sort of evidence for truths addressed to one faculty, which is available only in regard to truths addressed to another. By insisting on these topics, it is not improbable that many apparent atheists may be reclaimed. "In days of crisis and agitation," says an eminent French philosopher, "together with reflection, doubt and scepticism enter into the minds of many excellent men, who sigh over and are affrighted at their own incredulity. I would undertake their defence against themselves; I would prove to them that they always place faith in something. . . . When the scholar has denied the existence of God, hear the man; ask *him*, take him at unawares, and you will see that all his words imply the idea of God; and that faith in God is, without his knowledge, at the bottom of his heart."[1]

As for the rest, the propagandists of atheism, the men who *love* atheism from eccentricity, or misanthropy, or deadness of soul, — I say it with submission, but I say it with the utmost possible confidence in the wisdom of the course, *Let them alone.* Conversion by the ordinary modes of instruction and argument is precluded. Gratify them not with a few short days of that notoriety which they so much covet. Leave them to the natural influences of their system; leave them to the silent disgust which their excesses must awaken in a community not absolutely savage; leave them to the cant and priestcraft of a few ignorant and interested leaders; and it is not perhaps entirely past all hope that, in this way, some of them may be so far reclaimed as to become ashamed of their cause, ashamed of one another, and ashamed of themselves.

Meanwhile let us hope that a better philosophy than the degrading sensualism, out of which most

[1] Cousin's *Introduction to the History of Philosophy*, pp. 179, 180.

forms of modern infidelity have grown, will prevail; and that the minds of the rising generation will be thoroughly imbued with it. Let it be a philosophy which recognizes the higher nature of man, and aims in a chastened and reverential spirit to unfold the mysteries of his higher life. Let it be a philosophy which comprehends the soul, — a soul susceptible of religion, of the sublime principle of faith, of a faith which "entereth into that within the veil." Let it be a philosophy which continually reminds us of our intimate relationship to the spiritual world; which opens to us new sources of strength in temptation, new sources of consolation in trouble, and new sources of life in death; nay, which teaches us that what we call *death* is but the dying of all that is mortal, that nothing but life may remain. Let it be a philosophy which prepares us to expect extraordinary manifestations of our heavenly Father's love and care, and which harmonizes perfectly with the sublime moral purpose and meaning of the gospel, "casting down imaginations and every high thing that exalteth itself against the knowledge of God, and bringing into captivity every thought to the obedience of Christ."

1834.

IV.

PROVIDENCE.

"*Are not two sparrows sold for a farthing? and one of them shall not fall on the ground without your Father. But the very hairs of your head are all numbered.*" — Matthew x. 29, 30.

THESE words will suggest the subject of my discourse; namely, the immediate and universal providence of God.

At first sight we might presume that every sincere and earnest student of nature would devoutly recognize the Creator in his works. But distinguished names in the history of science will occur to every one, which remind us that it is not so; and there is a well-known principle of the human mind, which will help us to explain the fact. It is the business of the physical inquirer to trace phenomena to what are called *the laws of nature*, and there stop. This, in time, begets *a habit of mind* which controls not only his curiosity, but his *associations;* every phenomenon he beholds suggests the law which explains it, but nothing beyond the law. This habit of mind will also be very apt to affect his modes of expression, and all his scientific expositions; when he has referred an event to the laws of nature, he will think that he has gone as far as it is his province to go.

Now we have no right to say of such a person, that he is an atheist; we have no right even so much as to *suspect* that he has taken up and considered the theological question, and come to the conclusion that there is no God. The most that we have a right to say is, that the religious references in the case *have dropped out of the chain of his associations.* Still this alone is enough to show that, in one respect at least, the progress of science has been unfavorable to religious views of the universe. Formerly, when every unusual and startling phenomenon was referred directly to God, God seemed to be nearer to men than now; he was more on their lips, he was more in their thoughts, than now. These laws of nature, which are referred to so frequently, have to a certain extent usurped his place. "All things," we say, "take place according to the laws of nature;" as if nothing more was to be said about it; as if these laws were to be rested in as an efficient and ultimate cause; as if they could explain any thing, until they are themselves explained; as if they made the instant agency of the Deity any the less necessary, without whom not a sparrow falleth to the ground.

What *are* these *laws of nature*, which are thus allowed to form themselves into a sort of cloudy screen between us and God? When we reason from adaptation to contrivance, and say that the world supposes a maker just as much as a watch, there is one point where the analogy fails. The watch-maker has the materials furnished to his hands. He does not make the laws of nature: he only makes use of them. He ascertains what these laws are; and, knowing this, he puts the parts of the mechanism together, and the laws of nature do the rest. Accordingly we may say with sufficient propriety that the watch *goes* by virtue of the laws of nature, and not by the continued agency of the man who made it. But in the making and sustaining of the world it is otherwise. God not only framed the stupendous mechanism of the universe, but created the materials, and impressed upon them their respective laws, so that each might perform its part in the vast whole. With the mere mechanic, mechanism is every thing; that is, the form, connection, and relative proportions of the parts: with God it is as nothing. He might have adopted a different mechanism, and still, by altering the laws of the parts relatively to each other, he might have brought about the same result. Every thing depends, therefore, on these laws; but what do the laws themselves depend upon? Are they any thing but *the constant and immediate action of God on every particle of matter in the universe?*

This is the conception which seems best to accord with the nature of things, and the facts to be explained; and accordingly it has been adopted not only by many divines and metaphysicians, but by some of the most earnest and single-minded of physical inquirers, with Sir Isaac Newton, himself a host, at their head. In the observations on the nature of the Deity, with which that wonderful man closes his "Optics," he declares that the various portions of the world, organic and inorganic, "can be the effect of nothing else than the wisdom and skill of a powerful, ever-living Agent; who, being in all places, is more able by his will to move the bodies within his boundless uniform *sensorium*, and thereby to form and reform the parts of the universe, than we are by our will to move the parts of our own bodies." This conviction would also seem to be gaining ground from the countenance it has received of late from several of the leading minds in the scientific world. Thus Sir John Herschel, after speaking of certain fixed qualities and powers with which God has impressed the materials of the universe, is careful to add: "We would in no way be understood to deny the *constant exercise* of his *direct power* in maintaining the system of nature, or the ultimate emanation of every energy which material agents exert from his *immediate will, acting in conformity with its own laws.*"[1] Professor Whewell is still more explicit: "A law supposes an agent and a power; for it is the mode according to which the agent proceeds, the order according to which the power acts. Without the presence of such an agent, of such a power, conscious of the relations on which the law depends, producing the effects which the law prescribes, the law can have no efficacy, no existence. Hence we infer that the intelligence by which the law is ordained, the power by which it is put in action, must be present at all times and in all places where the effects of the power occur; that thus the knowledge and the agency of the Divine Being pervade every portion of the universe, producing all action and passion, all permanence and change."[2]

With such authorities in favor of this conception, I suppose I might take it for granted, and go on; but, as the subject is an important one, I am tempted to add a suggestion or two, which

[1] Study of Natural Philosophy, p. 37.

[2] Bridgewater Treatise, b. iii. c. viii. p. 185.

may help to familiarize minds unaccustomed to the subject with the idea, and dissipate half-formed objections and doubts.

The phrase, "laws of nature," is a figure of speech borrowed from human legislation; and, by pushing the analogy further than it will properly go, many slide into the belief that these laws were decreed once for all, like human laws, to exist and be in force ever afterwards *of themselves.* So it might have been, if, as in the case of human laws, there were minds to understand, remember, and apply them; but nothing like this is true of inert matter. "Yes, but cannot inert matter *be made* to obey them?" Certainly it can; and that is just what we are maintaining. We only say that our conceptions of matter will not allow us to suppose that *it can make itself* obey them. It can do nothing whatever of itself; it can move only as it is moved. All this holds good even of what are called the mechanical laws of matter: how much more clearly and manifestly of the countless forces of life and growth, which we cannot conceive of, even in thought, except as dependent on the Force of all forces, in and through which they exist and act! Here, as it seems to me, the reasoning of Dr. Clarke is conclusive. "Matter is evidently not capable of any laws or powers whatsoever, any more than it is capable of intelligence, excepting only this one negative power; that every part of it will always and necessarily continue in that state, whether of rest or motion, wherein it at present is. So that all those things which we commonly say are the effects of the natural powers of matter and laws of motion, — of gravitation, attraction, or the like, — are indeed (if we will speak strictly and properly) the effects of God's acting upon matter *continually and every moment*, either immediately by himself, or mediately by some created intelligent being."

It is hardly to be expected that any one will revive the old Epicurean objection to this doctrine, that such continual overseeing and interfering must disturb the divine *tranquillity*. On the contrary, adopting the theory that the world was made in the beginning, and then wound up like a clock, and left to run on until it runs down, is it easy to repress the inquiry, What is the Creator doing meanwhile? According to the common acceptation, it is *essential* to spiritual natures to be knowing and active. If so, must we not believe that God, who is an Infinite Spirit, exists at every instant of time in every point of space, knowing and active? Can we separate from the common, from the only true and legitimate, from the only possible, conception of an Infinite Spirit the conviction that he is the universally diffused, all-sustaining, and all-directing Energy? I think not. Reasoning then from the nature of God, we come to the very same conclusion as in reasoning from the nature of matter. "The universe exists in God; and every change in its state, from the extinction of a system of worlds to the falling of a feather from a sparrow's wing, is his act." It would save many minds from much perplexity and embarrassment on this subject, if they would give over thinking to assign to the Infinite Spirit a local centre of thought and activity. If they must have a *sensorium*, let it be Newton's "boundless uniform *sensorium*." God, as it has been sublimely said, is a circle whose centre is everywhere, whose circumference is no where: "overseeing" and "interference," therefore, are words which in respect to him have no meaning.

Another objection to the religious view here taken of the divine agency, is sometimes insisted on by a different class of minds. It would detract, they think, from the *skill* of the Divine Architect, to suppose that in the fabric of the universe he has put together a piece of mechanism which requires mending or interposition of any sort. Undoubtedly it would, but nothing like this is said or intended. Here I might protest, if it were necessary, against this practice of drawing illustrations of the divine agency almost exclusively from the slight and inadequate analogy of mechanical contrivances; but it is not. Let it be that the mechanism of the universe is perfect; that it never wears out; that it never needs readjustment. One thing, however, should be remembered: it is essential to the very idea of mechanism that a force be applied, — some weight, or spring, or other *power* which is continually acting upon it, and from which all its motions are derived. Now, in the case of the mechanism of the universe, where is this moving force to be found but in the universally diffused, all-directing, ever-active energy of God?

But it may be asked again, is it not derogatory to the *dignity* of the Supreme Being, that he should "set his hand to every thing," — even to things mean and unimportant? This objection is as old as Aristotle. "If," said he, "it were not congruous in respect of the state and majesty of Xerxes, the great king of Persia, that he should condescend to do all the meanest offices himself, much less can this be thought suitable in respect of God." How paltry and insignificant do these distinctions of earthly pride appear, when viewed in relation to the divine presence and agency! Who shall say what things *are* "mean and insignificant," when it is considered that every link in the chain of events is alike indispensable to the mighty results which an all-wise Providence is slowly unfolding? Besides, what are differences of the finite to the Infinite? Grant that He stoops to take care of the solar system, and I find no difficulty in supposing that he also stoops to take care of man, of an insect, of a worm.

Accordingly I hold, that in the natural world the hand of God is everywhere in every thing, holding the sun in its place, and also the mote in the sun's beam: the volcano and the bursting flower equally announce his presence. We talk about laws and mechanisms and organisms; and no one can object to this, for such they are to *our minds:* but when we ask ourselves what they are in themselves, what gives life and force to the whole, the veil is lifted, and the constant and immediate agency of the Infinite Mind stands revealed. Suppose this all-sustaining, self-sustained agency to be withdrawn for an instant, and the law, and the mechanism, and the organism would cease to act, would cease to be; the universe itself rush back into its primitive nothingness. The error of the pantheists consists in *identifying* nature with God; the error of the mechanical philosophers consists in making nature *independent of* God, at least in its present existence and operation. Both errors are to be avoided; the latter as well as the former: otherwise we shall lose ourselves in the phenomena, the *appearances*, and make no account of the *reality*. It was not without reason that Newton "thought it most unaccountable to exclude the Deity *only* from the universe," — the Deity by whom it is upheld and filled. Speculations are going on at this moment respecting the nature of light, and the profound affinities of electricity and magnetism, and even life itself, which seem to point to laws of nature which transcend matter. We may presume that these will have a tendency to lead science to take a more spiritual and religious view of nature itself. The office of science will still be to trace phenomena to the laws of nature; but when to the eye of faith these laws are seen to resolve themselves into the direct agency and control of the Lord of Nature, instead of forming a cloudy screen between us and him, they will help us to feel and to know that everywhere and at all times we are in his immediate presence.

If this conception of the laws of nature be accepted as the true one, what need is there of a labored argument to prove an immediate and universal Providence without which not a sparrow falls to the ground? *Nature itself is providence, and nothing but providence;* its laws are not merely the work of God, they are God working; and, as we have seen before what the character of the Lord of

Nature is, we may infer what the character of this providence must be.

But there are two or three points of view under which the doctrine of providence, as here unfolded, deserves and requires particular notice.

In the first place, when rightly understood and applied, it will banish for ever the thought of *chance*, *accident*, or *fortune*, as having nothing whatever to do with the course of events. And here the error is deeper and more widely spread than many are willing to suppose. As it has been justly said: "Some things *look* so like chance that we have difficulty in connecting them with the notion of Providence. We think the sparrow not formed by chance; we argue a Creator there: but by chance we think it may fly hither and thither. In human life many occurrences have a very fortuitous appearance. We cannot trace either their causes or their consequences. They are as the tree which, we say, *happened* to fall in one direction and not in another. They are as the wind which, we also say, *happened* to blow from one point of the compass yesterday, and from another to-day." "Our language is framed on the supposition of a mingling of accident with order, of chance with design. It is framed on a false supposition. We are often aware of this on reflection; and yet we are so familiarized with such language, that we perhaps unconsciously delude our own minds by its use, and keep up a notion of the incompatibility of a Providence with the particular events so described."[1]

Looking back on the past history of mankind, it is easy to see that two opposite tendencies have been at work, at different stages in the development of human thought, to impair or dim the doctrine of a strictly immediate and universal Providence. At first men saw the hand of God only in strange and startling phenomena, — in the whirlwind, the lightning, the earthquake. Afterwards, as these also fell, one after another, under the domain of order and law, and were explained and accounted for by science on mechanical principles, men began to see design *in the whole*, but not the instant and constant presence and influence of the Designer in the whole and *in every part*. Now we must not expect that science will go back: this would be to contradict and falsify the experience of ages and the nature of truth itself. Let science go on, and demonstrate that every thing is *ordered*. It is not by chance that a bird flies hither or thither; the tree does not *happen* to fall, or the wind to blow, this way or that: all is *ordered*. But we must go one step further. We must enter into the sublime conception, that the life and soul of this order, the all-

[1] Fox's "Christ and Christianity," i. 177.

sustaining, ever-active energy without which the whole would be nothing, without which not a leaf in the forest stirs, is God.

Again, it has been customary to lay a good deal of stress on the distinction between a *General* Providence and a *Particular* Providence, especially as regards the efficacy of prayer: but in the doctrine here maintained of an immediate and universal Providence, this distinction disappears, and with it many difficulties both speculative and practical.

If by *a general providence* nothing more is meant than the general provision which God has made for mankind in the laws and constitution of nature, as framed by him in the beginning and set in motion, to go on afterwards of itself, — I can easily see that this view of Providence cannot and ought not to satisfy the longings of the soul. If this were all, man would feel himself to be standing amidst the play of a vast and complicated machinery, which is working out his destiny and that of all other beings, — it knows not, and it cares not, how or why. Should he pray, it must be on the ground that he himself and his prayers make a part of the machinery just mentioned, which was foreseen and provided for when the whole was first put together. But with what heart, with what truth or naturalness of feeling, could he utter his supplications, if he believed that the prayer he is making now was granted or denied six thousand years ago?

Not satisfied with this, the religiously disposed have turned instinctively to a *particular providence.* But here again we meet with difficulty. If by a *particular* providence is meant a special interposition of the Deity; if it is meant that God occasionally breaks into the course of nature, and acts directly and immediately, *when otherwise he would not act at all,* — it supposes a violent change in the mode of the divine agency in favor of the individual, which those who most deserve it would have too much humility to expect; or, if they did, I am afraid its effect on their humility and on their whole character would be any thing but good. There is much force in a remark of Dr. Brown: "There are many minds, perhaps the greatest number, in which the constant habit of ascribing every little beneficial event to some interposition of the Divine Power in their particular favor, tends to cherish a sort of isolating selfishness, which, in its own peculiar relation to events that are supposed to be out of the common course of things, almost loses the comprehensive and far more important relation of Nature to the whole human race."[1]

To the doctrine of a Providence at once immediate and universal, none of these objections

[1] Inquiry into the Relation of Cause and Effect, p. 538.

apply. As it is absolutely *universal*, its tendency cannot be, like that of a belief in special interpositions, to nourish an egotistic or clannish spirit, under the impression that God is *our* God in a way in which he is not the God of all mankind. At the same time, as it is *immediate*, it entirely meets and satisfies that want of the soul out of which, as we have seen, the doctrine of a particular and special providence arose. It opens the way by which every individual soul can be brought into instant and immediate communion with the Living God. We no longer feel ourselves to be standing amidst the play of a vast and complicated machinery which is doing it knows not what: every motion, every breath around us proclaims the instant presence and instant action of the Divinity. You kneel beside the pallid and wasted form of one whose malady baffles all human skill, and pray that his life may yet be spared. You feel, you know, that you are not speaking into the air: you feel, you know, that the event is still in the hands of one who is acting now, who acts consciously and freely, who hears every word you say. That any remedy has any effect whatever is wholly owing to the conscious and instant agency of God; and what that effect shall be in any particular instance will depend on the law which his unerring Wisdom prescribes *at the time* to his Omnipotent Will.

There is also another aspect under which this doctrine recommends itself, at least to Christians; it scatters to the winds the common philosophical objections to the credibility of miracles. A miracle has been variously defined by Christian writers. Sometimes it has been made to be "a violation of the laws of nature;" sometimes, "an extraordinary effect of an extraordinary cause," God acting *immediately* in this case, and in this case only, as "*one* of the powers of nature." But some minds find a difficulty in believing that there is, or can be, any thing like *violation* or *interposition* in the laws of nature, or the providence of God. Understand, then, that all events, common as well as miraculous, are caused by the constant and immediate agency of Divine Power: in this respect there is no difference; one is no more of the nature of an *interposition* than the other. Understand, likewise, that what we call "the laws of nature" are nothing but the uniformity of the divine action; and again, that God observes this uniformity as a general rule, not on account of any thing in the uniformity itself, but simply and solely because he sees, *in each particular instance*, that it is best for his creatures. The law of his own nature, the law of infinite wisdom and goodness, moves him to do, in each particular instance, what he sees to be best for his creatures: this is the only law which has any thing to do with the divine conduct. Suppose now an exigency to arise (as in the case of the first promulgation of the gospel), when it is manifestly best for his creatures that he should deviate from his customary uniformity of action, — do you not perceive that in this case all the reasons and all the law which move him at other times to observe this uniformity, must move him now to depart from it? The miracle, therefore, is not a violation of the only law on which the uniformity of nature depends, but necessary to its fulfilment.

To the Christian, therefore, I repeat it, this view of nature and providence must recommend itself, because it takes from the miraculous evidence, on which in part at least his faith must rest, the anomalous character it has sometimes been made to wear. A real miracle is not of the nature of an interposition, neither is it a violation of the law of the Divine Nature. All events are what they are, through the constant and instant action of the Divinity; and, if in any case they deviate from the customary uniformity of nature, it is only because it is necessary to the immutability of God; for this immutability, as every one must perceive, does not consist in his acting in the same way under an essential change of circumstances, but in his acting in all circumstances from the same eternal principle of love. It must, also, recommend itself to Christians as being what the Saviour and his apostles taught. The doctrine of Providence, which I have been endeavoring though feebly and inadequately to set forth, is pre-eminently the Christian doctrine. "Are not two sparrows sold for a farthing? and one of them shall not fall on the ground without your Father. But the very hairs of your head are all numbered." "Of Him, and through Him, and to Him are all things." "In Him we live, and move, and have our being."

Thus far I have spoken of the providence which God exercises over the material world, over nature, and over man only in so far as he is related to nature and influenced by it. But it would hardly do to pass from this subject without saying a few words on what is at once the most interesting and the most difficult part: I mean the providence which God exercises over the spiritual world, over *minds*.

Here there is a marked difference growing out of the essential distinction between matter and spirit. The distinguishing characteristic of matter is *inertia:* it moves only as it is moved; it acts only as it is acted on. The distinguishing characteristic of spirit is *self-activity:* it moves itself; it is a free cause. Herein, perhaps, more than in any thing else, man resembles his Creator; he is, in short, a kind of limited and dependent creator: he creates his own volitions; he can begin a new series of events. God has seen fit to invest him with a freedom *which he himself respects:* hence man's responsibility, glory, peril. The planets are not free to move in their orbits, or not; the flowers of the field are not free to expand their leaves and diffuse their fragrance, or not; even the animals are not free to follow out, or not, those mysterious instincts which have been wrought into their organization, as a kind of vision or dream. But man — the soul — is free; free to do or not to do; to obey or disobey, to yield to or resist even divine influences and suggestions.

Here, as I have said, is a remarkable peculiarity; how is it provided for? As Dr. Price observes: "It would be denying the doctrine of Providence entirely, and making the universe in a manner forlorn and fatherless, to suppose that all that the Deity does, is to endow beings with powers and affections, and then to turn them out into a wide theatre, there to scuffle as they can, and do what they please, without taking any care of them, or presiding over their affairs. We cannot be more sure of the moral perfections of the Deity, than we are that this is false."[1] But man's condition in this world would not be very different from that which

[1] Four Dissertations, p. 98.

is here described, if God's providence extends no further than to his outward circumstances, leaving him to be affected by them as he may. Indeed, on the most general grounds, I cannot divest myself of the conviction, that the Infinite Spirit must act in and through his spiritual creation, by virtue of an intimacy far more profound than any which does or can exist between him and unconscious nature. Then, too, the inward experiences of every man that lives, — the sense of dependence, the instinct of prayer, the effort to raise himself above himself, the aspiration after the perfect and the infinite, — what are these but so many intimations that we were made to be sustained and filled by a strength and a light which are not our own? That this doctrine springs up naturally in a pious and thoughtful mind, even without the aid of revelation, appears from the following statement of it, as given by one of the most spiritually minded of the ancient sages: "Let your soul receive the Deity as your blood does the air; for the influences of the one are no less vital than the other. This correspondence is practicable; for there is an ambient, omnipresent Spirit, which lies as open and pervious to your mind as the air you breathe does to your lungs. But then you must remember to be disposed to draw it."

Provision is here made as well for the freedom

as for the frailty of man. God does not break into the soul against its will, or without its consent: the most that he does is, in the expressive language of Scripture, to "stand at the door and knock." Man can open his soul by holy exercises, by humility, by prayer, by love; or he can keep it shut. God is everywhere present and everywhere active in nature; we cannot help being surrounded at all times by the universally diffused light and energy. Not only good men, but bad men, the worst of men, are immersed, if I may so express it, in the Divine Presence: still the rebel spirit can keep himself utterly false and dark. The reason is, that this Presence finds entrance into the soul only in so far as the soul is brought into harmony with it, or humbles itself before it.

This I suppose to be the philosophical basis of the Christian doctrine of Divine Influences. Of course it is not pretended that there is any thing supernatural or miraculous in the ordinary influences of the Spirit. They result from the constitution of things as determined by the Creator; and, so far as we are concerned, they appear to result from that constitution according to general and fixed laws. They are not arbitrarily bestowed; they are not offered to one, and not to another, on any principle of partiality or selection. They are offered to all, — absolutely to all; and they can be, and are, made available by all of every kindred and tongue, of every faith and worship, just in proportion as by holy exercises, by love, by self-surrender, by humility and prayer, they put themselves into a condition to receive the needed Presence. Still, there would seem to be no good reason why an attempt should be made, from fear of extravagance and fanaticism, to confound the ordinary influences of the Spirit with the operations of our own minds. We cannot be reminded too often that under paganism, and also under Christianity, the most debasing and revolting forms of extravagance and fanaticism have prevailed among the ignorant, precisely at those times when a cold, sceptical, and rationalizing spirit found most favor among the better informed. This Divine Presence, this spiritual and heavenly succor, is shed abroad in our hearts as an influx of light and peace and joy, — a confidence, an energy, an impulse; and hence it is not to be regarded as mental action of our own, but rather as the foundation of a better and higher mental action of our own. Even Cicero could say, "there never was a truly great man without divine inspiration." In one word, what we mean is simply this: as a man may be filled with the spirit of selfishness, and in this case will act from selfish influences; or, with the spirit of the world, and in this case will act from worldly influences, — so may he also, in the same proportion as he makes himself like God, or humbles himself unreservedly before him, be filled with the Spirit of God; and in this case he will act from Divine influences.

I meant to say something of the place which prayer holds in this view of the providence which God exercises over the spiritual world; but I forbear. When we undertake to reason about what does not belong to the reasoning faculties, but to the affections, we soon find ourselves involved in inextricable difficulties. It is not that the thing itself is not reasonable: we feel that it is reasonable; but we feel, at the same time, that it is not a matter of *reasoning*. And the difficulty is complicated still further, when what we have to consider not only belongs to the affections, but is a spontaneous tribute of those affections. The moral and religious affections are in themselves essentially disinterested; and of course what they do and say is essentially untranslatable into the language of selfishness. Thus it is, as a general rule, that the heart alone can understand itself, and the reasonableness and the profit of its own offerings. To be able therefore to answer the question, What profit is there in prayer? we must enter into its spirit; and, as soon as we do enter into its spirit, we shall cease to take much interest in the question.

Time also fails me to speak as I should of the

spiritual discernment, and earnest and living faith, imparted to those in whom the Spirit of God dwells. A foreign writer has said of that great light which has lately gone down among us: "All true light he regarded as proceeding from the higher sentiments of the soul, receiving and manifesting God's spirit. To keep his own nature pure, reverential, loving, unstained by the passions, unsullied by appetite and sense, so that God might find it ready for his impulses, and be able to breathe his Holy Spirit through it, — this he regarded as the highest and surest preparation for the reception of Spiritual Truth. And the sense proceeding to him from such states, of the goodness of God, of the destination and true happiness of man, of an all-embracing love as the only principle of a beneficent connection with one another, or with the universe; of the blessedness of obeying conscience; of the sure triumph and eternal vindication of Righteousness and Mercy, — was not to him a mere human or fallible impression, but the solemn affirmation of Almighty God."[1]

If what I have now said is true, God is really present and active throughout nature and in all good men, in a sense and to a degree much beyond what the common opinion, or the common speech, seems to recognize. The promise of philosophy has

[1] Christian Teacher, vol. v. p. 106. Jan. 1843.

always been to give us back the simplicity of wisdom as a substitute for the simplicity of ignorance, which it has taken away ; to give us back simplicity of life, simplicity of manners, simplicity of faith. May we not hope that it will make this promise good ? The child listens to the thunder as the voice of God ; the savage listens to the sighings of the wind through the primeval forests as the breathing of the Great Spirit. Both are right, according to their apprehension of things. Philosophy, a devout and Christian philosophy, would only extend this solemn and awful recognition of the Divine Presence, and " see God in every thing, and every thing in God."

1843–1856.

V.

SPIRITUAL DEATH.

"I know thy works, that thou hast a name that thou livest, and art dead." — REVELATION iii. 1.

SINNERS, in whom the better principles of human nature are entirely overpowered by evil habit, are said in Scripture and elsewhere to be spiritually dead. I purpose to speak, in this discourse, of the nature, the causes, and the remedy of spiritual death.

In speaking of this state, let us take care, in the first place, never to mistake for spiritual death what is not that, though it may resemble it in some respects. There are those, everybody knows, who are *constitutionally* cold and phlegmatic, — cold and phlegmatic in every thing, — who are never excited, who are never warm. Look at them in all their relations; follow them into all their occupations. They are not ardent in their friendships or their enmities, or in the pursuit of knowledge, or of gain, or of pleasure. Now it would be preposterous to expect such persons to be otherwise than phlegmatic in religion, when compared with Christians of a more sanguine temperament. And yet, they are not spiritually dead. They are as much alive to religion as they are to any thing. Besides, there is nothing in their constitutional coldness and phlegm to hinder them from acting habitually on religious principles; or from being swayed on the whole by a religious spirit: which is all that is absolutely indispensable to a religious life. It is true, they are not likely to have enough of earnestness and devotion, to counteract strong antagonist feelings; but then, it is also true of the persons now under consideration, that by the very constitution of their nature they do not have *strong* antagonist feelings to be counteracted. They may be said, therefore, to require — they can get along with — less intensity of religious feeling than other people, because in them the passions, propensities which are apt to come into conflict with religious feelings, are also proportionably less intense. And what say the Scriptures? "Thou shalt love the Lord thy God, with all thy heart, with all thy soul, and with all thy mind, and with all thy strength." Here you will observe, that the abstract amount of affection required is not stated; one fixed and absolute standard is not set up for all persons; it is not said, with precisely *how much* heart, soul, mind, and strength we must love the Lord our God: it is enough if we love him, each one with *all* the heart, and soul, and mind, and strength that *he* has.

Again, we must not mistake for spiritual death that *outward reserve on religious subjects,* which sometimes springs from the very intensity of the feelings, or at least from an extreme and morbid delicacy of the feelings. Our Lord says, it is true, "Out of the abundance of the heart the mouth speaketh. A good man, out of the good treasure of his heart, bringeth forth good things; and an evil man, out of the evil treasure, bringeth forth evil things." That is, a man's conversation, if he says any thing, will be likely to be pure or impure, according to the predominant bias of his affections and inclinations. But it is by no means asserted or implied here, and it is by no means in accordance with experience and observation, that those men are always the most *talkative* whose hearts are the fullest. The direct contrary to this would be nearer the truth. As a general rule, people everywhere hesitate to say much, or to speak freely, about their deepest and most delicate feelings: partly from a difficulty to find words adequate to express them; partly from a fear that they will not meet with a hearty sympathy in other minds; and partly from an almost invincible repugnance to lay bare to vulgar gaze the mysteries of the inner man. Occasionally you may meet with those who are fond of talking about their religious experiences; and it is not for me, or for you, to judge, or even to call in question, their sincerity, or the reality of their experiences. But this we think we may say: with sensible people, the indications of suppressed feeling weigh more, a thousand times more, as evidence of real and deep emotion, than having the same feeling uttered and exaggerated.

But surely I need not labor this point. As some men are constitutionally cold and phlegmatic, so others, who are far from being cold and phlegmatic, are yet constitutionally reserved and uncommunicative, — reserved and uncommunicative in matters of business, as well as in the things of the Spirit. Now I do not say that this *habitual reserve*, this indisposition to free communion of thought and feeling on religious subjects, cannot be carried too far. I do not say that it never amounts to a fault. On the contrary, I believe that it is often a very great fault, and that Christianity has suffered as much from this fault in its enlightened friends, as from almost any other. Still I maintain, and after what has been said I hope it is sufficiently obvious, that outward reserve as regards religion is not in itself, and does not of itself, necessarily argue or imply spiritual death.

What, then, is spiritual death? It consists in the absence of that sensibility of soul by which men are made capable of feeling and appreciating spiritual things. Sometimes this arises from the fact that the spiritual element in our nature has *never* been excited and developed; the man has never been spiritually *born*. But it is more frequently owing to a torpor or palsy which, from some cause, comes over the spiritual faculties after their partial development, to such a degree as, in some instances, entirely to destroy and suspend their vital and legitimate functions. He still is alive to other things,—alive, and perhaps intensely alive, to the pleasures of sense, to the pursuits of gain, to a love of power and fame; to every thing, in short, which does not involve the presence and activity of the moral and spiritual faculties: but so far as these are concerned he is dead. When we say that a man is spiritually dead, we do not mean that his body is dead; nay, we do not mean that his mind is dead, so far as it is capable of being occupied exclusively on things of time, and sense, and self. He may even be eminent as a mathematician, or naturalist, or statesman; and yet as regards all those feelings and exercises which involve the consciousness and the agency of his higher nature, and his relations to the spiritual world, he may be as dead as the drunken vagabond about the streets.

This, then, is what we understand by spiritual death. Not a general and constitutional coldness in regard to all things, but a particular deadness and insensibility to every thing which is addressed to our spiritual nature; not a mere outward reserve, but a torpor and palsy of the spiritual faculties.

The Scriptures sometimes represent this under the figure of a "second death;" for as there is a second birth, indicating that the body is born at one time and the spirit at another, so also is there a second death, indicating in like manner that the body may die at one time and the spirit at another. But there is this difference: though the spirit is never born first, it may die first, so far at least as it is susceptible of death. So far, I say, so far as it is susceptible of death; for we must not urge the language of Scripture, or this analogy between the death of the body and the death of the spirit, too far. The death of the body is an utter and final dissolution of the body; but the death of the spirit is nothing more, strictly speaking, than the inaction and temporary suspension of faculties which are in their own nature indestructible. Nay, it does not follow, because the soul is dead to every thing which constitutes its *proper life*, that it is dead to the want and misery occasioned by what may justly be termed a living death. However this may be, it is certain that the soul, so far as it can die, may die before the body ; that causes may now be in operation to destroy the proper life of the soul, and that the individual himself may voluntarily contribute to this effect, to his own spiritual self-destruction. It is, indeed, an appalling thought, that, where there is one suicide of the body, there are probably twenty, may I not say a hundred, suicides of the soul.

Let us now advert briefly to some of the causes conspiring to induce that indifference and insensibility to spiritual things, which constitutes, as we have seen, spiritual death.

And first, I would say, that less is to be feared, in this connection, from erroneous than from lifeless training. A writer, of whom our country and the age may justly boast, has said: "I do not think that so much harm is done by giving error to a child, as by giving truth in a lifeless form. What is the misery of the multitudes in Christian countries? Not that they disbelieve Christianity, or that they hold great errors, but that truth lies dead within them. They use the most sacred words without meaning. They hear of spiritual realities, awful enough to raise the dead, with utter unconcern ; and one reason of this insensibility is, that teaching in early life was so mechanical, that religion was lodged in the memory and the unthinking belief, whilst the reason was not awakened, nor the conscience nor the heart moved. According to the common modes of instruction, the minds of the young become worn to great truths. By reading the Scriptures without thought or feeling, their minds are dulled to their most touching and sublime passages; and, when once a passage lies dead in the mind, its resurrection to life and power is a most difficult work."[1]

A kindred thought was presented long ago, by Dr. Priestley, in a sermon on "The Danger of Bad Habits," — cold and philosophical throughout in manner, yet one of the most solemn appeals ever made to the conscience; the object being to prove that to many the day of judgment may be said to come before the day of their death. "A person," he observes, "who has studied, or who fancies he has studied, any particular subject, sooner or later *makes up his mind*, as we say, with respect to it; and, after this, all arguments intended to convince him of his mistake, only serve to confirm him in his chosen way of thinking. An argument or evidence of any kind, that is entirely *new* to a man, may make a proper impression upon him; but if it has often been proposed to him, and he has had time to view and

[1] Dr. Channing's "Discourse on Sunday Schools," Christian Examiner, vol. xxii. pp. 74, 75.

consider it, so as to have hit upon any method of evading the power of it, he is afterwards quite callous to it, and can very seldom be prevailed upon to give it any proper attention. This consideration accounts, in some measure, both for the great influence of Christianity on its first publication, when the doctrines were *new* and *striking*, and also for the absolute indifference with which the same great truths are now heard in all Christian countries." [1]

It is high time that all, and that intelligent Christians especially, should wake up to the importance of these suggestions. We are for ever extolling the power of truth, the value of sound and just views, and a rational and consistent faith; and all this is well, provided the whole be instinct with a living spirit. But of what avail will be the truth itself, if held, I do not say "in unrighteousness," but in indifference and apathy? We have, I know, the warrant of Scripture for believing that it is *the truth* by which men are to be sanctified and made free; but who has yet to learn that the truth which is to do this, is not truth contemplated as an abstraction, truth set forth in propositions, truth locked up in creeds? It is living truth. It is truth in action,

[1] Discourses on Various Subjects. Birmingham, 1787, pp. 374, 375.

truth considered as wrought into the very life, the truth which we *live* from day to day. But that this sort of truth may be dispensed, it is necessary that both preacher and hearer should *reproduce it*, each one in his own mind and heart. It is not enough that we receive it passively as a tradition, or adopt it passively on authority; we must make it matter of inward experience, of spiritual consciousness, and thus reproduce it, as it were, in our own minds and hearts. And in this way, let me observe in passing, the oldest truths may again become as fresh and new *to us*, individually and personally, as when they first fell from the lips of the Great Teacher.

Give us the living truth; but, if we cannot have that, give us, in God's name, *living* error. As liberal Christians we are, beyond question, over-critical and fastidious in this matter. It may not be so with other denominations, but our chief danger grows out of an under current that is continually setting towards a dead rationalism. Give us, I repeat it, *living* error, rather than *dead* truth; for the same maxim holds good in regard to our higher as well as our lower nature: "so long as there is life, there is hope." Besides, do we not know that a ship under sail, though a little off from its course, can get into it again *in half the time* it will take another vessel at anchor under a headland, or waterlogged in a calm, to get under way?

Again, so far as religious indifference and insensibility are concerned, there is less to fear, as it seems to me, from the influence of an *avowed* and *active* scepticism than from the influence of a scepticism which is *unacknowledged and merely passive.* Well and truly was it said by Archbishop Leighton: "Where there is a great deal of smoke, and no clear flame, it argues much moisture in the matter, yet it witnesseth certainly that there is *fire* there; and therefore dubious questioning is a much better evidence than that senseless deadness which most take for believing. Men that know nothing in sciences have no doubts. He never truly believes who was not made first sensible, and convinced of his unbelief. Never be afraid to doubt, if only you have *the disposition to believe*, and doubt in order that you may end in believing the truth."[1] If we must have an active or a passive scepticism, give us the first. An active scepticism will often cure itself, work itself clear of its difficulties; but there is no hope whatever for a man who will neither believe nor inquire. An active scepticism, moreover, does not imply an indifference to truth, nor prevent men from discriminating; so that, while it leads them

[1] Coleridge's "Aids," p. 64.

to deny this thing and doubt that, it leaves their confidence in other things unimpaired, and perhaps strengthened and quickened. But it is of the nature of a latent and passive scepticism, by confounding the true with the false, and the certain with the doubtful, to spread itself gradually over the whole subject, involving natural as well as revealed religion in the same doubt, and causing them to be regarded with a like indifference. Under the influence of this spirit, the best that men can be expected to do is to settle down at last into the conceited and supercilious conclusion, that Christianity, whether true or not, is a good thing for society, and especially for the lower classes, and must not be disturbed.[1]

Yes, I earnestly contend that any thing is better than that senseless deadness here referred to, which sometimes passes for believing. Accordingly I do not participate, to any considerable degree, in the regret or alarm expressed by some at the tendency of modern scepticism to come forth into the light of day, and to put on a form of light and activity corresponding to the magnitude of the principles at stake. It is no evidence that scepticism and infidelity are *on the increase:* both have always existed to an extent far beyond what is generally supposed; but it is the consequence of that spirit

[1] Christian Examiner, vol. xi. p. 191.

which is abroad, leading men to sift all subjects to the bottom, and religion among the rest, with a determination to find whether it is founded in reality or not. And I, for one, welcome the change. Indeed, when I see deists, like Lord Herbert, praying on their bended knees that God would give them a sign from heaven to end their doubts; when I see atheists shedding bitter tears over the conscious desolation which want of faith has brought on their whole inward being,—though the iron has entered into their souls, I feel that still, while there is pain, there is life; and, while there is life, there is hope. Nay, I am almost tempted, under such circumstances, to pronounce a *living* scepticism better than a *dead* faith, as doing more to agitate and wake up a man's moral nature, to make him alive to the deep wants of his soul, and thus to put him into a condition to be affected and impressed by exhibitions of divine truth, from whatever quarter they may come. And I am much mistaken if it does not appear in the end, that the design, the final cause, in the providence of God, of the recent development of what are called the sceptical tendencies of the age, is to purify, by means of a reaction, the dull, close, and suffocating atmosphere in which, to so great an extent, the selfishness and the worldliness, and the low and earthly utilitarian-

ism of the times, have wrapped so large a portion of the Church. If there is no other way of regenerating nominal Christianity, — if there is no other way of raising men out of this state of passive, latent, unacknowledged scepticism, which is doing so much, gradually and insidiously, to waste away the heart and moral life of humanity, but by passing through a process of active scepticism, — I, for one, welcome the ordeal. And, under the sway of a God of omnipotence and truth, I have no more fear that religion itself is to go down, than I have that civilization is again to be engulphed in barbarism, or that the wild beasts of the desert will rise on mankind, and depopulate the earth.

Once more, I need say but a word in illustration of what you all know, that sin, under any and all its thousand forms, leads to spiritual death. But it may be of more importance to observe here, that less perhaps is to be apprehended, so far as indifference and utter insensibility are concerned, from open, flagrant, and passionate crime, than from that worldliness and self-seeking which finds but little difficulty in disguising itself under a decent exterior, and keeping on good terms with itself and with society. Fanatics, as you are aware, have sometimes said that thieves and drunkards are nearer the Kingdom of Heaven than merely moral men; and there is just enough of truth in this statement to give currency in some circles to the radical and pestilent error it conveys. It is true, beyond all doubt, that the man who has killed within himself the *principle* of virtue, without having cast off its most indispensable outward forms, or adopted those of gross vice, is less likely to be startled in his downward course, is less likely to awake to the imminent peril of his situation, than one whose every-day scenes and every-day actions are of a nature to bring up before him visions of hell.

Moreover, it is not enough considered that mere levity and frivolity may superinduce an impenetrable callousness upon the human heart; and in time, through the power of habit, may render it absolutely unimpressible by the weightiest and most interesting objects in the universe. And what shall I say of sensuality? "She that liveth in pleasure is dead while she liveth." Self-surrender to the animal passions, — it is the grave of every thing that is pure, and noble, and good; converting man, by a sort of living metempsychosis, into the beast in whose tastes and propensities he grovels. Neither does the curse stop with the torpor and palsy of the soul, but pursues him at last, under the form of a sated appetite and a withered heart, even into all his forbidden indulgences. Who has yet to learn that there are none who in effect extract so little happiness from pleasure as those who look to it as their sole or their highest gratification? Excess blunts every faculty and every sense until the man of pleasure becomes as dead to animal as to spiritual enjoyment; as dead to pleasure and the world as he is to religion and to God.

But it is time to conclude. You will remember that spiritual death is not absolute death. It is but the inaction or suspension of faculties which are in their own nature indestructible. Under the government and providence of our Heavenly Father, and with the powerful aids and appliances of a spiritual faith and worship, despair is unpardonable sin, — despair either for ourselves or for others. It is only necessary that we should be apprized of our danger, and avail ourselves of the means of resuscitating or waking up our moral and spiritual nature. Evoke its latent energies, and put them forth in deeds of philanthropy and mercy; commune with your own soul, and stand in awe of its mysterious revelations of the unseen and the infinite; study the lives and cultivate the society of those whose faith and piety at once excite and attract all who come within the sphere of their influence; resort as you may be able, and as you feel yourselves prepared, to earnest, heartfelt prayer, in which man is said, by a most expressive figure, to wrestle with God. Above all, have faith in him, at whose powerful word the grave gave up its dead; have faith in him that he can also work the kindred miracle of raising your soul from the death of sin to the life of righteousness. Wherefore it is said, — and their line is gone out through all the earth, and their words to the end of the world, — "Awake, thou that sleepest, and arise from the dead, and Christ shall give thee life!"

1837–1858.

VI.

MEANS OF STRENGTHENING AN INFIRM FAITH.

"*And straightway the father of the child cried out, and said with tears, Lord, I believe: help thou mine unbelief!*" — MARK ix. 24.

THE state of mind which the Evangelist ascribes to the father of the lunatic child is not uncommon. It is the condition of one who has faith; but yet is conscious at times of doubts by which his faith is weakened and disturbed.

Such being the condition of many minds, perhaps of most thinking minds, it may be well to inquire how this temptation or tendency to doubt may be prevented. In other words, What are some of the best means of strengthening an unsettled or infirm faith?

First of all, we should eradicate from our minds what may be called *the conceit of scepticism.*

I do not suppose that all the scepticism in the world originates in one cause, or in causes all of which imply guilt. Something, doubtless, depends on organization; something also on education, society, public opinion, and other extraneous influences for which the individual is, at most, but in part responsible. Still I cannot help suspecting that a principal consideration which *reconciles* many to being sceptical is the thought, that it argues more than usual strength or activity of mind; that it is because they can see through what others cannot, and so are made less easy to be convinced. Whatever may be said of their doubts in a moral and religious point of view, they are fain to look upon them as the sign, perhaps as the penalty, of intellectual superiority.

But is this conceit well founded? I allow that doubting is commonly the result of thinking; but not of successful thinking: it is the result of *baffled* thinking; and is baffled thinking a sign of intellectual power? Again, the *objections* to a doctrine are generally obvious, palpable, on the outside, — anybody can understand them; while the *answers*, for the most part, lie deeper, and so require more information, or greater reach of mind, in order to be appreciated, in order that their full force may be felt. For this reason, in a community where it is the fashion for all to think for themselves, no small portion of the actual scepticism, secret or avowed, may be referred to the single circumstance, that multitudes have enough of intelligence to understand the objection, but not enough to understand the answer. Certainly, therefore, it is not true of *all* scepticism, that it supposes mental superiority.

Furthermore, a propensity to scepticism does not betoken the best style or cast of mind. Minds may be divided into two classes: some are constructive, others destructive; some apt to discover analogies and harmonies, others quick to detect defects or discrepancies; some always trying to build up, others always trying to pull down. Now I suppose that most persons will go along with me when I say, that the first mentioned sort of mind is on every account to be preferred; yet the sceptically disposed belong to the last. I might illustrate and confirm what I mean from history. Compare Socrates with the sophists of his day; compare Bacon with Bayle; compare Locke with Hume; compare Newton with Laplace. I have no wish to detract aught from the acknowledged eminence of the last named in these several comparisons, as regards what fell in with the peculiar bent of their genius. If acuteness and subtilty of intellect, if a power to analyze and dissect, to criticise and find fault and pull to pieces, were all that is required, some of the great sceptics might be set down, I suppose, as second to none. Unquestionably these men stand among the highest in the order to which they belong, but the order itself is not the highest. The habit of attending to minute distinctions and mere details unfits them more and more for making up a confident opinion respecting any large and complicated subject. They belong to a class of ingenious persons, who are for ever liable to be ensnared by their own ingenuity. They are so ready with their difficulties and objections as to be more than a match even for themselves; and hence their scepticism.

Again, therefore, I say, let no one hug his scepticism, or entertain it with complacency, from a conceit that it is the price he has to pay for his intellectual superiority. So far is this from being the case, that in a large majority of instances scepticism is the sign of nothing but a limited and baffled understanding; and, even when it must be admitted to pertain to extraordinary powers, they are still, for the most part, the powers of a subtle and captious mind, but not those of a large, generous, comprehensive, and effective mind. Exceptions there may be; but the general rule is as I have said. A man is not great because he can see difficulties, but because he can see through difficulties; or, because he believes in what makes difficulties of no account, so that he can go on as if they did not exist. Accordingly we find that those who have been looked up to in all ages as lights and guides, — the great discoverers and inventors, the great legislators, the great reformers, the great benefactors of the race, — have not been men of doubt, but men of faith.

Having thus discarded every vestige of the conceit of scepticism, the next rule to be observed by those who would cure themselves of a tendency to unsettled opinions, in morals and religion, is to abstain from *dwelling unduly on the difficult and perplexing aspects of the subject.*

Every subject has its difficult and perplexing aspects. Take the simplest fact in Nature; consider it in all its connections and relations, and it will be found to run out into questions which all the triumphs of modern science leave as much in the dark as ever. Now where will you stop? Most persons, however sceptically inclined, would be willing to say, I suppose, that they should be content if they had as good evidence for the existence of the soul, as they have for that of the body; or as good evidence for the existence of the spiritual world, as they have for that of the material world. Yet, even in respect to the body and the material world, doubts and difficulties have been raised which have made the strongest minds waver; nay, books have been written, in all seriousness and good faith, to demonstrate not only their non-existence, but their impossibility. And so in morals. Few things, I suppose, are clearer to the great bulk of mankind, or more universally recognized, than the great primary distinctions of right and wrong. Here again, however, uneasy and distrustful minds may push their questionings into that perplexing field of inquiry which has to do with hereditary biases, differences of organization, and the power of circumstances, or with the insolvable mystery of the Divine prescience and human free agency, until what before was as clear as noon-day becomes hopelessly obscured and confused; until they are ready to doubt whether there is any such thing as proper responsibility, whether conscience, after all, is not an empty name, or at best an unauthorized prejudice, — a mere figment of the brain. Thus, by dwelling exclusively on the difficult side of things, a man may lose all confidence even in what the world, whether infidel or not on the subject of religion, have agreed to set down among the best established conclusions of sense and reason. How it is that such a result should follow from such a course is easy of explanation. By dwelling on the difficult and perplexing aspects of any subject, the mind is continually exposed to a twofold cause of mistake. In the first place, the points of objection and difference may be very few, compared with the points of general consent; still, if we give a great deal more attention and thought to the former than to the latter, we shall be tempted to believe that the proportion is reversed. Besides, the practical effect of objections to any doctrine depends much less on their number or weight than on the place we give them in our thoughts; on the amount of attention we pay to them. If, in other words, we think of them and nothing else, then it is plain that we shall know nothing about the subject but its difficulties and objections, and we shall be doubters as a matter of course. The law is, that our minds are affected by what is present to them, and not by what is absent from them, whether it exists or not. This law manifests itself in many things which have nothing to do with morals or religion. For example: we almost always over estimate the merits of our friends, and under estimate the merits of our enemies. Why? The reason is, that in thinking of our friends we are apt to think only of their virtues, while in thinking of our enemies we are apt to think only of their defects and faults. Here, too, we find the origin of much that goes under the name of party rancor, with all its meannesses and injustice, and particularly its disposition to impeach the motives or question the sincerity of opponents. Wonder is often expressed that really good men, in proportion as they become zealous partisans, are so ready to lend themselves to these abuses; but it is only another application of the above-mentioned law. When they think of their own party, they are apt to think of its good side only, but when they think of the party opposed to them, they are apt to think of its bad side only; and, doing so, the effect of this on their own minds is just the same as if *their* party really had no bad side, and the other no good side.

So likewise in respect to Christianity. If we never recur to it except to dwell on its difficulties and perplexities, and on the dark side of its history, it is plain that the effect on our minds will be the same as if these constituted the whole of Christianity. Christianity has a multitude of other aspects which recommend it immediately and irresistibly to the reason and the heart; but these are nothing to one who will not think on them, or, which is the same in effect, allows his mind to be wholly taken up with the difficult and perplexing aspects of the subject.

What makes it worse in the case of Christianity is, that, when persons fall into doubt respecting it, they naturally turn to *books on the evidences*, and the burden of these books is still the difficulties and perplexities. Considering what these books are intended for, it cannot be otherwise; they are written in order to make clear and plain, not what is clear and plain already, but what is not so. They may, therefore, be consulted with profit by those who wish to view the subject on all sides, or whose faith labors on particular points. But where scepticism does not originate in want of information, and is not confined to particulars, but takes the form of a general distrust in regard to the whole subject (and this is the common character of modern scepticism), a resort to books on the evidences will often be found, I think, to aggravate rather than remove the evil. Modern scepticism resembles in one respect that disordered state of the affections called *misanthropy*, which justifies itself on the ground that men are the proper objects of *a general distrust:* both are *general distrusts*, and both are to be dealt with in the same way. Now would you think to cure a person laboring under the delusion of misanthropy, by advising him to dwell on the cases of real or supposed deception and treachery which have made him distrustful of everybody, in the hope that these will be cleared up to his entire satisfaction? No: on the contrary, you would advise him to treat these cases as being at the worst but few and exceptional, and therefore as not fairly representing human character; and you would try to draw away his attention and his thoughts from these, and fix them on the bright side of human nature as represented by the multitude of good and upright men whom he has known.

For the same reason, the same or a similar course should be taken with those who have become infected in any way with religious scepticism as a general habit or disease. Let me not be misunderstood. I do not mean that men should be *afraid* of the difficulties and objections in the way of faith, or try to hush up the controversy respecting them. All I contend for is simply this, that, in so vast and complicated a subject as religion, having to do at every step with the unseen and eternal, difficulties and objections must be expected; and, as some of them are incident to the limitation and imperfection of the human faculties, they never can be entirely done away: so that we must believe, if we believe at all, *in spite* of these difficulties and objections.

Having in view this state of things, all I ask of the sceptic is, that he would not give way to a morbid tendency of his mind to dwell on these difficulties and objections *alone*, but enter on a generous and comprehensive survey of the whole subject; in which it will appear that the difficulties and objections are exceptional cases, the best answer to which is found in the cumulative, and to most minds overwhelming, evidence on the other side. The sceptic may hold, if he will, that to all human observation there are spots on the sun's disc; I only ask him to admit, — and it would not seem to be an unreasonable request, — I only ask him to admit that the sun shines, nevertheless.

I will now suppose the sceptic to have cast away the conceit of scepticism, and also to be willing to survey the subject on all sides; that is, to consider what he believes and knows, as well as what he doubts. If still he does not believe enough, and is anxious to believe more, his next step should be *to make the most of what he does believe;* and this in two ways, *logically* and *practically.*

In the first place, *logically;* that is to say, he should consider not only how much he believes, in express terms, but also every thing which this implies or presupposes. This is the way, I suspect, in which thinking and independent minds commonly expand themselves; not by borrowing a fragment here and a fragment there, but by unfolding more and more what they already know. A striking example of what I mean is met with in Descartes, the founder of modern metaphysics. Wishing to establish human knowledge on a basis beyond the reach of attack, he began by doubting every thing which could be doubted, and went on this way, rejecting one thing after another, until he came to his own existence. This he found he could not doubt, because the very act of doubting supposed him to exist in order to doubt. Behold him, then, reduced in his faith to belief in his own existence! This he could not help accepting as an incontestable fact, and with it, of course, whatever it involved, implied, or presupposed. His next step was, therefore, to unfold this fact to see what it did involve, imply, or presuppose; which he found to be every thing he had formerly been in the habit of taking on trust. Emanuel Kant is another example among the great thinkers who have recovered their faith in the same way. After having ruined by his criticism, as he thought, the common arguments for morality and religion, he still felt himself to be confronted by conscience, the authority of which he could neither deny nor call in question. Practically, he could not help admitting that he was bound by the moral law; and, consequently, he could not help admitting what this on reflection was seen to involve, imply, or presuppose: to wit, liberty, immortality, and Divine Providence. The faith, therefore, which his speculative reason had shaken, was restored by his practical reason, so that he could go on with as much confidence as before. Here, I hardly need say, we have nothing to do with the soundness or unsoundness of the positions taken by these philosophers. They are referred to merely as showing how men of unsurpassed speculative power, joined to strong sceptical leanings, may begin with believing little and go on to believe more and more, merely by considering what is involved, implied, or presupposed in this little; that is to say, by making the most of this little.

I am also reminded in this connection of Bishop Butler's "Analogy of Religion to the Course of Nature," which a competent judge[1] has pronounced "the most original and profound work extant in any language on the philosophy of religion." The argument in this treatise is not addressed to atheists, but to semi-theists, like Bolingbroke, who admitted the existence of an intelligent Author and natural Governor of the world. Thus much being conceded, Bishop Butler proves that they cannot consistently stop here; by showing that what they already believe involves the analogy — that is, the verisimilitude or probability — of every thing else which religion teaches, together with all the difficulties and objections by which the subject is embarrassed. Some have complained that this celebrated work, from its peculiar structure and drift, is likely to raise more difficulties and objections than it removes. This remark may hold good in respect to a certain class of minds; Mr. Pitt told Wilberforce that it was so with him; still the general rule is unquestionably on the other side. Besides, even in those cases where more difficulties and objections are raised

[1] Sir James Mackintosh.

than removed, it does not follow that the book fails of its leading purpose. This purpose is not to prove that there are no difficulties and objections in religion, but to show what we ought to believe and do, and what a *wise man* will be disposed to believe and do, *notwithstanding these difficulties and objections*, — a point of view under which, as it seems to me, the argument is unequalled, and in many parts absolutely irresistible.

We have now seen in this way how much may be gained by logically making the most of what we already believe. It remains for us to consider, as being indeed of vastly greater importance at least to the bulk of mankind, how much may also be gained by *practically* making the most of what we already believe.

Religion, I hardly need say, is not so much a matter of speculation as of practice. Confessedly it is the great practical concernment of human life, and therefore should be judged of by analogies borrowed from practical affairs. Now it may be doubted whether a single great practical interest or measure can be named, which has not its difficult and unsettled questions. Take politics, for example; who will pretend that he has entirely made up his mind on every question connected with this subject? Yet uncertainty on some points hinders him not from *acting* in respect to others, or even from taking *a decided stand*, if he conceives the interests or honor of his country, or his own duty as a citizen, require it. If it were a matter of knowledge merely, then it would be a matter of inquiry merely; and our whole duty would consist in *continuing to inquire.* But it is not so. It is matter of practice; we know, *merely* that we may put what we know into practice; so that any measure or degree of knowledge, not reduced to practice, fails of its purpose and end, and is therefore in a moral view worse than total ignorance, because it is so much light sinned against by not being acted out. Hence in practical matters, — and again I say, these include religion as the greatest practical concernment of all, — every one must perceive the inconsistency of adopting the rule that we will *do nothing* until we *know every thing.*

To return, then, to the sceptic in religion. There are few, I suppose, who carry their scepticism to the extent of believing *nothing at all.* On some subjects they have their doubts; on others none. Now all I ask of such persons is simply this: that they would be consistent, and reduce to practice what they do believe; carry into effect the principles respecting which they have really made up their minds; or, which is the same thing, live up to that measure of light to which they have actually attained. And let it not be thought that this, in a practical point of view, will turn out to be a small matter. It would be difficult to name a single important doctrine of Christianity, which alone, to be faithfully and entirely carried out, does not require the whole Christian character. Nay, more. We will suppose a man's scepticism to reach the very foundations of Christianity, making it necessary for him to fall back on natural religion, — our argument is still the same. Let him begin by reducing to practice what he does believe, be it little or much. If as yet he believes but little, let him begin by bringing his life into faithful and strict accordance with that little, as a condition of believing more. And here let me remind you again, that a faithful and strict conformity to this little, to one or two doctrines of natural religion, will not turn out to be a small matter. Suppose a man's faith narrowed down to believing that there is a God who is just and good: he is bound, I say, for consistency's sake and for conscience' sake, to live as if in the presence and under the government of such a Being; and if he really does so, hardly a duty enjoined by Christianity will be left unperformed.

Some may object to this reasoning, that I misconceive the nature of scepticism in making it to consist in the narrowness or brevity of a man's creed. It will be said that modern scepticism shows itself, not so much in the small number of the articles which compose a man's creed, as in the general distrust or misgiving with which the whole creed and all creeds are regarded. The sceptic cannot make up his mind whether religion is a reality at all, in any sense or degree; whether there is, or is not, a spiritual world, or any world but this. And in this state of his convictions, or rather of his want of conviction, he may think that to act as if religion were a reality would be a kind of untruthfulness, a seeming to believe what he does not believe; or, at any rate, an inconsistency.

But why so? Because a man cannot make up his mind as to what he ought *to believe*, it does not follow that he cannot make up his mind as to what he ought *to do*. Let it be that he needs more evidence to assure him of the truth and reality of religion; let it be that the evidence is only probable evidence, — nay, that to his mind there is not more than one chance in twenty, or one in a hundred, that religion is true, — I still insist that both duty and consistency require that he should live as religion directs; that is to say, on the assumption of its truth. For, in the first place, it is plain that in life, in conduct, he must take one side or the other, notwithstanding his doubts. In opinion, a man may be in the condition of one who neither believes nor disbelieves; but in life, in conduct, he cannot be in the condition of one who neither obeys nor disobeys; for not to obey *is* to disobey. As regards practice, therefore, the question with the sceptic resolves itself into this: is it wiser and better to act on the assumption that religion is true, and run the risk of its turning out to be false, or to act on the assumption of its being false, and run the risk of its turning out to be true? When the alternative is put in this form, and as regards practice it is the only alternative, I cannot help thinking that all must be of one mind.

From not understanding the position here taken, some may ask, Is not this to expect that the sceptic will act without a motive? Certainly not. His motive is the hope of obtaining an *infinite* good, or the dread of incurring an *infinite* evil: the magnitude of the stake being such as to make up for any real or supposed deficiency of evidence; so much so, that a bare possibility of the event should be sufficient to determine our conduct. Hence, in the words of Bishop Butler: "Considering the infinite importance of religion, revealed as well as natural, I think it may be said in general, that whoever will weigh the matter thoroughly may see there is not near so much difference, as is commonly imagined, between what ought to be the *rule of life* to those persons who are fully convinced of its truth, and to those who have only a serious doubting apprehension that it *may be* true." And again. From these things it must follow, that *doubting* concerning religion "implies such a degree of evidence for it, as, joined with the consideration of its importance, unquestionably lays men under the obligation before mentioned, to have a dutiful regard to it in all their behavior."

But this is not all. I do not count on the power of the sceptic to persevere in a righteous course on the strength of his doubts, supposing his doubts to continue. My argument is, that he should make the most of the measure of faith he already has, as the appointed and necessary condition of his having more. The habit of obedience, the habit of piety, the habit of prayer, generates a conviction of the reality of moral and spiritual things, which nothing else can give. Who has not found that, in his best moods, — when, for example, he is in the midst of a good work, or when his heart is full of generous affections and purposes, or when he is under the influence of good and holy men, — he finds no difficulty in believing what religion teaches? We have, therefore, but to make our best moods our constant moods, and our doubts would never return.

In this discourse I have supposed a person to

resemble the father of the lunatic child mentioned in the Gospels, who "cried out, and said, with tears, Lord, I believe: help thou mine unbelief!" It is the condition of one who has faith, but yet is conscious at times of doubts by which his faith is weakened or disturbed. As a remedy for this defect, it is natural and right to recommend what is called the study of the evidences; a study, however, which will be to little purpose unless the three inculcations insisted on above are regarded. Dismiss from your minds every vestige of the conceit of scepticism. Do not allow your minds to dwell exclusively or unduly on the difficulties of the subject; or be willing, at any rate, to consider that, if there are difficulties in the way of believing, there are greater ones in the way of not believing. Above all, begin, begin to-day, to live up to the measure of light and faith to which you have already attained. Thus will you be in a frame of mind which will dispose you to *wish*, at least, that the gospel may be true; and, if you superadd earnest and devout prayer, your hearts will be open to receive the needed illumination from above. "Jesus answered them, and said, My doctrine is not mine, but his that sent me. If any man will do his will, he shall know of the doctrine, whether it be of God, or whether I speak of myself."

1848–1858.

VII.

NOMINAL CHRISTIANS.

"*Not every one that saith unto me, Lord, Lord, shall enter into the kingdom of heaven; but he that doeth the will of my Father which is in heaven.*" — MATT. vii. 21.

OUR Saviour speaks here of *nominal* Christians, in contradistinction to *real* Christians. Enough has not been made, as it seems to me, of this distinction; nay, the distinction itself has often been misstated and misunderstood. It is common to say of men who live in a Christian community, but are themselves indifferent to the subject of religion, that *they* are nominal Christians. The truth is, however, that such persons are not Christians in any sense; they are neither nominal Christians, nor real Christians; they do not pretend even to the name. Nominal Christians, properly so called, are those who feel an interest in the general subject of religion, and are sincerely and perhaps zealously devoted to the Christian sect, as a sect; that is to say, they are

Christians in contradistinction to Jews, or Pagans, or Mahometans. They are Christian *in sect;* they are Christian *in name;* they have a right to *the name;* but they are not Christians in reality, because they do not breathe the Christian spirit. *Nominal* Christians differ from those who are *not Christians in any sense*, by being sincerely and perhaps ardently attached to the Christian sect and name. On the other hand, they differ from *real* Christians, because though sincerely and perhaps ardently attached to the Christian sect and name, they do not as individuals breathe the Christian spirit. They are *nominal* Christians, but they are not *real* Christians.

According to this distinction, it is obvious, in the first place, that a man's *zeal as a nominal Christian* may sometimes operate to prevent him from being a *real* Christian. Thus when some of the early Christians sought by pious frauds to bring over the pagans to their views, many of them were actuated by a sincere zeal for the Christian sect and name. So likewise after the Christians had gotten the civil power into their own hands, and began to turn it against the pagans and heretics, many of them were unquestionably actuated by a sincere zeal for the Christian sect and name. And again in more modern times, when Christians have lost their reason and temper in the heat of theological controversy, there can be no doubt that many of them at least have been moved to it by a sincere zeal for the Christian sect and name. In ways like these, a man's sincere devotedness to the Christian sect and name will sometimes push him into measures that will have the effect to estrange him more and more from real Christianity. A man's zeal for the Christian sect and name, though perfectly *sincere and disinterested*, will sometimes induce a spirit the very opposite to that which real Christianity breathes. Paradoxical as it may seem, therefore, it is a sincere zeal for the Christian sect and name, that sometimes operates to hinder him from being a real Christian himself.

Secondly, the distinction here insisted on will also lead us to observe, that Christians in all ages have been always more anxious to extend the Christian name and sect than to spread the religion itself. In other words, they have been more anxious to make nominal Christians than real Christians. Take, for example, the conversion of the Franks under Clovis, about the beginning of the sixth century. Clovis and his people were idolaters, but in the distress of the battle of Tolbiac he loudly invoked the God of the Christians, and appears to have ascribed the victory he gained on that occasion to the interposition of the Christians' God. While in this state of mind, the Catholic missionaries found but little difficulty in persuading him and his followers, to the number of three thousand, to submit almost immediately to the rite of baptism. This, the missionaries thought, was to make them Christians. But what sort of Christians must we suppose that the sprinkling of a little water would make out of these fierce and ruthless barbarians, especially as we learn that their conduct and character afterwards were not preceptibly improved? Many centuries afterwards, when the Jesuits first set in motion their scheme for converting South America, we know that they succeeded beyond all parallel, converting the natives by thousands, and by hundreds of thousands. What sort of Christians, however, are we to give them credit for making, it being understood that they did not so much as attempt to cure them of their superstitions, but only sought to give these superstitions another and, in some respects, a worse direction, by turning them to the use of the Church? At one period the English government, moved doubtless by humane considerations, directed that measures should be taken for bringing the negroes on some of the West India Islands within the Christian pale, by the usual initiatory rite. But as the work still went on heavily, a law was passed in 1817 giving the clergyman a bounty of 2*s*. 6*d*. a head for every negro he should baptize. This bribe had such effect, that one of the clergy wrote home soon afterwards, that he had already baptized five thousand negroes, and was making arrangements for baptizing, before the close of the year, all the rest on the island, amounting to about twenty thousand more. Now, I ask again, what sort of Christians we can suppose that sprinkling a little water would make out of these wronged and degraded beings, instruction and every other means of moral and religious edification being systematically withheld?

I am aware of the essential difficulties in the case. I am aware that it is in order *first* to convert men to nominal Christianity; that it is in order *first* to induce them to join the Christian sect and adopt the Christian name, in the hope that, being thus brought under the influence of Christian doctrines and institutions, they may in time become real Christians. The apostles themselves proceeded in this way; and there was no other way in which they could proceed. What we object to is, that any should feel chiefly anxious to convert men to nominal Christianity; that they should feel satisfied with converting men to nominal Christianity; that they should think their work done, or half done, when men are induced to join the Christian sect and submit to its outward rites, and assume the Christian name. Men are not real Christians because they are nominal Christians, because they belong to any one of the Christian sects, or because they are ever so sincerely devoted to the Christian name. Men are not real Christians because they are Calvinists, or Unitarians, or Baptists. They are not real Christians until, as individuals, they breathe the Christian spirit, and live a Christian life.

Again, we sometimes hear of Christian communities, of Christian States; but the distinctions pointed out in this discourse between nominal and real Christians make it clear that there is no State, and that there never has been one, which can be pronounced Christian except in name. Christianity may be perhaps the popular worship, its truth and importance may be recognized by the laws, and provision may be made for its institutions by public enactments, and perhaps at the public charge. Still this does not prove that the State, considered as a whole community, is penetrated throughout with the Christian spirit, and determined and governed in all things by Christian principles. It only proves that the State, in its public capacity, has joined itself to the Christian sect; that it calls itself Christian; that it is to be regarded as part of Christendom; that it is a

Christian State and not a Mahometan State: in one word, that it is *nominally* Christian. Name, if you can, the State in any age, or in any part of the world, which, considered as a whole community, can be pronounced really Christian! Where is the nation in which the laws, the customs, the institutions, — in which literature, public opinion, and public amusements, — are uniformly or generally in accordance with the spirit and precepts of the New Testament? Where is the government that is administered by none but real Christians, and invariably or generally according to Christian principles, and in the Christian spirit? Where is the people on the face of the earth, who, as a whole people, love God supremely, and one another as themselves? Not one, not one! I suppose that without undue national vanity we may say of the moral and religious condition of our own country, that it will compare favorably with that of any other. When we look around, however, and observe how little there is amongst us of a truly Christian spirit; what vague and imperfect notions prevail of the Christian character, of Christian philanthropy, and even of Christian honesty; and behold also the jealousies and the chicanery, and the mean and bad passions which trouble the course of human affairs, and the consent in great public wrongs, — I fear it would be a mere compliment to say even of the people of this community, that they are as a body, that they are universally, or even generally, real Christians. Doubtless in every Christian community individuals may be found who are real Christians; but, I repeat it, the community, considered as a whole community, is Christian only in name. History has not, as yet, furnished us with a single example of a truly Christian people, of a whole community pervaded and governed throughout by the spirit and law of Christ.

I go further than this. I have spoken of States, and I would now speak of religious sects. I believe there is no sect, and that there never has been one, which can be pronounced Christian except in name. I make no exceptions, for I believe in my conscience there is none. Doubtless there is no considerable religious sect in which individuals cannot be found who are real Christians; and in some religious sects there may be more real Christians than in others; and the views held by some sects may be, in themselves considered, peculiarly favorable to the nurture of a truly Christian character. Still, when we come to read the history of these sects, I fear we shall find that, without a solitary exception, they have been swayed, as sects, by a spirit oftentimes not only not Christian, but positively antichristian. I fear it will be found that, without a solitary exception, they have borrowed their notions of policy, as sects, from the world, and not from the New Testament. We may think that it was different formerly, but history does not confirm this impression. Cardinal Barberini being present at Rome, at the canonization of a saint whom he had himself personally known, and known to be unworthy of that honor, could not help whispering to a bystander, that these new saints put him in strange doubts and difficulties about the old ones. I fear it will be found, moreover, that those especially who take the lead in religious sects, and stamp the character of the party, are not commonly men very remarkable for the Christian virtues of charity, meekness, and heavenly mindedness. In common parlance, we call all these sects Christian sects; and it is proper that we should, for they have a right to the *name*. As sects, they are probably sincere in their profession of attachment to the Christian name, and belong therefore to the Christian denomination; in other words, they are nominally Christian. They have a right to the name, all of them. They are Christians in contradistinction to atheists or deists, to Jews or Mahometans. They have a right to the name, — all of them; but still they want the reality. They are not, as sects, pervaded throughout, and influenced and determined in all their measures, by the spirit and example of Jesus.

Thus have I endeavored to point out and illustrate the true distinction between nominal and real Christianity. I have also shown that it is nominal Christianity only, which can be said as yet to prevail even in Christendom, in Christian States, and in Christian sects. One great revolution has been wrought in converting men to nominal Christianity. Another and still more important revolution remains yet to be wrought, in order to convert them, as a body, to real Christianity.

From this doctrine there are two practical inferences which I must entreat you to ponder well.

In the first place, it supplies us with a full and perfect answer to the popular objection to Christianity, derived from the inconsistencies and vices of *professed* Christians. They are not the inconsistencies and vices of real Christians. Now it is manifestly absurd to make Christianity answerable for the conduct of those who, by the very terms of the proposition, have not as yet been converted to real Christianity. Bring me a man who is thoroughly imbued with the spirit of the gospel, and who has brought his whole life and mind into subjection to the law of Christ, and I admit that it would be perfectly fair to try the merits of the religion by the conduct of the disciple. Point me to a community that is pervaded and governed throughout by the spirit and maxims of the New Testament, and I admit that it would be perfectly fair, in such a case, to try the merits of the religion by its actual results. But in the name of reason and common sense, why would you charge on Christianity itself the inconsistencies and vices which originate in a want of Christianity? With what show even of plausibility can you make real Christianity responsible for the inconsistencies and vices of those who are not real Christians, but only nominal Christians?

My second inference from the doctrine of this discourse is still more personal and direct in its application. Amidst the immense number and variety of nominal Christians, where are we to look for real Christians? And yet it is only in proportion as men become real Christians, that they can hope to be saved. Submitting to ordinances will avail us nothing; assenting to propositions will avail us nothing; being clamorous for what we deem *the truth* will avail us nothing; giving our bodies to be burned will avail us nothing, — without the temper and life of a real Christian. How many thousand martyrs have poured out their blood like water in the name of Christ, and yet have not breathed his spirit, and therefore were none of his! The world stands in need of another regeneration, deeper and more spiritual than the first, converting men from nominal Christianity to real Christianity. We want something more than mere profession; we want something more than mere belief, however sincere; we want something more than mere zeal, however disinterested and self-sacrificing; we want something more than a mere external sobriety and virtue. We must pray to be imbued with the Christian spirit; we must resolve to live a Christian life. "Not every one that saith unto me, Lord, Lord, shall enter into the kingdom of heaven; but he that doeth the will of my Father which is in heaven." "Many will say to me, in that day, Lord, Lord, have we not prophesied in thy name, and in thy name have cast out devils, and in thy name done many wonderful works? And then will I profess unto them, I never knew you; depart from me, ye that work iniquity."

1830–1861.

VIII.

THE DAILY CROSS.

"*And he said unto them all, If any man will come after me, let him deny himself, and take up his cross daily, and follow me.*" — LUKE ix. 23.

IT is often mentioned, and not without reason, as one proof of the *honesty* of the first Christians, that they did not hold out before their followers the lure of an easy or self-indulgent life. "Then," said our Saviour, "they shall deliver you up to be afflicted, and shall kill you, and ye shall be hated of all nations for my name's sake." "They shall lay hands on you, and persecute you, delivering you up to the synagogues, and into prisons; and ye shall be betrayed both by parents and brethren and kinsfolk and friends." "But these things have I told you, that when the time shall come ye may remember that I told you of them."

All must admit that this was dealing fairly and honestly with men. At the same time, I am bound to say that I think it was also dealing wisely with them. Men of a strong, earnest, and resolved spirit, the only men to be relied upon in building up a new religion, if convinced of the importance of a cause, are only won to it the more by the difficulties and dangers which environ it. To the interest of the duty is thus added the interest of the struggle. The only minds which are likely to be repelled are timid, distrustful, unsteady minds; these however are not the strength, but the weakness of a struggling cause. They constitute the unsound part of the army, which at some critical moment of the battle starts a panic, or goes over to the enemy; and by this treachery of weakness, if not of purpose, betrays all. For a forlorn hope, a hundred picked men, without an individual who knows what it is to hesitate or falter in a noble enterprise, are stronger by far than ten times that number if mixed with here and there a faint heart, sufficient to infect the whole with irresolution, with even so much as the thought of turning back. The first Christians were *picked men.* It was necessary this should be so; and that they were so, we owe it, under God, to the whirlwind of persecution which met them everywhere, winnowing the chaff from the wheat; and not only the chaff, but all the light and imperfect kernels.

In process of time, power passed out of the

hands of the pagans into those of the Christians: and, after that, none but heretics could aspire to the glory of martyrdom; and even in respect to them, the fires of persecution began to burn lower and lower. The Christian world was soon made to feel how much it had lost, in losing the purifying influence of suffering; and, to supply the defect, they very naturally resorted to artificial means: partly to self-inflicted tortures, and partly to the fasts and penances of the Church.

Of the self-inflicted tortures it is hardly possible for us, at the present day, to speak as we should, because it is hardly possible for us to enter into the thoughts and feelings of the persons whom we undertake to judge. They believed, — that is, those at least who were most active in introducing ascetic practices into the Church, believed, — that matter was wholly evil; that all our natural affections and desires were sinful, and sinful only, and that continually; that the war between the flesh and the spirit was a war of extermination; that the body was not something to be subdued and regulated, but something to be spurned, mortified, killed. With these views their duty was plain. It would be well for us if we lived up to our idea of what makes a good man, as nearly as they did up to theirs.

Of the fasts and penances of the Church I cannot say as much. Imposed, but not self-imposed, they have always been liable to be used as the instruments of tyranny and oppression on one part, and to beget nothing better than hypocrisy or formality on the other. Among a rude people, in order to tame their ferocity and turbulence, and bring them under subjection to a spiritual rule, this discipline may sometimes have answered a good purpose; but even here I suspect that the benefit has been almost always overrated. It is a required, a coerced, and therefore for the most part an outside penitence. It has no living root, like the self-tortures of the anchorite, in the moral aspirations of the sufferer himself. However this may be, it is certain that Church fasts and penances in these last days, except with the very ignorant and a few devotees, have sunk into a byword for their insignificance.

These are some of the ways in which the Christians of other times were called upon, or thought themselves called upon, to crucify "the flesh with the affections and lusts;" but it is plain that *we* must look elsewhere for occasions to prove our faith and constancy.

But the times just referred to have been, and have passed away. Persecution, in the sense in which that word used to be understood, is no longer to be expected in the ordinary course of events. Neither are any of us likely, with our notions of life and duty, to think it necessary or wise to submit to ascetic practices, whether self-imposed, or imposed by the Church. Still, what our Lord says in the text must be considered as applicable to all times: "If any man will come after me, let him deny himself, and take up his cross daily, and follow me."

Never was the earnest inculcation of this precept more needed than at the present day. Surrounded, as many Christians now are, by ease, security, and abundance, they are tempted not only to neglect the self-denying virtues, but almost to forget their obligations and the important place they hold in the Christian life. When a cross is actually laid upon us by Providence, when it cannot be averted, all I suppose will agree that it ought to be borne, and borne with firmness and a calm trust; but that we are frequently called upon to submit to self-denial not from necessity but from choice, or, in other words, to take up our cross *voluntarily*, and to take it up *daily*, is not so generally conceded. To some it may even sound as no better than a futile attempt to revive the self-inflicted austerities of the cloister, which the age, as all Protestants at least will allow, has outgrown.

What, then, is meant by that self-denial which is so frequently enjoined upon all men, in the New Testament? Every one is required to take up his cross daily; but *what to crucify?*

There is the more need of some explanation here, because the term *self-denial*, if literally understood, might mislead. We are not to deny *ourselves* in the sense of denying our *whole* selves; for this would be to deny what is good in us, as well as what is bad. What then, I ask again, are we to deny?

Every one must be conscious of being under the influence of two orders of propensities and desires: *the higher*, or those which belong to him as a rational and moral being; and *the lower*, or those which belong to him as a sensual and selfish being. Even the lower tendencies of our nature are not bad *in themselves;* they are bad only when they interfere with the proper development, or with the proper gratification, of the higher. Here then it is, that Christian self-denial begins and ends; we are to deny the solicitations of our lower nature, whenever they interfere with the aspirations of our higher nature. Christian self-denial does not require us to deny our nature as a whole, but only to be true to our nature as a whole; that is, to take care that the rightful subordination amongst its various springs of action shall be maintained.

Christian self-denial does not require us to deny our *happiness;* that is to say, our *highest* happiness; but only to be true to *that* happiness, by repressing every appetite or passion which puts itself in opposition to it, or which tends to frustrate or endanger it.

Again, neither reason nor the New Testament makes the moral value of self-denial depend on the *pain it costs.* This *pain* is the measure, not so much of what we *have done*, as of what we have *yet to do*, in order to make ourselves thoroughly good men. It is manifestly the sign of an unformed or of a half-formed Christian character, to find it *hard* to keep under the lower propensities of our nature, when they stand in the way of moral progress. If we cannot give up without reluctance or regret any appetite or desire, as soon as we see it to interfere with our highest good, so much the worse for us; but we can hardly set down such reluctance or regret, or the pain it gives us, to the score of merit. Who would think that a man ought to be praised or rewarded for the pain it costs him to keep himself from lying or stealing? He would feel none of this pain, if his nature had been properly disciplined; and the moral value of self-denial consists in its tendency to bring about this discipline: to teach every part of our nature to know its place, and keep its place, and thus to co-operate harmoniously and spontaneously in promoting the highest good of the individual. The moral value of self-denial does not consist in the pain it costs, but in its tendency to induce a *habit of virtue*, under the influence of which the practice of virtue will become *agreeable and easy;* so as, in the end, that is to say in heaven, to dispense with the necessity of self-denial altogether.

Self-denial, therefore, is not an end but a means; the end being to convert, through the power of habit, a painful and constrained obedience into a joyful and free obedience. The highest form of virtue is not the virtue of self-denial, but of earnest and irrepressible love; when duty has ceased to be a task and become a pleasure, a kind of necessity. Hence that sublime doctrine of the New Testament. "Whosoever is born of God doth not commit sin, for his seed remaineth in him; and he cannot sin, because he is born of God."

Not entirely satisfied with this view of the subject, some may still ask, "What! is there not more moral worth in an action requiring great self-denial, than in one requiring little or none? For example; is not a choleric man more meritorious for keeping his temper, under great provocation, than he would be if by nature or habit mild and self-possessed? Is not a man who abstains from intoxicating drinks, though he hankers for them, more meritorious than he would be if he did not hanker for them, if he loathed them?"

These questions are often put in a tone which would seem to imply that they must be answered in the affirmative; yet such an answer will be found to involve consequences which nobody, I suppose, would care to admit. It would follow that, just in proportion as a man succeeds in subduing and extirpating his evil inclinations, the merit of his obedience must become less and less, until at last it entirely disappears. Thus, to recur to the examples just given; were a man to succeed in entirely overcoming a choleric temper, or a hankering for intoxicating drinks, — as a good man is very likely to do, or at any rate aims to do, — after that he would be gentle or temperate as a matter of course; but there would be no merit in it, because there would be no difficulty in it: it would be worth nothing, for it would cost nothing. Or take a case of a somewhat different description. Suppose a man to begin to attend church from a sense of duty, though it is extremely irksome to him. For a while, on the principle assumed above, there would be great merit in it, because it would call for great self-denial. But suppose the man, in process of time, to become deeply interested in religion and in religious services. Of course he will still continue to attend church. Now, however, instead of its being irksome to him, he finds the greatest delight in it. But if so, then, on the principle assumed above, there would be no merit in it; attending church would be no better than a kind of self-indulgence.

Obviously, therefore, it will not do to estimate the deserts of a Christian by the degree of self-denial which accompanies his conduct; certainly not by the degree of self-denial which *now* accompanies his conduct.

Most of the error or perplexity on this subject has probably grown out of not distinguishing between the judgment passed on *single actions*, and the judgment passed on the character of *the agent*. In pronouncing judgment on a single action we are influenced and determined, I allow, in no small measure, by the amount of self-denial it costs. We admire an act of self-sacrifice; we cannot help admiring such an act, whatever we may think of the agent in other respects; that is to say, whatever we may think of his character generally. We cannot help admiring a generous or just action when performed in the face of great difficulty and great opposition; because it was less to be expected on this account; because it supposes great effort, and this, again, great strength of purpose; because it is a triumph of the *human will*, a triumph in which we can all sympathize, and one in which we all seem to share. Hence, I suppose it is, that our Saviour has said, "Likewise joy shall be in heaven over one sinner that repenteth, more than over ninety-and-nine just persons which need no repentance." It is not meant that the new convert is an object of more favor or confidence, in himself considered, than a man of tried and confirmed virtue; undoubtedly he is not an object of as much of either. Still there is something in the single act by which the sinner breaks away from his old habits, and tramples under foot his evil inclinations, and turns unto God, — something so unexpected, so auspicious, so heroic, — that it cannot fail to excite at the moment in all good beings, on earth and in heaven, a peculiar joy and admiration, — a momentary burst of exultation.

But the joy and admiration inspired by a single action, at the moment of its performance, have nothing to do, at any rate nothing to do definitely, with what will become of the agent himself at last, or with the sober and just estimate to be made of his deserts on the whole. As men we are to be judged, as the Scriptures say, according to our deeds; but not according to our deeds taken singly and abstractly, and without reference to the influence they have on ourselves; nor yet according to any real or supposed preponderance of our good deeds over our bad deeds, or of our bad deeds over our good deeds, taken abstractly and numerically. We are to be judged according to our deeds in this sense only: we are to be judged according to the moral state or condition in which all our deeds, taken together, have left us. "God looketh on the heart." Every man is to be judged according to what he is in himself; according to what he has *become*, — his past actions having nothing to do with his present or his future prospects, except in so far as they have contributed to make his dispositions and character what they now *are;* or, in other words, have contributed to make him what he has *become.*

Hence it appears that the rule, according to which we pass judgment on *actions* taken singly and abstractly, is very different from that according to which we pass judgments on *men.* The glory of an *action* depends on its unexpectedness, on its difficulty, on the moral force or moral courage it displays, sometimes even on the general degradation of the agent; for the glory of the single action may be, that one so degraded in other respects should suddenly raise himself to so noble a thought, to so high an endeavor. But, when we speak of the worth of a *man*, we always make it to depend on what he is *in himself;* that is to say, on the habits he has formed; not on the amount of discipline which he has undergone, simply and abstractly considered, but on the *effect this discipline has had* on his character; on the degree of harmony, purity, and elevation of soul which he has actually gained; in one word, to adopt the language in which the Scriptures express the change, on his having been "born again," on his having become "a new creature." We think better of an action in proportion to the difficulty and self-denial it involves; but, when we turn from the action to the man, we think better of *him* in proportion as he is in a condition to do the same thing *without* any difficulty at all, *without* any self-denial at all. The best man, the perfect man, if we could find one, would be a person with whom, in ordinary circumstances, it would be as easy and natural to fulfil all righteousness, as to breathe.

This distinction being understood and admitted, we see at once that self-denial is not the Christian character, nor an essential part of it, but only one of the instrumentalities by which the Christian character is formed. Self-denial does not belong to us as Christians; that is to say, as *perfect* Christians: for, in the perfect Christian, duty and pleasure become one; no place is therefore left for self-denial: it belongs to us as persons who *aspire* to be Christians, who are *learning* to be Christians.

In saying this, however, I do but say that, in point of fact, it belongs *to us all;* for what can be truly said of the best of us, except that we are *learning* or *aspiring* to be Christians? — some in the midst of the process, some just beginning, others only thinking about beginning, if indeed so much as that. In respect to all such persons without exception, the gospel teaches that it is only by self-denial, — that is, by crossing, restraining, and subduing the lower tendencies of our nature whenever they interfere with the higher tendencies of our nature, — that each one can bring his character into harmony with itself, and subject the whole to the law of Christ.

The fact that we have fallen upon easy and prosperous times, and are tempted by abundance and opportunity on every side, only makes this discipline *so much the more indispensable.* In a barren and poor country the people are abstemious and frugal, not from self-denial, but from necessity. And so in the case of individuals. An ambitious young man, starting in life with nothing to depend upon but his own exertions to make his way in the world, is comparatively in no danger from the love of ease or pleasure: if his conscience or his ambition do not restrain him, his want of means will. It is not until luxury abounds, and the means of self-indulgence are brought within the reach of all, that degeneracy is likely to prevail; for it is not until then, that the vices of self-indulgence become *possible*, — I mean, generally so, and to a ruinous extent. This, then, would seem to be the law: As any people advance in wealth and refinement, *the restraints of necessity* are gradually taken off; after which, it is only in so far as their place is supplied by *the restraints of self-denial*, that the national decay and ruin are stayed. History tells us how it was with the civilizations which were founded on paganism. *They* stood the trials of adversity; but under the trials of prosperity they all fell. If a better fate awaits the civilizations founded on Christianity, it will be mainly owing, under God, to its doctrine of the cross; to the fact that these civilizations are thoroughly penetrated with the spirit of him who has said, "If any man will come after me, let him deny himself, and take up his cross daily, and follow me."

Not only is self-denial becoming every day more necessary, but also *more difficult*. Much is said of the self-denying virtues of our fathers, under the hardships and privations of the early settlement of this country, and in their struggle for independence; and I heartily concur in the honor in which they are held on this account. Still all must agree, that it is not as hard to bear restraints which our condition has laid upon us, and which we know we cannot throw off if we would, as it is to bear restraints which we have laid upon ourselves, and which we know we can continue to bear, or not, as we please. No doubt it is hard to perform a task set us by an inevitable Providence; but it is harder still to set the same task to ourselves, and still be faithful to it. In the former case, we have but one thought: *it must be borne;* in the latter, we have the alternative, duty on one side, and indulgence on the other. We can bear it or not as we please; and it is the knowledge of this *alternative*, more even than hunger and nakedness, more even than prisons and scaffolds, which tries men's souls. We often hear it said, that the spirit of martyrdom is dying out. I believe no such thing. I believe that, if persecution *for opinion's sake* were to be revived to-day, there would be as many who would be burned at the stake, rather than deny the faith, as at any former period. The spirit of this form of martyrdom is latent merely because the exigency does not exist to call it forth. Meanwhile we have our own peculiar cross to bear,—a cross, too, which in one respect is harder to bear than that of persecution; for it is not laid upon us by others, but we are required to take it up of our own accord and lay it on ourselves, and bear it with unshrinking fortitude, with untiring constancy.

What adds to the difficulty of self-denial at the present day is, that it requires not only self-control, but *self-knowledge.* Every man is called upon in the text to take up his cross daily; but what to crucify? I answer, *His bosom sin.* As was said before, self-denial does not consist in denying our whole selves, but in denying any and every propensity of our lower nature which comes in competition with our higher nature. It is to deny the body, that we may be true to the soul; it is to deny what is worldly in us, that we may be true to what is heavenly in us; it is neither more nor less than a practical recognition of the sovereignty of reason and conscience and faith over passion and appetite. But the rebel which is to be denied and subdued in your heart is probably very different from the rebel which is to be denied and subdued in mine. With one man it is the love of ease; with another it is the love of pleasure; with another it is an irascible temper; with another it is the love of money; with another it is a selfish ambition. Nay, we may have aspirations, which, in their proper connection and subordination, are among the most amiable and commendable, — such as a thirst for knowledge, a desire of honorable distinction, — but which turn traitors when they tempt us to be unfaithful to virtue and religion. Our Saviour has said, "He that loveth father or mother more than me, is not worthy of me; and he that loveth son or daughter more than me, is not worthy of me." Every one therefore must be willing to *know* the cherished idol of his own heart, whatever it may be, though aware that his object in knowing it is, that he may deny it and put it under his feet.

Remember also what has been already intimated more than once. We are not merely to deny, we are to *subdue*, our rebellious inclinations, — the lusts and desires that war against the soul. The moral worth of self-denial does not consist in the pain it costs, but in its tendency to curb the lower propensities of our nature, to restore a lost symmetry and harmony of character, to induce the habit of natural, easy, and spontaneous obedience to the Divine will. A man may fight against his sins all his life long, and fight bravely, and die fighting; if however he does not *conquer* them, it is plain that he will die in his sins. The battle is necessary; the battle however is not for the sake of the battle, but for the sake of the victory. The life of God in the soul of man *begins* in struggle and self-denial; but it *ends* in love and repose.

What then, in conclusion, does Christianity require of us under the name of self-denial? Not *self-mortification;* which is nothing but the folly of morbid consciences. Not *austerities* of any kind; which are nothing but the despotism of a proud spirit playing the tyrant over its own tastes and inclinations. But she warns us, that our condition in this life is not constituted on the plan of ease and safety, but on that of difficulty and conflict. She warns us that our nature, if left to itself, will go to destruction. She warns us that the first duty incumbent on every man that lives is the duty of ruling his own spirit, and putting every rebellious principle under his feet. Under these circumstances, what religion requires of us is the firm and sure step of one who has gained the mastery over himself, and uses this mastery in the pursuit of the noblest ends by the noblest means. And she requires it of us all. She requires it of us as *men;* above all, she requires it of us as *Christians.* She holds up before us the sacred symbol of our faith, and proclaims the law: *By this you are to conquer.* And, knowing our weakness and our need of help, she conjures us, she beseeches us, to bow meekly and humbly before the Crucified One, whom we acknowledge as our Example and Lord, that we may arm ourselves with the same mind that was in him. She also comforts us by repeating his words: "In this world ye shall have tribulation: but be of good cheer; I have overcome the world."

1851–1858.

IX.

ON KEEPING THE PROMISES WE MAKE TO OURSELVES.

"*And Jacob vowed a vow, saying, If God will be with me, and will keep me in this way that I go, and will give me bread to eat and raiment to put on, so that I come again to my father's house in peace, then shall the Lord be my God.*" — GENESIS xxviii. 20, 21.

THIS is the first formal vow on record, though the practice itself appears to have existed from the earliest times. It had its foundation in human nature. In the infancy of the world men did not look on God as we do; they did not regard him as a Spirit, or think that those who worship him should worship him in spirit and in truth. They reverenced him, it is true, as a superior Being; but still as having like interests and like passions with themselves, — susceptible to attentions and flattery, expecting favor for favor, and therefore to be propitiated by votive services and offerings. The Jewish lawgiver, finding this custom in existence, adopted it into his code, though, as it would seem, not so much to recommend it, as to subject it to proper regulations, and to prevent abuses. According to him, vows when made were, as a general rule, to be kept; still he is careful to say, "But if thou shalt forbear to vow, it shall be no sin."

In our days vows have fallen into disuse, partly, no doubt, from the spread of a more rational faith; and partly also, I am afraid, from a less worthy cause, namely, a growing neglect on the part of many to recognize their personal relations to God in the affairs of life, or to appeal to the sanctions of religion in aid of duty. I do not mean that men have given up, or are likely to give up, promising what they will do in the future. The change consists in this: instead of making these promises, as they once did, to God, they now make them to one another; or, more frequently still, to themselves. Hardly an individual can be found who does not at times promise himself, that, in certain contingencies, he will take a certain course or do certain things which he believes to be right. Thus a large portion of the most solemn promises which we make consists of those which we make to ourselves; and my object in the present discourse will be to set forth our duty in respect to this class of promises, — *the promises which we make to ourselves.*

Even the schoolboy, mortified at the poor appearance he has made after having neglected his lesson, promises himself that he will be more attentive in future, and avoid the recurrence of a like disgrace. An ingenuous youth, betrayed into imprudence or crime by his inexperience, or by bad counsels, promises himself that in future he will be more on his guard. A man of a quick and hot temper says or does, in a fit of unrestrained anger, what he afterwards sincerely regrets; he therefore promises himself that in future he will keep a harder curb on his passions. A man is led on little by little in play, until he finds that he has gained or lost a considerable sum, — in short, that he is fast becoming a gambler; and, alarmed at the tendency of these things, he promises himself that no temptation shall ever induce him again to take a card into his hands. A man awakes after the debauch of the last night, feverish and sick, ashamed and penitent, and promises himself that from that moment he will break for ever from the scenes, company, and amusements which have so often had power to overcome his best resolutions. A man begins a new study, engages in a new and difficult undertaking, enters upon new and important relations in life; and, made serious by the uncertainty of the future, he promises himself that nothing which he can do or dare shall be wanting to his success. A man is interrupted in a worldly and thoughtless career by a dangerous sickness, and being forcibly led by his situation to review his past conduct, and consider his unfitness for eternity, he promises himself that, should he recover, he will commence a new life.

I might go on multiplying illustrations without end, but enough has been said to indicate the number and variety of the promises which men are continually making to themselves. They constitute, as I have said, a large proportion of the best considered and most solemn promises which any of us make. Nobody will deny that they are made, for the most part, in good faith, and with a serious purpose of fulfilling them; that they are entered into in our best moods, that they are the dictates of our best judgment, and that it would be best for us on every account to keep them. Yet the readiness and frequency with which they are broken has become a proverb. Why is this?

Some may think it not only accounted for, but justified or at least excused, on the ground that the promises which we make to ourselves are merely secret purposes or resolutions, which we are at liberty to change when we please. But I cannot agree to either part of this statement. Let it be that the promises in question are only another way of saying to ourselves what we propose to do in particular cases; in other words, that they are nothing but another name for *good resolutions*. Even in this view of the matter, I deny that we are at liberty to change them *when we please*. No matter whether we regard them as promises properly so called, or merely as good resolutions, we have no right to forget them, or set them aside, when the moment for action arrives. We have no right *not to make* the good resolutions; much less, to break them after they have been made.

But I do not concede what has just been assumed. A clear distinction can be drawn, as it seems to me, between *general* resolutions to do well, and specific promises made to ourselves that we will pursue a particular line of conduct. You know how it is in our dealings with others in analogous cases. If I merely say, in general phrase, that I mean to serve a friend, but do not promise any particular service, he cannot claim any particular service at my hands. If, on the contrary, my expression of good wishes takes the form of a specific promise to do this or that, he can hold me to my word. And so in my intercourse with myself. So long as I can put myself off with good resolutions; that is, with general purposes to repent and do well hereafter, — I may postpone fulfilling them day after day, and month after month, and year after year, and yet not feel that I have abandoned them. I may still hold and cherish the same good resolutions to repent and do well hereafter. But if I solemnly promise myself that on a certain occasion, or at a certain time, I will do a particular thing, and fail to do it, I know and feel that I have broken my word. I know and feel that I cannot be relied on; and, what is more and worse, that I cannot rely on myself. Again, a particular and specific promise is more even than a particular and specific resolution for another reason. In all such cases, the promise is the resolution *begun to be carried out.* I have proceeded so far as to give my word to that effect; and if this is nothing, it must be because my word is nothing.

Again, others may hastily conclude that promises made to ourselves are not binding, because they are not *published;* because they are known to ourselves alone; because there is no witness. But here, as before, I cannot admit either the fact, or the inference from the fact. What is it, I would begin by asking, that makes any promise binding? Not human laws; for all human laws might be struck out of being, without making our promises any the less binding on our consciences. Nor yet the *mere* fact that by publishing the promise *we have raised expectations in others;* for a promise extorted from us by force, or obtained by false pretences, will have the effect to raise expectations *in others:* but this will not make such a promise morally binding. A promise is binding, when in a fair and full view of the subject we voluntarily enter into engagements, by which we stand pledged to regulate our future conduct. Now all this holds true of the promises in question. For example, when a sick man promises that, should he recover, he will amend his ways; or the conscience-stricken oppressor, that he will repent of his misdeeds and make reparation for the wrongs he has done, — in all such cases it will not be denied that a promise is really made, and made voluntarily, and in a fair and full view of the subject, and with an expectation of performing it; and that such will be our duty. But there is no witness! Suppose, for a moment, there were none; this might affect the means of proving or enforcing the promise, but not its moral obligation. If you were at a loss whether you had made the promise or not, it might be of importance to call in witnesses to satisfy you on that point; but what need is there of witnesses to prove a fact which is not doubted? Besides, this supposition that there is no witness, is wholly gratuitous. There is a witness, — that Being whose eye is everywhere, on the evil and on the good, — there is a witness whose presence is felt and acknowledged at the time of making the promise. Moreover, it is the witness of *that* Eye, and not the witness of the many eyes of the world, which is the foundation of our responsibility in all cases, even for our most public acts. That Eye is upon us in all places, at all times. It penetrates into our most secret thoughts; it is acquainted with our most secret promises; it remembers them whether we do or not, and it will call them into judgment at the last day.

There is also another ground for evading our duty in respect to the promises we make to ourselves, which is likely to occur to some minds. It may be said that, when a man makes a promise to himself, he is both parties to the contract; not only promiser, but promisee; so that should he afterwards conclude to break it, he can do so without blame on obtaining his own consent: for this, as in the present case it comprehends the consent of both parties, is authority sufficient to annul the most solemn compact. But, in the first place, whoever should reason thus forgets, — no, he does not forget, but he refuses or neglects to consider, — that when such promises are entered into it is distinctly understood on the part of the promiser's conscience, that they shall never be made the subject of this sort of tampering. No one, I suppose, will pretend that the promiser, at the time of making such a promise, *means* to leave himself at liberty to keep it or not as he sees fit; for if so, why make the promise? He would do what he sees fit when the time comes round, without the promise, just as well.

Moreover, though the promise is made to the same person who makes it, it is not made to the same person in the same capacity. It is the self in both cases, but the self considered as divided into two, — the acting self and the judging self. It is the *will* making a promise to the *conscience*. Make the most, therefore, of this right to release ourselves from the obligation of such a promise, it is a right which belongs exclusively to the conscience; for it was to the conscience that the promise was originally made. But who will say, that, when we break the promises we have made to ourselves, it is commonly from the calm and unbiassed consent of our consciences? Who does not know that, in nine cases out of ten, our unfaithfulness to such promises is owing to the re-ascendancy of the very passions against which the promise was directed, and which it was intended to restrain, but which are again allowed to bear down conscience, and the promise too? Indeed, I might insist that in most instances the promise is not so much made to ourselves, as to God. It is, to all intents and purposes, the reproduction, under a modern form, of the ancient vow.

Even though *in form* we make the promise to ourselves, we often do it looking to God as the witness and guaranty of our sincerity ; which virtually involves a promise *to Him*, that we will be faithful to the promises which we make *to ourselves*. And He will hold us to such promises.

When therefore, in a moral and religious view of our responsibilities, we promise ourselves to fulfil a particular duty, it appears to me that this promise is of the nature of a bond on the soul. It is an engagement voluntarily entered into, in a fair and full view of the circumstances ; and there is also a witness, or rather there are witnesses, to the engagement, — God and our own consciences, — to whom we are pledged for its fulfilment, and often under all the solemnities of a religious vow. Habit or custom may make it *seem* a light thing to trifle with such engagements ; but in morals it is not a light thing ; in the sight of God it is not a light thing. Neither human laws nor public opinion have any thing to do with the making or the keeping of these solemn engagements ; it is enough to know that they will be judged at the bar of eternal justice, and that any attempt to evade their strict fulfilment by casuistical distinctions will be regarded like the kindred one in social morality, — that of attempting to avoid the payment of an honest debt by a legal quibble.

Apart also from these clear and solemn inculcations of conscience and religion, I might appeal to every man's *self-respect*, as a motive to fulfil the promises he makes to himself. Is it not an humbling and mortifying thought, that we cannot depend on our own word for our own good? As for the promises of others, we expect they will often fail us. We expect to be often deceived, cheated, betrayed by other people; but has it come to this, that we cannot rely on ourselves? If we could believe that our infidelity to the promises we are now considering grew out of a real change of opinion as to the wisdom of them, it would be different. But it is not so. When the drunkard returns to his cups, or the gamester to his haunts, after having solemnly abjured them in his own thought, do you suppose, does anybody suppose, does he even suppose himself, that it is because he has altered his mind as to the ruinous tendency of such conduct? No! it is mere weakness and irresolution; the bondage of evil habit. With his eyes open to the folly of his course, and perfectly aware of the promises he is violating, he returns to practices which he still, in his better judgment, condemns and abhors as much as ever. Who, I ask again, is willing that this should be said of him, that it should be a faithful picture of his own life, even though we were to leave out of view duty and religion, and look only to self-respect? Yet *it is* a faithful picture of every one's life, who cannot rely on the promises he makes to himself.

Shall we then abstain from making such promises, lest we should incur the guilt and shame of violating them? There are many, I know, who contend against all making of promises respecting the future, on the plea that we ought to do what we think to be right at the time, taking care to leave ourselves as much untrammelled on moral questions as possible. But this reasoning proceeds on the mistaken notion, that our greatest danger is either that we shall not *know* what is right, or that we shall not do it from the *highest* motive. On the contrary, our greatest danger in point of fact is, that, though we know what is right, we shall fail to do it from *any* motive; being turned aside by passion, or some supposed present interest, or mere indifference or apathy. Hence it follows that what we most need is, to fortify *beforehand* our general purpose to do well, especially in respect to those dangers and temptations which we have found to have the greatest power over us.

Behold, then, the occasion and use of the open pledge and the secret promise! They do not displace a sense of duty, and the fear of God; but they reënforce these motives, and often give them the victory. Having pledged ourselves beforehand to our own souls that we will take and pursue a certain course, when the moment of trial arrives we shall feel, in addition to all the other motives, the motive growing out of having solemnly entered into such an engagement. Frail and uncertain as this dependence is, it is *something;* and it is not for beings, weak and tempted as we are, to reject or to slight any auxiliary to virtue. Nay, nothing truly great and excellent can be attained in any profession or calling, unless a man prescribes to himself a particular line of conduct, and adheres to it with constancy. Yet this is to promise himself what he will do; and having done so, if he has not truthfulness and stability enough to keep the promise, he is born to inferiority as certainly and irrevocably as if it were stamped on his forehead.

Besides, in our present circumstances we cannot refrain altogether from making promises to ourselves, even if we try. When we look abroad on the works of God, and behold them everywhere marked with the traces of Divine benignity, how is it possible for us not to promise ourselves to lead a life of grateful obedience to the Giver of all good? When we open the Scriptures and read there the story of the merits and sacrifices of the sinless One, and dwell on his example of unearthly purity and peace, and are touched by his redeeming spirit, how is it possible that we should not promise ourselves to become his disciples, — if not to-day, at least at some future time? When we turn our eyes inward on our own hearts, and see there the ruins of many, many broken resolutions, and the dark and deep stains which passion and frivolity, and the world, and the beginnings of many crimes have left on our undying souls, how is it possible that we should not promise ourselves, in our intervals of serious reflection, that we will turn from evil to good? It is but the spontaneous and, I had almost said, irrepressible effort of an awakened mind to put itself into an attitude to begin obedience to the dictates of reason and conscience, and the requisitions of a just and holy God. The worst men need not make themselves worse than they are; even they have their intervals of serious reflection. Amidst all its seeming thoughtlessness, amidst all its real degradation, the human heart still yearns for better things, aspires to better things, promises itself better things. We cannot help these promises, if we would; we ought not to try to suppress them, if we could: but we should concentrate our whole moral strength on the purpose to keep them.

Religion itself is not more exacting of us than we often are of ourselves. Were we to listen now to all the good resolutions we have at any time formed, all the clear, distinct, and solemn promises we have made to ourselves, we should find that nothing is required of us in the gospel, except to keep our own word. This wonderful consent and harmony between the Bible and the aspirations of the human soul in its best moods is, perhaps, to most minds the strongest, or at least the most convincing, evidence of the heavenly origin of both. There is nothing in the warnings and counsels of God which sounds strange or unfamiliar to our better nature, to the inner man. "For that which I do, I allow not: for what I would, that do I not; but what I hate, that do I. If then I do that which I would not, I consent unto the law that it is good." There is nothing which the teachings of Christ, or the example of holy and devout men, or the exhortations of loving friends call upon us to do or become, which many of us have not promised ourselves to do and become a hundred times. Where is our consistency, where is our self-respect, where is our reverence for truth, or our fear of God, that we should promise and not perform? May that grace, which alone is sufficient for us, turn our hearts anew to these promises, and help us to fulfil them! May that mercy which never faileth have pity and forgive, whenever we come short of it, from weakness and frailty, or the sudden and unforeseen stress of temptation! And, in the judgment of the last day, may we all find pardon and acceptance, not for our promises alone, but for our honest and unremitting endeavor to fulfil them in life and in death!

1846–1858.

X.

JESUS CHRIST MADE PERFECT THROUGH SUFFERINGS.

"*For it became him, for whom are all things, and by whom are all things, in bringing many sons unto glory, to make the captain of their salvation perfect through sufferings.*" — HEBREWS ii. 10.

THERE is so much sadness and mystery mingled in human life, that one is often tempted to think it well with those with whom it is well over. If innocence were a shield, if all the suffering in the world could be clearly seen to be retributive or corrective, the suffering would remain the same, it is true; but it would not be so difficult to account for its being permitted under the divine administration. How can we account for the fact, that Jesus Christ, the purest and most exalted of the children of God, "the holy one," should live a life of sorrow, and die at last prematurely to all human apprehension, and amidst torture and ignominy?

The declaration in the text will help us to resolve this difficulty in the providence of the All-

Wise and the All-Good. Jesus suffered, it appears, that he might be *made perfect.*

Because *a man* suffers, it does not follow necessarily that his sufferings are to be regarded as a retribution for his sins, or as a means of correcting his sins, or that they are inflicted in consequence of his sins, or even that they imply in any way that he is, or has been, a sinner. He may be a good man already, one of the best of men, "unspotted from the world;" and yet he may suffer, not that he may be made good, but that he may be made better, that he may be made perfect.

So it was preëminently with Jesus Christ, whose sufferings had nothing to do with sin, but they led to higher degrees of moral and spiritual excellence and glory. Every trial he underwent had this design and tendency, to make him *perfect;* perfect *in himself;* perfect *in his office as Mediator;* perfect *as an example to his followers.* "For it became Him, for whom are all things, and by whom are all things, in bringing many sons unto glory, to make the captain of their salvation perfect through sufferings."

The sufferings of Jesus Christ were necessary, in the first place, to make him *perfect in himself.*

Affliction, it has often been said, is like fire; what it does not melt, it hardens. If trials and disappointments do not make a man visibly better, they are apt to make him visibly worse, by making him reckless, or by inducing a misanthropic temper, or perhaps a gloomy fatalism. As a general rule, however, it will not be denied that adversity makes men more thoughtful and considerate, and gives them juster views of human life, and quickens their sense of dependence on a higher Power. Some qualities especially, which yet are essential to a perfect character, — such, for example, as patient endurance, a submissive spirit, and magnanimous self-devotion, — are only to be acquired and exercised under the discipline of that stern and rigid nurse of human virtue.

And, in reasoning on this subject, we must not suppose that these means were less necessary to our Saviour than to others, for the full development of his mind and soul. Whatever views may be entertained of his relationship to the Divinity, all Christians agree that he had a human character; and this character was formed like that of his followers, *gradually*, by adding excellence to excellence, as circumstances or the occasion drew it forth. That our Lord differed from all others in being "without sin" from the beginning is admitted; but to confound mere sinlessness with absolute perfection, to suppose he was perfect *from the beginning* in the same sense in which he actually became so afterwards, would be to contradict the express teachings of the Evangelists, who represent his piety and virtue as a *gradual* acquisition. "The child," they say, "*grew and waxed strong* in spirit, filled with wisdom; and the grace of God was upon him." And again, "Jesus *increased* in wisdom and stature, and in favor with God and man." So much then is certain. If the Bible is to be believed, his character was formed *gradually*, like that of any other person; and depended, as we must presume, in the same sense, though not perhaps in the same degree, on discipline, and cultivation, and external influences. At any rate, his character *appeared* as occasion called it forth. Hence it follows, that if the discipline of adversity is necessary, as we have seen, to the perfect unfolding of the spiritual nature of "such as are saved," it was equally so to the perfect unfolding of the spiritual nature of him who is every where set forward as "the captain of their salvation."

In reading the accounts which the sacred writers give us of the life of our Lord, I think we can perceive the effect which his sufferings had on his character in making him more and more an object of veneration and holy trust. His *first* public acts were sometimes marked with a sternness and severity, and he sometimes expresses himself with an indignation, which we do not find amidst that subdued and serene submission and benignity which throw such a melancholy interest and grandeur around the closing scenes of his earthly labors and trials. Compare his conduct at the opening of his public ministry, when with a scourge of small cords he drove out the money changers and other traffickers who had intruded themselves into the precincts of the temple; and the manner when, at least in one instance, he turned round "*in anger*" to rebuke the obduracy of his countrymen; and also the woe upon woe which through a whole chapter he thundered on their vices and their hypocrisy, — compare, I say, his conduct in these instances with his conduct afterwards; with the tears he shed over the devoted city; with his last and most affecting interview with his disciples; with the manner in which he received the kiss of Judas, though he knew it was to betray him, and in which he bore himself at his trial, amidst the insults and mockery of his judges and the soldiery; above all, with his prayer on the cross, "Father, forgive them, for they know not what they do." By studying the character of Jesus Christ under this single point of view, we shall see, I think, that it underwent a gradual change, and became more tender, more unearthly, more godlike under the afflictions he endured. Many qualities in his character which command our highest admiration, our deepest reverence, would have had no opportunity for exertion or manifestation, perhaps would not have existed, but for the sufferings which called them forth.

Besides, the constancy and moral sublimity, which our Lord could only have evinced under the severest trials, supply us with one of the strongest internal evidences of his *miraculous* character and the *divinity* of his mission. I am aware that the cross of Christ, notwithstanding the more than human magnanimity with which it was borne, created many doubts and difficulties even in the honest minds amongst his contemporaries; for they reasoned that, if he had really been the Son of God, God would not have given him over to such humiliation. But it was because they had associated with the expected Messiah the vulgar notions of greatness, and could not conceive of one as great who was not surrounded with the usual circumstances of greatness; the pomp and blazonry cf earthly power and renown. With us, however, it is different. We know that the only *true* greatness is greatness of *soul;* and that the circumstances, whatever they may be, which have the effect to display the highest degree of *this* greatness, are those which vindicate a man's claim to real superiority. Let history tell of her hero who in the day of his triumph bestrode the world like a colossus, and was worshipped as a god; but when a reverse came on his fortunes, and he was hurled from the eminence he had occupied, where then was his glory, or the qualities by which it had been won? If Jesus Christ had merely been a successful adventurer, or a mighty conqueror,—another Solomon, or another Judas Maccabæus; another Alexander or Cæsar,—his ascendancy might easily be accounted for by natural causes. But when we look on him as an obscure Galilean, educated in all the prejudices of his country, unsustained by any of the excitements or illusions which do so much to bolster up the vulgar great; betrayed and forsaken by the few he had counted on as friends; left alone, absolutely alone, to watch the gathering of that black and portentous cloud which was soon to break in thunder on his naked head; and yet with a soul unshaken, unappalled,—well, indeed, may we exclaim with the Roman centurion, who witnessed his last sufferings, "Truly this was the Son of God!" Jesus Christ might have been great, as other men have been great, and it would have *proved nothing;* but the circumstances of extreme trial in which he was placed afforded him an opportunity for displaying a greatness to which there is no parallel; a greatness not more remarkable for its degree than for its entire *originality.* Every mind capable of profound thought will appreciate this argument for Christianity; because the entire originality of our Saviour's character makes it as much a miracle that the Evangelists, with all their prejudices, should have drawn it from the imagination, as that the character itself should have really existed for them to describe.

Again, the sufferings of Jesus were necessary *in his character of Mediator*, to be as a ground of mutual sympathy between him and his followers.

One of the principal reasons which make the idea of a Mediator so grateful to the human heart is, that with our frail and imperfect natures we can feel no proper sympathy with the mysterious and awful Power, the Infinite One, we wish to propitiate. Hence the deep and inextinguishable longing of humble and devout minds for some one of a like nature, between whom and us there can be something like a fellow-feeling, on whom our religious affections may repose, and who will intercede for us before the throne of that incomprehensible Being, to us unapproachable even in thought. The great purpose and benefit of a Mediator would be compromised and lost, if he were not a Mediator who could be touched, and who had been really touched, by a sense of our infirmities. Wherefore, to borrow the words of the apostle, "In all things it behoved him to be made like unto his brethren, so that as he himself hath suffered, being tempted, he is able to succor them that are tempted."

It is also this mutual sympathy, a sympathy growing out of a consciousness of common trials and sufferings, which gives to *the example* of our Lord almost all its applicability to human conduct. If he had been made in the nature of angels, if "in all things" he had not been made like unto his brethren, to be tried as they are tried, and to suffer as they suffer, we might be told what he did, but it would not follow that it was possible for us to do the same, or even that it was proper for us to aspire to do the same. If Jesus Christ were a superior being, he might be an example to superior beings like himself, but he would not be an example to men. The very idea of an example supposes not only that we ought to imitate it, but that we can imitate it; and, of course, that we possess in general the same powers and capacities with the person by whom it is set. If Jesus Christ were a superior being above all human sympathy, his very virtues would no more be an example to us in any proper sense of that word, than the flight of an eagle or the strength of an elephant is an example to us. The whole force and pertinency of the example of Jesus consists in supposing, that he was a sharer with us in the same dangers and sorrows, that he was tried as we are tried, that he suffered as we suffer, that he triumphed as we might triumph. Unless we begin by assuming this, his *virtues*, much as we may admire them, are no more an example to us than his *miracles*.

Add to this, that the sufferings of Jesus have given a peculiar cast to his religion, and fitted it permanently to become a *religion of consolation*. Go to the various religions of paganism, if you want a religion to fill and captivate the imagination with the fictions of a beautiful mythology. Go to the religion of Mohammed, if you want a religion merely to stir the blood of warriors and voluptuaries. Go to the religion of a Socrates or a Seneca, if you merely want a religion for sages and philosophers, in which to bewilder themselves in subtle and endless speculation. But if you want a religion to assuage human woe, and wipe away the starting tear, and light up even the darkness of the tomb with a light from heaven, go to that which was dispensed by one who was himself a man of sorrows and acquainted with grief.

It is to this circumstance, I suppose, that we owe that vein of tender melancholy running through all his discourses, and his propensity to dwell on those topics which are most grateful to a bruised spirit, and also the fondness with which those who have neglected his religion in prosperity often turn to it, and cling to it, in the dark hour of peril or bereavement. Again, we submit more readily to be advised and consoled by one who has felt the same or a similar distress, because we know that he can enter fully into all our feelings, and will make allowance for the infirmities of which he has been painfully conscious in his own person; and because he has a peculiar right to insist on a submission and constancy which he has himself so signally displayed. It is to the suffering Jesus much more than to the triumphant Jesus, to his cross much more than to his crown, that the bowed spirit of an afflicted race turns with hope and trust.

What, then, is the practical use of these observations?

They teach us, in the first place, that we ought never to question or doubt the justice or benignity of the Supreme Disposer in permitting the sufferings which Jesus endured. These sufferings, we have seen, were necessary to carry out the great purposes of his mission; and of course the same wisdom and mercy which prompted the mission sanctioned also the means by which alone it could be made effectual. On the part of our Saviour himself, too, the same pure and expansive benevolence, which led him to assume his high and responsible office, made him willing also meekly to acquiesce in the sacrifices it required.

Let us rather learn, from the sufferings of Jesus, the meekness and constancy with which the chastisements of God are to be borne by all. We greatly err, if we imagine that our Lord's pain and misery were in any sense less real or less exquisite than the pain and misery of others, or that he had supports other than those which are open to us,— an approving mind, and reliance on the Divinity. The same angel which was sent to strengthen him is sent to strengthen us, if we ask for it aright. Having therefore the same consolations and supports, let it be our constant endeavor to bear the ills and sorrows of life with the same composure and dignity, and the same entire acquiescence in the will of the Supreme. After considering the sufferings of Jesus, we certainly cannot think it a strange thing that we also should be afflicted; rather let us remember that, if we suffer with Jesus, we shall also reign with him. And is it too much to expect from the afflicted, even while the hand of God is heavy upon them, to feel that the sufferings of this life are not worthy to be compared with the glory to be revealed in those who continue faithful to the end?

Let us then reflect often on the sufferings of

Jesus, and ponder them well; and especially when in the presence, as now, of the symbols intended to commemorate these sufferings, and the undying love with which they were borne, and of which they tell. We should do so that it may increase our faith, and fill us with gratitude towards him who is the resurrection and the life. Above all, we should do it that we may catch something of that spirit of constancy and self-devotion, which could say, "Father, not as I will, but as thou wilt;" "Father, into thy hands I commend my spirit." "For consider him that endured such contradiction of sinners against himself, lest ye be wearied and faint in your minds. Have ye forgotten the exhortation which speaketh unto you as unto children, My son, despise not thou the chastening of the Lord, nor faint when thou art rebuked of him; for whom the Lord loveth he chasteneth, and scourgeth every son whom he receiveth."

1828–1860.

XI.

HE KNEW WHAT WAS IN MAN.

"*For he knew what was in man.*" — JOHN ii. 25.

THERE are two kinds of knowledge which are often confounded together: a knowledge of the world, and a knowledge of human nature; a knowledge of men as they are, and a knowledge of men as they might be; a knowledge of what man has put forth, and a knowledge of what is *in* man, to be put forth if he would.

Knowledge of the world, or of men as they are, supposes one to be conversant with affairs, with the shifts and turns of fortune, and with the various humors of men. It can hardly be acquired in much perfection except by large and frequent commerce with society, by mixing with all sorts of people in all sorts of ways. This kind of knowledge, if possessed in an eminent degree, fits one to get on in the world. It makes what is called a good business man, and is more essential, perhaps, than any other quality to success in public life. It is also important to some forms of literary success. A writer or speaker, to be immediately and generally popular, must be thoroughly imbued with the prevailing opinions and sentiments, and not much in advance of them; — a little in advance of them, perhaps, that he may be looked up to as an authority; but not much in advance of them, lest he should lose the public sympathy, or fail to be understood. Even the popular statesman differs from others chiefly in this, that he can see what the multitude are going to think and do a little sooner than they can themselves; and thus is often in a condition to take ground a little in advance of the public opinion of to-day, in the assurance that it will be sustained by the public opinion of to-morrow.

But this knowledge of the world, or of men as they are, however important and necessary, is often found to exist in great perfection in persons who have but little knowledge of *human nature* properly so called; that is to say, of what is *in* man, to be put forth if he would, — of what is latent in man. And, as they have but little knowledge of it, they commonly have but little faith in it.

Jesus Christ, "in whom were hid all the treasures of wisdom and knowledge," "knew all men, and needed not that any should testify of man, for he knew what was in man." He knew at the same time what was in the world, and what was in human nature; man as he was, and man as he might be.

His knowledge of the world, of the ways of men, of men as they are, appeared in all his intercourse with the men of his day,—penetrating at a glance the half-formed purpose or thought of friend or foe. Though surrounded from the beginning by powerful and subtle enemies who were continually plotting his destruction, he was never, in a single instance, taken by surprise. Even when he went up to Jerusalem for the last time, he knew what awaited him there; he went up because his time had come. And this knowledge was necessary. In much of his conduct, and to a certain extent even in his mode of teaching, and in his teaching itself, it was necessary that he should understand and adapt himself to the ways of the world around him, to the habits and prejudices of the people with whom he had to deal.

But a more difficult and more profound knowledge than this was also required to fit him to become the Great Teacher; a teacher not of the Jews alone, but of all mankind; not of one age only, but all ages. To fulfil his high mission as the Divine Word to man, it was necessary that he should know what is *in* man, and *all* that is in man, though much of it had never before found adequate utterance; nay, had never before been revealed to the consciousness of any living being. He knew what was in man; as well what had not been put forth, as what had been put forth. He addressed himself not merely to the men he saw around him, to the *actual* man, but also to the *possible* man. He knew the immeasurable capacities and resources which were *latent* in man. And this it was which qualified him to legislate for all nations and all ages. Hence also it is, that, so long as man continues to be man, his religion will continue to meet the wants and be adapted to the condition of man. It will never become obsolete; it will never grow old: it will be "the same yesterday, to-day, and for ever."

That our Lord "knew what was in man" appears, first, in the doctrines which he taught; and, secondly, in the means by which he would have them established and propagated in the world.

In the first place, look at the doctrines which he taught. And here I speak, as my text actually leads me to do, of the doctrines which he taught *respecting man.* The doctrines respecting man, which may be said to be in some sense original with Christ and peculiar to him, are these three: First, that duty in man consists not in an outward conformity to prescribed rules, but in an inward and strict fidelity to great principles. Secondly, that true greatness in man consists not in wealth or station, nor even in intellectual gifts, but in public service and in dignity and elevation of soul. And lastly, that the secret of the highest form of influence over man is found, not by acting on his self-love or his fears, but by overcoming evil with good.

No doubt the narrow and worldly-minded Jews, when they first listened to inculcations like these, were tempted to regard them as the extravagances of a young and inexperienced reformer who did not know what he was about. But it was by falling into the error mentioned above; it was by mistaking a knowledge of what is in the world for a knowledge of what is in human nature. The great prophet of the new dispensation was able to see through, at a glance, the sevenfold disguises of worldly prejudice and worldly habit. Underneath all this he saw what was in man; he saw there the elements of a new obedience, the elements of a higher form of moral, social, and spiritual life, which the ancient civilizations, whether Jewish or pagan, had not awakened or recognized, but which it was his mission to appeal to and call forth.

Take, for example, the first of the doctrines above mentioned; namely, that duty consists not in an outward conformity to prescribed rules, but in faithfulness to great principles. We question not the wisdom or the necessity of governing the childhood of the world, as children are governed now, by outward rules arbitrarily imposed and blindly followed. And no evil is likely to ensue in such cases; for the same authority that imposes the rule can modify it, from time to time, to suit the exigency; and the modification will be accepted with the same trustful and blind acquiescence as the rule itself. But as society advances, and the human mind is unfolded more and more, man gradually passes from this state of pupilage, making it necessary that he should be governed in another manner. He is now able to understand not only the rule, but the reason or principle of the rule; and hence becomes responsible not merely for his obedience to this or that received rule, but also in some sense for the soundness of the rule itself, or at least for its right application in particular instances. In one word, he is no longer under a schoolmaster as in the primitive times, but under Christ, who has said, "Henceforth I call you not servants, for the servant knoweth not what his lord doeth; but I have called you friends, for all things that I have heard of my Father I have made known to you."

Compare the decalogue, which constitutes the

basis of the morality of the Old Testament, with the beatitudes which constitute the basis of the morality of the New; and you will readily understand what I mean by the distinction between a morality of dead rules and a morality of living principles. "Blessed are the merciful;" "blessed are the peace-makers;" "blessed are the pure in heart." Here no unbending formula is prescribed. We are not commanded to do this or that particular thing, — to force through, for instance, a particular measure without regard to circumstances or consequences; but the *disposition*, the *inward principle*, is indicated from which we are always to act; the way, the means, being left to be determined by an enlightened Christian conscience in view of all the circumstances and foreseen consequences of the act. It is a law, but it is a "law of liberty." We are not treated as slaves, nor yet as children, but as the Lord's freemen. The spirit, the reason, the principle of the law is given, and it is left for us to consider, under the light of the gospel, and under a solemn sense of our responsibility to God, in what way this principle can best be carried into effect in the condition in which we are placed. And the excellency of this wisdom consists herein: as the reason of the law is better understood, as the principle of the law unfolds itself in the individual and in society more and more, its form rises to meet it, becomes clothed with a higher significance; and thus, as I have said before, never becomes obsolete, but renews itself, and reaffirms itself at every step of human progress.

The same is also true of the second Christian doctrine, above mentioned; namely, that greatness consists not in wealth or station, nor yet in intellectual superiority, but in public service, and in dignity and elevation of soul. We must expect that a man will be *called* great in any community according as he excels in those particular qualities which are held there in the highest account. Hence, among savages the great man is a man of gigantic strength and stature; among a warlike people the great warrior is the great man; in proportion as the civic virtues come to be appreciated and honored, the great statesman begins to be looked up to as a great man; if intellect is the standard, the great thinker; if usefulness and integrity, — the public benefactor, the moral hero. Thus we see that, as civilization advances, human greatness is determined by a continually ascending scale; and what I wish to impress upon you here is, that Christianity began by taking this scale at the highest.

Thus, when a strife arose among the Twelve which of them should be accounted greatest, Jesus said: "The kings of the gentiles exercise lordship over them, and they that exercise authority upon them are called benefactors. Let it not be so with you; but he that is greatest among you, let him be as the younger, and he that is chief as he that doth serve." He who spoke thus must have known not only what mankind had become, but what they were capable of becoming; and also by what means they were to be led on. He knew that the first thing to be done was to hold up before them the *idea* of true greatness. The idea, the conception, must go before the reality. For a while the light shone in darkness, and the darkness comprehended it not. But the darkness never entirely extinguished the Christian idea of true greatness. Nothing is more remarkable of what are called by way of distinction the Dark Ages, than the inconsistency, the contradiction, between what the Christians of that time *really were* and what in moments of high spiritual exaltation *they aspired to be;* in one word, between the moral practice and the moral thought in that benighted period of the Christian world. By means of the Scriptures, sacred hymns, and the symbols of the Church, the *idea* of what God required still lived. Over the confusion and license and ferocity which prevailed, there still hovered a *conception* of the true Christian life, to command the respect and win the love of all, and slowly and silently to draw all men unto it.

Again, the third and last of the above-mentioned Christian doctrines — namely, that the secret of the highest form of influence over man is found, not in interest or fear, but in self-devotion and love, in overcoming evil with good — is equally in accordance with a profound knowledge of what is in man. In taking this stand we do not shut our eyes on the many weaknesses, follies, and extravagances which have been and still are recommended and practised under fanatical notions of devotion and self-sacrifice. Nevertheless we must not abandon an important and sound principle from disgusts occasioned by the misunderstandings or exaggerations to which it has sometimes led, or by the ill-repute into which the principle itself has sometimes fallen in consequence. It is still true that love has more power over man, to induce real and lasting change, than either hope or fear. I have no doubt that Christianity has done much good through its distinct and authoritative annunciation of a future life; but it is a mistake to suppose that this is the sole, or the chief, secret of its influence. Its peculiar and distinctive excellence and power do not grow out of its being a new revelation of God's omnipotence, nor yet of his justice, but of his love. Its doctrine is, "God is love; and he that dwelleth in love dwelleth in God, and God in him." "*Therefore*, if thine enemy hunger, feed him; if he thirst, give him drink: for in so doing thou shalt heap coals of fire on his head. Be not overcome of evil, but overcome evil with good."

Strange that the professed followers of Jesus should be so slow to find out what is so clearly laid down as being at the bottom of all genuine Christian influence. But they are beginning to find it out at last, and to reap the fruit of the discovery, in the wonderful success attending those attempts to reclaim the erring and lift up the fallen, where men trust wholly to the accents of human sympathy, speaking in the name of him who loved us and gave himself for us. *Moral* miracles might still be wrought, if men would only have faith in that ever open and ever flowing source of Divine power. "For I am persuaded, that neither death, nor life, nor angels, nor principalities, nor powers, nor things present, nor things to come, nor height, nor depth, nor any other creature, shall be able to separate us from the love of God, which is in Christ Jesus our Lord."

Finally, that our Lord "knew what was in man" appears not only in his doctrines, but also in the means by which he would have them established and propagated in the world.

The history of Christianity, read by one who mistakes a knowledge of the world for a knowledge of human nature, presents an inexplicable enigma. Go back to the day of the crucifixion; follow the feeble and fainting steps of the Victim as he passes through the streets of Jerusalem on his way to Calvary; witness the scene of torture and ignominy which followed. Is this the King that was promised? Is this his coronation? All experience, all history, all our affections answer, "It is." To a suffering and not to a triumphant Christ the thoughts of a tempted, perplexed, and sorrowing race instinctively turn. It is the memory of that love which was stronger than death, mingled with the consciousness that the sacrifice had become necessary to our reconciliation with God, that has enthroned the Crucified One for ever in the heart of man. What is there in mere worldly greatness to be followed by results like these? What care we at this day for Herod the Great, or Alexander the Great? It is one of the eternal laws of nature, that every thing which is personal and selfish perishes; that only which contributes to the spread of light, and the progress of truth and virtue, endures.

There are three ways in which a religion can be established and propagated;—by force, by authority, or by individual conviction and heart-felt love. The first two are ever likely to recommend themselves to those who mistake a knowledge of the world for a knowledge of human nature, because the outward success attending them is more immediate and more apparent. Thus we see Mohammed and his successors, the scimitar in one hand and the Koran in the other, with the stern and brief argument, "Believe or die!" But is this the way to win souls? Again, after the great Christian apostasy, the Church opposed and exalted itself above all that is called God, or that is worshipped; and began to claim for human authority what is only due to the Divine. Men were called upon to consent to be blindly led. Was this the way to bring about an inward and moral change? The only righteousness which the gospel accepts, or knows, is the righteousness that is by faith, the righteousness that has its root in personal conviction, the righteousness that proceeds, not from a blind and slavish assent to what is said to be true, but from a knowledge, acceptance, and love of what is felt to be true.

Thus it is that real Christianity has spread. Hence also, I may add, the explanation, at least in part, of a difficulty which troubles many minds. I mean the fact that the progress of real Christianity has been so slow, and that so much still remains to be done before its triumph is complete. Christianity is not a mere development of human nature; it is a divine element communicated to that nature, by which the nature itself is to be renewed and transfigured. It is not the nature itself, but is intended to act on it; still its action must be in accordance with the laws of that nature, and also in proportion as the nature itself is developed in obedience to those laws. The divine seed is planted; the result is to be not a mechanical displacing of the parts, but a living growth; and growth *requires time.* Therefore it is that God waits; therefore it is that the Saviour waits; and we also must labor and wait, until the tree takes deep root, until it sends out its boughs unto the sea, and its branches unto the river, and fills the whole earth.

We have now seen how entirely and profoundly the gospel is adjusted to human nature, both in its moral teachings and in the manner of its action and success. Two general remarks must sum up what we have to add by way of application.

In the first place, we find in the doctrine of this discourse a striking confirmation of the divine origin of Christianity. We have shown that its Founder understood human nature better than any philosopher of antiquity, and knew how to mould this nature to his purposes better than any lawgiver or statesman of antiquity. The question is therefore forced upon us: "Whence hath this man all this wisdom?" It is idle to talk about training and discipline; for he had neither: and, besides, any instruction he might have received in this way would only have had the effect to give his mind a more decidedly Jewish or Oriental bent, and so have been fatal to that breadth and universality of view on which, as I have said, his chief distinction and glory depend. Neither is it to any purpose to say, that we have no measures by which to determine beforehand what unassisted genius can do. I grant this, but with one important and necessary qualification. We must confine the remark to what properly pertains to *genius;* to poetry for example, to some of the forms of eloquence, or at most to native sagacity; but this makes it inapplicable in the present case. For we find here what we are accustomed to expect only as the result, not of genius, but of *profound study, and wide and various observation.* True, we have no means of ascertaining precisely how far the unassisted forces of the human mind might enable an individual to go in any direction. For example; if the attention of a savage were accidentally turned to the study of the heavens, we cannot tell precisely how far he would be competent to master the rudiments of astronomy. But one thing is certain; he never would be able to produce such a work as the "Principia" of Newton. Yet even this would feebly represent the marvel to be explained, when we are told that a Galilean peasant not only undertook to legislate for the conduct of all ages and countries, but succeeded so well as to leave not a single error to be corrected, and not a single defect to be supplied.

Finally, if Christianity is so nicely adjusted to human nature as has been shown, it follows that whoever puts himself in contradiction to it, puts himself in contradiction to his own nature. You blame the drunkard, not only because he has violated the laws of his country and the laws of God, but because he has violated the laws of his own physical nature. Now we all have a *moral* and *spiritual* nature to consult and provide for as well, dependent also on our observing its eternal and unalterable laws; which laws it is the mission of the gospel, as we have seen, to inculcate and enforce. If this be so, then whoever disowns or neglects the gospel, disowns and neglects his own proper nature; refuses to accept that peace of soul to which he might aspire, by refusing to submit to the conditions on which alone that peace can be built. All that the gospel requires of us is, that we should be true to our own nature; but in order to be so we must accept those principles which alone are able to reach, arouse, and call forth the inmost elements of that nature, — elements, however, which are essential to the highest form of the soul's life. The perfect Christian is neither more nor less than the perfect man. Hence the language of Divine Wisdom is ever the same: "Whoso findeth me findeth life, and shall obtain favor of the Lord. But he that sinneth against me wrongeth his own soul: all that hate me love death."

1850–1856.

XII.

SPIRITUAL DISCERNMENT.

"*But the natural man receiveth not the things of the Spirit of God; for they are foolishness unto him: neither can he know them, because they are spiritually discerned.*" — 1 CORINTHIANS ii. 14.

BY what means and faculties can man become acquainted with the realities of the spiritual life and the spiritual world, and know them, and be affected by them, as realities? We learn from the text that "the natural man receiveth not the things of the Spirit of God; for they are foolishness unto him: neither *can* he know them, because they are spiritually discerned." But what is this *spiritual discernment?* Why is "the natural man" incapable of it? What are the changes he must undergo, in order to become capable of it?

These are the questions which I now propose to take up, and, if possible, to resolve; and this, too, on the basis of a general doctrine, which is at once rational, and Scriptural, and eminently practical.

The general doctrine to which I refer is, that

every kind of knowledge supposes a mind *prepared to receive it*, and this preparation of mind may be regarded as the appropriate and indispensable condition of such knowledge.

Let me illustrate what I mean, at considerable length, beginning with the simplest and most elementary kind of knowledge, that which we obtain by means of the senses, — *external perception.* As all knowledge begins here, it might be presumed that it requires no preparation; in other words, that what one man can *see*, all can see, that what one man can *hear*, all can hear. But it is far otherwise. A large proportion of what we know by external perception, we know by what is called *acquired* perception; so much so, that, if a man were now created with all his senses in their entire physical development, they would be at first of but little or no service to him as knowing faculties. He would still have to *learn* how to see, how to hear, and even how to feel, in order to distinguish and know; and his capacity to distinguish and know in this way would be in proportion as his senses were *educated up to it.* How much more a blind man can distinguish and know by hearing alone than other men! How much more an artist can see in a picture or landscape than the unpractised and unskilful eye! It is not that the senses themselves are different, or more perfectly developed; but because the mind, through changes which it has itself undergone, is able to recognize, in what is manifested to the senses, a new significance.

So likewise in respect to that form of knowledge which goes under the name of *common sense*, as if it were common to all men, and the same in all. But here, too, in point of fact, it is far otherwise. Common sense, in the usual acceptation of that term, comprehends two elements: first, the primitive judgments of the human mind, for which, as the name denotes, the mind can have no other evidence except that which it finds in itself; and, secondly, such generally received deductions from experience as have taken the form of maxims, and in this form are adopted and transmitted without question as the common heritage. Now even in respect to the primitive judgments, considered as actual knowledge, we cannot say that they are either common to all, or the same in all; for we must make a distinction between principles of knowledge and a knowledge of these principles. Because there are truths which the mind knows *at once*, when it is sufficiently developed to know them *at all*, it does not follow that every mind is sufficiently developed (for example, in infancy or in extreme barbarism) to know them *at all.* And this is still more obvious as regards the other element of common sense, the maxims deduced from experience. Evidently there was a time when these maxims were in process of formation, and when of course they had not as yet been incorporated into the common sense of any people. Hence we are not surprised to find that the common sense of savages is a very different thing from the common sense of civilized men; and, furthermore, that it is essentially modified by the *kind* of civilization which prevails. For example, the common sense of the Chinese is not the same with that of the English or the French.

This, then, is our conclusion even in respect to the earliest and simplest steps in human intelligence: they all depend on a previous preparation of mind; this previous preparation of mind being an indispensable condition of the knowledge, — wanting which, the knowledge fails.

The general doctrine gains in clearness and impressiveness when applied to the more advanced and complicated efforts of science and the arts. In the infancy of society, in the early stages of human progress, the steps were short and simple, consisting for the most part of *a single thought turned to some single and special purpose;* these, therefore, might have been suggested to one, almost as well as to another, if placed in like favorable circumstances. But it is far otherwise now. At the present day we may discover or invent things over again; but, to take a step really in advance, we must begin by mastering what has been done before by the best minds in the same field of inquiry: and this, too, not merely that we may be in a condition to solve the new problem, but that we may be in a condition even so much as to accost it, or comprehend it. I know how common it is to refer some of the most important discoveries and inventions even in modern times to casual events, to a hint dropped unawares, to a transient glimpse vouchsafed the favored aspirant; as if the whole depended on accident, or at best on a kind of inspiration, which as it happens to one might happen to all. But no such thing. It was not the swinging of a lamp in the cathedral of Pisa, nor the falling of an apple in the garden at Woolsthorpe, but the fact that the first was observed by a Galileo, and the second by a Newton, which has made them so fruitful of consequences in the history of science. The hint is nothing, except to those who are in a condition to take it and unfold it. Accident may do a little towards determining the time when, and the place where of a great discovery, but the discovery itself must come from the mind of the discoverer; that is to say, from the fact that his mind has been previously educated up to a level with the problem to be solved.

Thus far I have spoken of acts of the pure intellect; but the illustrations of the doctrine most in point are drawn from those acts of the intellect which are blended with feeling; as in matters of taste and conscience. Here a twofold preparation is necessary, a preparation of the head and the heart: we must know in order to feel, and we must feel in order to know; which requires that we should be in a condition to do both.

Take, for example, æsthetic sentiment, or what is sometimes called *taste*, meaning thereby the faculty to know and appreciate what is sublime or beautiful in Nature and art. I do not deny that the *germs* of this faculty are innate, or that, in various proportions, they are common to all men, making part of what constitutes the essential distinction between the *human* and the *animal* mind even in its undeveloped state. Still it is only in proportion as the faculty itself is developed in the human mind, either by growth, or experience, or culture, that it can be expected to manifest itself in the life of the individual. An undeveloped faculty is not a faculty in use, but only in prospect, the possibility of a faculty: it does not speak of what a man can do as he is, but only of what he might be made capable of doing.

Hence there is no inconsistency in saying that man may have so little of his proper humanity *developed*, as to be almost as incapable of appreciating the works of Raphael or Mendelssohn as the inferior animals. Like them, as regards what is sublime or beautiful in such works, seeing he would see, but not perceive; and hearing he would hear, but not understand.

And here it is to no purpose to object, that the *simpler forms* of beauty, a simple air in music, for instance, is understood by one as well as by another. For, in the first place, this is true in respect to those communities only which are more or less advanced in civilization; and besides, even where it is true, the doctrine resolves itself, after all, into a question of degrees merely. It shows, what indeed might have been taken for granted, that *less* culture is necessary in order to understand and enjoy simple forms of beauty than such as are complicated and refined; and, furthermore, that this degree of culture needs not be above that which is common or universal in a particular community. But because this degree of culture happens to be common or universal in a particular community, it does not follow that it ceases to be culture; so that the objection falls to the ground. It is still just as true as it was before, that *some degree* of culture is indispensable to the knowledge and appreciation of what is beautiful in nature or art.

The same is also true of *conscience* or *the moral sense*. There can be no doubt that man is constituted a moral being: that is to say, his moral judgments and feelings are not a factitious or accidental creation, the work of government, or education, or self-interest. Though stimulated and unfolded by influences from without, it is always in accordance with an *innate and internal law* — a law of his own nature. This law may be said to be "written in his heart;" so that, failing all other law, he would become "a law unto himself." But this law takes effect in the case of this or that individual in so far only as his moral nature, which determines it, is developed; and his moral nature, like his physical or intellectual nature, is developed gradually, step by step. Thus is laid a foundation for the possibility and the necessity of moral progress in individuals, and in whole communities. It is not merely or mainly that men should become more *conscientious*, meaning thereby more observant of what conscience dictates; but conscience itself must become more tender, more enlightened, more discriminating: it must dictate a higher and purer morality. We are wont to speak of our Puritan ancestors as eminently conscientious; and so they were. With all their errors in doctrine, and all their faults in manner and temper, they were probably more strictly conscientious — that is, lived more strictly according to their convictions of duty — than any other people who can be named. Nevertheless they could countenance not only slavery as an existing institution, which is done by many good men now, but the *slave trade;* nay, some of the best of them scrupled not to engage, directly or indirectly, in that nefarious traffic. And the reason is obvious. They did not and they *could not* see such conduct in the moral light in which we see it; partly because this particular subject had not as yet been cleared up, as it has been since, by discussion; and partly because their general conception of human rights was less just and comprehensive then than that which prevails at the present day: to which must be added what has been gained to public sentiment from the humanizing influence of a progressive Christian civilization.

Let me not be misunderstood. I neither say nor mean, that the notion of right in itself, of right *as such*, differs in different places, at different times, with different men. Men do not differ as to the regard which is due to right, *as right.* All men — that is, all men whose moral nature has begun to be developed ever so imperfectly — agree in this, that they *ought* to do what is right. But they differ on the question what *is* right; a question the solution of which does not depend, like the preceding, merely on their having a moral nature, but on the manner and degree of its development. Moreover this doctrine affords no color of pretence for doubting the reality of moral distinctions; that is to say, for insinuating that there is no such thing as right independently of our opinion of right. You might just as well maintain that there is no such thing as *truth*, because men, though they agree in their notion of truth itself, differ on the question, what *is* true. The doctrine, as here laid down, merely supposes that our moral, as well as our intellectual, faculties are capable of being enlightened, improved, and enlarged. In other words, because man, in a high state of moral progress, sees at once, and, as he is apt to think, intuitively, a particular action or class of actions to be right or wrong, it does not follow that he could have done the same at the beginning or lower state of his moral progress. I say *could*, and not *would;* for it is not enough to say of a man who has made but little moral progress, that he *does* not see difficult and refined moral distinctions: he *cannot* see them; that is, he cannot, until his moral nature is educated up to a level with the moral question proposed; or, in other words, until *the eye*, as well as the object, is given to him.

One word more in this connection. Theorists are fond of seeking the *ultimate test* of morals; and some have thought to find it in intuitions of reason, others in instinctive feelings, others in expediency, and others in the will of God. But make the *ultimate* test of morals what you will, it does not alter the fact as to the *immediate* or *proximate* test, which is the conscience of the individual; and this, again, is not an absolute or even a fixed standard, but varies with the moral progress of the individual from day to day; nay, is neither more nor less than the measure and expression of this progress for the time being.

I have been purposely slow in my approaches to the proper doctrine of this discourse; namely, the incompetency of unspiritual men to apprehend and appreciate spiritual truth. My reason for taking this course has been, that in respect to the high inculcations of the gospel the office of the preacher, as I understand it, is not so much *to prove the truth* of these inculcations, for their truth is supposed to be conceded, at least by Christians, to whom alone they are addressed; but rather to prepare and dispose his hearers to receive the truths in question *in their full significance*, by showing how they are to be reconciled and coördinated with all other truths; by showing, in short, how entirely they fall in with the whole of human experience. We have seen it to be a universal law of human intelligence, that it should be gradual, successive, step by step. No matter whether it be a question of common sense or the highest science; no matter whether it be a question of expediency, or of taste, or of morals, — we are not in a condition to pronounce upon it, until our minds by growth, or experience, or training are raised to a level with it. And in the case of taste and morals, where knowledge takes the form of sentiment, where we must love in order to know, as well as know in order to love, — in all such cases, including of course piety, religion, the preparation required is not merely a preparation of the intellect, but also a preparation of heart and life. This is the general, the universal law; and the text does but inculcate a single, though the highest, application of this law when it tells us, that "the natural man receiveth not the things of the Spirit of God, for they are foolishness unto him; neither can he know them, because they are spiritually discerned."

To return, then, to the questions proposed at the opening of this discourse; if asked, in the first place, what constitutes spiritual discernment; what gives the power of spiritual discernment? — I answer, in one word, — spiritual experience. Spiritual experience supposes, of course, the excitement and activity of the spiritual faculties, more or less of spiritual culture or growth, some degree of spiritual progress ; and our actual capacity of knowledge, or of living faith, in spiritual things depends on the degree of this progress. "Oh taste and see that the Lord is good!" exclaimed the Hebrew psalmist three thousand years ago; for it was as well understood then by heavenly minded men as it is now, that we cannot apprehend spiritual truth through the experience of others, but only through our own. And again, "Jesus answered them and said, My doctrine is not mine, but his that sent me. If any man will do his will, he shall know of the doctrine, whether it be of God, or whether I speak of myself." This and a multitude more of our Saviour's precepts clearly teach, that what is called spiritual insight depends much less on intellectual gifts, or intellectual culture, or learning of any kind, than on the state of the affections and our whole moral being. The same views were also inculcated and insisted on by his immediate followers. Thus, in the chapter from which the text is taken, we are expressly told that "the deep things of God" are revealed through his Spirit. "For what man knoweth the things of a man, save the spirit of a man which is in him? Even so the things of God knoweth no man, but the Spirit of God. Now we have received not the spirit of the world, but the spirit which is of God;

that we might know the things that are freely given to us of God." The apostle's meaning here would seem to be, that it is only through the agency of what is divine in our own regenerated nature that we are put into communication with the Divinity, and made capable of apprehending divine things. In other words, properly to know God, we must be in sympathy with him; we must have a portion at least of his Spirit. Accordingly we are exhorted to follow "holiness, without which," as it is expressly said, "no man shall *see* the Lord;" nay, the Scriptures call upon us, in so many words, to become "partakers of his holiness," clearly implying that sympathy and participation in divine things must precede a proper knowledge, that is to say a living sense, of divine things.

If then we are asked, in the second place, why "the natural man" is incapable of such knowledge; why he is incapable of spiritual discernment, properly so called? — the answer, again, is plain. It is because he has not put himself into a real, that is to say a living, communication with spiritual things. He is incapable of this knowledge, because he has not as yet put himself into a real and living communication *with the objects of this knowledge*. By "the natural man," in this connection, we understand the opposite to the spiritual man. The natural man is the *unspiritual* man.

It is not necessary that he should be addicted to atrocious crimes, or sunk in sensuality, or destitute of refinement, or intelligence, or worldly prudence; it is enough if he is unspiritual. He is, in the strictest sense of that word, a *worldly* man; one who looks not beyond or above the present world for his motives, encouragements, and consolations; one in whom the spiritual elements of his nature are not as yet awakened; and one, therefore, who neither feels nor recognizes his spiritual capacities, or his spiritual relations. This is "the natural man"; and, after what has been said, it is obvious that his incapacity of spiritual discernment results from his not being in a condition to know the things of the Spirit in the only way in which they can be known, — by actual experience, by personal consciousness. There is no miracle, no mystery here. It is what happens every day in analogous cases not immediately connected with religion, where men show themselves incapable of understanding parts of their own nature as developed *in others*, if they have not also been developed *in themselves*. Thus the man of facts cannot understand the man of imagination, nor the man of imagination the man of facts; the miser cannot understand the philanthropist, nor the philanthropist the miser. Each is a puzzle, an extravagance, a foolishness to the other; merely because their natures, though the same in essence, are so differently developed that they cannot reason from consciousness to consciousness.

If then matters of taste and conscience cannot be understood or appreciated by men, except in proportion as their taste and conscience are unfolded, why wonder that the same law holds in the kindred subject of religion? Why wonder that religious or spiritual truths cannot be understood or appreciated as such, except in proportion as men's spiritual faculties are unfolded, meaning by spiritual faculties a spiritual consciousness; that is, a state of mind which makes men alive and awake to spiritual things, and puts what is divine in their own nature into communication with its Divine Source. And this is what I understand to be the apostle's teaching in the text. "The natural man"—that is, one in whom all sense of the spiritual and divine still slumbers —"receiveth not the things of the Spirit of God, for they are foolishness unto him;" that is, they appear so to a mind which is the result of such experiences; "neither can he know them, because they are spiritually discerned,"—showing that the waking up of his own spiritual faculties is a necessary prerequisite.

Thus are we brought to the third and last question: What changes must the natural man undergo in order to become capable of spiritual discernment? And to answer it aright we must guard against two opposite extremes, — the extreme of supposing that nothing depends on ourselves, and the extreme of supposing that every thing depends on ourselves. Our faculties are our own, and it depends on ourselves whether we use or abuse them, and also whether we cultivate or neglect them, for self-culture is eminently a personal act. But it does not depend on ourselves under what influences, from around and from above, all this takes place, — influences which in point of fact have so much to do in shaping our characters as well as our fortunes. It does not depend on ourselves under what religion we are born, or under what instructions or institutions we are brought up, or, to a certain extent, into what connections or companionships we are thrown. For this reason the wise and good man, after his greatest moral triumphs, will always be ready to exclaim: "Not unto us, O Lord, not unto us, but to thy name give glory for thy mercy, and for thy truth's sake." Nevertheless it would seem that *for us* every thing has been done but man's part. "The day-spring from on high hath visited us," the Holy Spirit is promised to every one who will open his heart to welcome the heavenly Visitant; nothing more is required, even of the unregenerate, but to submit to the means, and co-operate in the work, of the great salvation.

The change in "the natural man," to which these means and this work look, and in which they are fulfilled, is the unfolding of his higher and better nature. The unspiritual man must become spiritual; he must bring out into activity and consciousness latent qualities of mind and heart; and then he will be in a condition to understand and feel the reality and the infinite worth of what strikes him perhaps as foolishness now. Nor has he any reason to despair of being able to do this. It is not as if the germs of the new life were not in him; they are in him, and only require to be unfolded and put forth. A humble sense of dependence and of his spiritual needs, the yearning of the soul after a better state of things, the prayer of faith, the various means which God has appointed, and the continual aids of his Holy Spirit will ensure the object. The change might be begun, and often is begun, in lisping infancy, through the power of a wise Christian nurture; it might be, and it sometimes is, carried on towards perfection in every step of advancing youth and manhood, through a life devoted from the beginning to the highest principles and the noblest objects. Oh, if from the cradle to the grave half as much pains were taken, or half as many appliances used, to bring out what is spiritual and divine in man as to bring out those qualities which pertain to worldly success, another day would dawn on this earth!

And his spiritual convictions and sensibilities will keep pace with his spiritual growth. To depend wholly or mainly on books, on nice and ingenious argumentation, on hearsay or authority, to clear up our doubts and difficulties in regard to the invisible things of God, is like seeking the living among the dead. A single earnest and hearty prayer, the actual putting forth of the spiritual life in deeds of benevolence and mercy, the living consciousness that we have become "partakers of the Divine nature," will do more to fill the soul with light and confidence, than years of unsanctified study. What is most wanted in order to still our doubts or dispel our perplexities in religion is, not that we may be convinced by argument of its reasonableness and abstract probability, but that we may be made to feel and know its reality from personal consciousness. I repeat it; the natural, the unspiritual man must become spiritual. His first satisfactory vision of heavenly things will be reflected back upon the depths of his own spiritual nature, excited, developed, regenerated by the power of the Christian faith. The Christian's doubts and difficulties on the subject of religion never trouble him when he is in his highest spiritual moods. And this is what our Saviour meant when he said in the passage which has been cited once before, "If any man will do his will, he will know of the doctrine, whether it be of God, or whether I speak of myself." He will have "the witness in himself." "There is," says one of the wisest and best of the old English divines, "there is a knowing of the truth as it is in Jesus, as it is in a Christ-like nature, as it is in that sweet, mild, humble, and loving spirit of Jesus, which spreads itself like a morning sun upon the souls of good men, full of light and life."

1854–1858.

XIII.

PUBLIC OPINION.

" Carried about with every wind of doctrine." — EPHESIANS iv. 14.

OUR free political institutions, the general diffusion of knowledge, and the facilities, particularly through the newspaper press, for acting on whole communities at once, have had the effect gradually to introduce among us a new instrument of influence and reform; or, at any rate, to clothe an old one with new power and activity. This instrument, I hardly need say, is Public Opinion.

In what I am going to say on this subject, let me not be understood to deny that public opinion, in its place and degree, is a legitimate principle and rule of human conduct. It is natural and fit that we should desire to stand well with our fellow-men. From our condition in society, and from the very constitution of our minds, it was obviously intended that we should be affected and determined, more or less, by praise and blame. Nor is this all. Public opinion, on all simple questions resting on a direct appeal to common sense and the moral sentiments, is generally right; at any rate, it is more likely to be so than the private opinion of interested parties. Look back on the history of human progress: almost every important step has been taken, not because *the few* advised it, but because *the many* demanded it. The history of reform in most countries is little else than the history of a series of concessions to public opinion. And so in other countries, even in the most despotic; for though in absolute governments there are no *legal* checks on the abuse of power, there is still the check of public opinion; to wit, a fear lest the people may be goaded into some desperate act. Then, too, the despot, at least if he lives within the pale of Christian civilization, cannot be wholly indifferent to the public opinion of other nations; he cannot help being restrained, more or less, by an unwillingness to incur the world's execration or contempt.

Some may object that conscience, enlightened by revelation, is the sole rule in the last appeal, and that to ask ourselves what the world will think, or say, is treason to this rule. But why so? With ordinary men, and in the ordinary course of things, what we call the individual conscience is little else than a reflection of the public conscience; that is to say, of the public opinion of right. In such cases, therefore, the appeal to the public opinion of right is not necessarily an appeal from conscience to some other standard; to that of expediency for example. It may be, and often is, an appeal from the uninstructed conscience of the individual to what is believed to be the better instructed conscience of the community; the public sense of right. Exigencies sometimes arise, as I shall have occasion presently to show, when each one should follow his own conscience without regard to public opinion; but, in the ordinary course of things, I cannot help thinking public opinion to be a safer rule than that conceit of private judgment, that extravagance of individualism, which it is now so much the fashion to recommend. Still, even here, you will observe, I do not suppose a man to defer to public opinion any further than his own conscience dictates; so that, after all, he does but follow his own conscience in following the consciences of other men.

Thus much in favor of public opinion as *a rule* of conduct: it is still more important as *a motive and sanction.* When a man is tempted to commit a fraud, or to be guilty of any meanness or cruelty or excess, his own conscience protests against it; and this alone ought to restrain him: often, however, we know it does not. Happily, in most cases public opinion protests as well; and the same person who is not restrained by his own sense of the wrong, or by a fear of self-condemnation, is restrained by a fear of disgrace, or of public condemnation. In other words, he does not stand so much in awe of *his own* conscience as he does of the consciences of other men. After all, however, the motive from which he acts is often at least of the nature of a moral motive: he is afraid of *moral* disapprobation; he stands in awe of the collective conscience of the community, which he looks up to as sanctioning and reënforcing his own conscience. For let me impress it upon you, that, when any one is restrained from wrong-doing by the public opinion of right *as such*, he is still restrained by conscience; that is, the public conscience: "Conscience, I say, not thine own, but of the other."

How little the best of us are in a condition to spare the restraints of public opinion, as a safeguard to morals and decency, appears from the effect it almost always has on the principles and habits even of good men, if they move into a neighborhood where a lower standard of public opinion prevails; or where, as in the case of new and border settlements, no effective public opinion has as yet been organized; or where the individual from any cause has reason to think himself unknown or unobserved. I speak not now of a few exceptional cases, of here and there one who seems born to influence others without being influenced by them in return. I speak of mankind as they arise, including what are called the better classes: I say of men in general, that in every tolerably constituted society *they help to hold each other up*. I am aware how apt public opinion is to be perverted or warped *on single points*. For example; in almost every community there are certain antiquated and widespread abuses, which the public opinion of that community, from prejudice or superstition or interest, is still disposed to uphold or connive at. Nevertheless, even there, on the great majority of topics in morals and humanity, public opinion is almost sure to be in advance of what men would be if left to themselves. Imperfect as public opinion is, there is not one man in ten thousand, whom a fear of offending it does not make more circumspect in many respects than he otherwise would be; more anxious not merely to appear, but also to be, worthy of public confidence.

And besides, why insist on what cannot be? Theorists may declaim, as they will, about the duty and the safety of disregarding public opinion as a practical principle, but a single glance at the actual working of the social constitution will show that, even with the theorists themselves, theory is one thing and practice another. No sane man ever did or ever will live in society, and yet be wholly indifferent to the opinion of society; for, however much he may be at issue with society on some points, he is never at issue with it in such a sense as to cast off all regard to appearances. The martyr, on his way to the stake, is not content with *being* sincere and brave; he would *appear* so, and *live as such in the memory and speeches of men.* And why not? Why not wish to stand well before the sense of right in other men, as we would before the sense of right in ourselves, or in God?

Let me, therefore, repeat what I said in the beginning: — public opinion has its legitimate place as a rule and sanction of human conduct, even in matters of right and wrong. Private conscience is not an absolute or all-sufficient rule, to the exclusion or neglect of the public conscience; much less is it of the nature of a protest against the public conscience. If it were so, where would be found that unity in men's moral judgment on which law is founded, and without which society could not exist?

Still it by no means follows that there is no occasion for the warning in the text, "that we henceforth be no more children, tossed to and fro, and carried about by every wind of doctrine." The character of the trimmer and time-server, whether from selfish notions or from mere weakness, is so odious, and of so frequent occurrence in modern society, that we can hardly be too much on our guard against the danger of which the Apostle speaks.

How then is this danger to be averted? How is it possible to pay a proper regard to public opinion, without allowing it to become inordinate,—a snare to our own integrity, to all manly independence and stability of purpose?

In the first place, we are to make sure that what we take for public opinion *is* public opinion;—a much more difficult thing to do than is commonly supposed. The writers and talkers constitute but a small minority of any community; yet we are very apt to reason and act on the assumption, that, what the writers and talkers *say*, everybody *thinks*. Nay, a very few writers if they write a great deal, and a very few talkers if they talk a great deal, and talk loudly and confidently and repeat themselves and quote one another, can easily create an impression, in regard to some subjects, that the world is on their side when it is not. And when to this is added the whole machinery of party and popular agitation,—pamphlets, periodical publications, newspapers, meetings, speeches, agencies,—it is astonishing how small a number of leading and active spirits can make their earnest cry, either for or against the project in hand, sound like the public voice. So it was with a knot of philosophers in the opening scenes of the first French Revolution. Even in our own days, a single newspaper in London aspires, we are told, to manufacture public opinion for the whole kingdom. So profound is my reverence for the will of the people, or of even a majority of the people, that, could I be sure it has been expressed freely and understandingly, I should hardly hesitate, in any case, to obey. But I must have better evidence that the people will it, than the reiterated and passionate asseverations of zealots or demagogues assuming to speak in their name. I remember that among the people are vast numbers who cannot be said to have made up any mind on the subject, and also that many among those who have made up their minds are kept back from expressing them by constitutional reserve, or by inability or distaste for controversy. I remember, too, Burke's often-quoted illustration: "Because half-a-dozen grasshoppers under a fern make the field ring with their importunate chink, whilst thousands of great cattle, reposed beneath the shadow of the British oak, chew the cud and are silent, pray do not imagine that *those who make the noise* are the only inhabitants of the field; that of course they are many in number; or that, after all, they are other than the little, shrivelled, meagre, hopping, though loud and troublesome insects of the hour."

There is nothing of which I feel more confident than I do of this: that what often passes for public opinion is *not* public opinion, but the passions and prejudices of a few heated, and it may be interested, writers and talkers. Happily, in almost every community making the smallest pretensions to intelligence and freedom, there is a powerful reserve of moderate and silent men, who seldom cause themselves to be heard or felt in public matters, but yet are known to exist, and, by creating a fear of reactions, operate as a check on violent and headlong counsels. I say, "by creating a fear of reactions;" for the liability to reactions, about which so much is said, would seem to resolve itself into the fact, that ordinarily a considerable portion of society take but little part in the great movements going on around them, until alarm at the waywardness or extravagance of these movements constrains them, contrary to all their natural tastes and inclinations, to speak out. When they do speak out, and not until they do, we are in a condition to know what the public opinion really is,—that which previously passed for it being but a counterfeit and a pretence. I hold therefore, that, in making up our minds as to what public opinion enjoins or forbids, we are not to look to the writers and talkers alone; but are to take into the account that powerful reserve of moderate and for the most part silent men, on whom, as I believe, in all great and trying emergencies God has made the order and stability of society in no small measure to depend. Truth and justice, as it seems to me, demand this at our hand. Besides, were we always disposed to take this course, I need not say how much it would do to save both Church and State from those panics and violent and disastrous convulsions, which have done so much, and are likely to do so much more, to trouble and retard the progress of humanity and civilization.

But supposing it to be conceded whither public opinion points, another question arises:—Is it an *enlightened* public opinion; that is, one formed on a *proper understanding of the subject, and freely expressed?* Who would, for example, give much weight to the public voice in despotic countries, where not a word is printed which has not passed under a rigid censorship of the press, nor a word uttered in favor of liberty or against the powers that be, even in familiar intercourse, but at the hazard of men's lives? Who, again, would attach much importance to universal consent in matters of faith among the Roman Catholics, where the principle is avowedly acted on of submitting all individual differences to the unity of the Church? In all such cases there is no proper public opinion; there can be none: the *voice* is the voice of many, but the *opinion* is the opinion of one or a few of a past age. In all such cases the consent of the multitude is not the result of opinion, but of arrangement and influence; men giving their suffrages as mechanically as if you heard the clatter of the machinery by which their hands are lifted up.

Then, too, there are mysterious states of mind as well as body, brought about we cannot always tell how, in consequence of which, as in the witchcraft times, whole communities, though comparatively enlightened and free, become liable to strange delusions. The delusion arises and spreads, and takes on the laws of an epidemic, and the people are mad, and not the less so because all are mad together. But what regard is due to public opinion when, as in such cases, it appears under the form of public frenzy?

Add to this that local or sectional interests or prejudices often have the effect to blind and pervert the judgment, so as to make it of little or no value as evidence of truth and right, though the almost unanimous judgment of a whole community. Have you never known a difficult financial, political, or moral question, respecting which those for whose supposed interest, convenience, or safety it is that it should be decided in one way, maintain almost to a man that it *ought* to be so decided; while those for whose supposed interest, convenience, or safety it is that it should be decided in the opposite way, are just as confident and unanimous that it ought to be so decided? Narrow-minded men may suspect and charge one at least of the parties to such a contest with acting against what they see to be right; but it is much more reasonable, as well as much more fair and magnanimous, to suppose that neither party is in a condition to see what is right in the particular question. If so, however, their united opinion on the subject, though honestly entertained and freely expressed, is not worth a straw. We can see this in our neighbors, and especially in our opponents; but, unhappily, we cannot see it in ourselves. The very idea that a man's judgment is blinded or perverted, by prejudice or passion, implies that he himself is insensible to the delusion; otherwise, I hardly need say, the delusion would not be.

Look, again, and observe in what manner consent in opinion and concert in action are often brought about, especially in politics and religion, and then tell me candidly how much such consent and concert are worth. If, indeed, the uniformity insisted on resulted from the free, independent, and unbiassed action of individual minds calmly deciding the question on its merits, and in view of all the evidence on both sides, and with a single eye to the truth, it would be a moral miracle if it varied much from the reality. But no such thing. Take away what early education has done, and what mere authority has done, and what sympathy and imitation have done, and what party spirit and party drill have done, and what addresses to the feelings, and especially to men's fears and jealousies, have done,—and what is there left? Public opinion, do you say? Ought it not rather to be accounted an illustration of the practicability of casting a multitude of minds in one and the same mould, wherever the proper apparatus for doing it exists, and the right sort of men can be found to work it? I do not mean that a wise man will slight or contemn, or needlessly defy even, such a public opinion; but he will hardly regard it as the fruit of profound research and free discussion, or as being in any way the effect of evidence, or as being itself of the nature of evidence that should weigh with the weight of a feather in making up his own conclusions. He knows that whoever supposes a multitude of persons can *really think*, and yet think *exactly alike*, has yet to learn what thinking means. Accordingly, so far as authority or argument is concerned, he will be more influenced by conclusions deliberately arrived at by a single individual of an honest and gifted mind, who has really examined the subject for himself under the best lights of an advancing science and civilization, than by the consent of many thousands, where this consent is obviously a matter of tradition, or policy, or sympathy, or drill, or a mere echo. What a noted writer has said is strictly true: "One man, who has in him a higher wisdom, or a hitherto unknown spiritual truth, is stronger, — not than ten men who have it not, nor than ten thousand, — but stronger than all men who have it not, and stands out among them with quite an ethereal, angelic power."

Let me call your attention to another circumstance. What gives to public opinion its chief and characteristic value consists in this: that it is understood to result from a great variety of minds, acting under a *great variety of influences and prepossessions*, and so tending to balance, qualify, and correct one another. It is understood to be an opinion in which the old and the young, the rich and the poor, the learned and the unlearned concur. Hence it follows, that the public opinion of a party as to the measures of the party, or of employers on one side, or of workmen on the other, as to their respective rights and duties, is not public opinion, properly so called. The same is also true of collections of persons living together in temporary or partial separation from the rest of the world, so as to have what is called a public opinion of their own, especially where community of age, or of prejudice, or of taste and pursuits inclines them all to look on subjects under one and the same point of view. Under such circumstances, what is sometimes appealed to as public opinion is not public opinion. It is not the opinion of the public, but of a minute and isolated portion of the public, — an opinion also generated and pronounced under special biasses of judgment, with nothing to balance, modify, or correct these biasses. So far from being the opinion of the public, it is the opinion of a class or clique. This, I know, *may be* right; let us hope that *it generally is so:* what I insist upon is, that it is just as liable to be misled by one-sided views of subjects as the opinion of an individual; and when it is thus misled, a sense of numbers will only have the effect to exaggerate and intensify the one-sidedness and the mischiefs growing out of it. For this reason, if a man expects aid to his conscience from public opinion, it must be from a large and comprehensive public opinion. It must not be the public opinion of his clique or party; and therefore it is well if what he sometimes calls public opinion, that is, the prevalent opinion among those immediately about him, is not continually tempting him to do what his own conscience, and the public conscience rightly understood, alike condemn.

One caution more. We are never to give way to public opinion, however formed and however well ascertained, in such a manner, or in such a spirit, as to be "like children, tossed to and fro, and carried about with every wind of doctrine, by the slight of men and cunning craftiness, whereby they lie in wait to deceive."

On a multitude of questions respecting the mere externals of life a wise man will do as others do; not because he has no opinion of his own, but because it is reason enough, in such cases, to take one course rather than another, if such is the common practice. Moreover, it is a great mistake to suppose that deference to public opinion is, in general, a temptation to inconstancy and fickleness, to innovation and change: on the contrary, it is the sheet-anchor of conservatism. Read the lives of such men as Chillingworth and Blanco White.

All admit their ability and general excellence of character; but all lament, at the same time, their melancholy instability of faith, which arose not from too much but from too little sympathy with the common mind. What was said of one of them applies to the whole class: "His frequent changes proceeded from too nice an inquisition into truth: his doubts *grew out of himself:* he assisted them with all the strength of his reason: he was then too hard for himself; but finding as little quiet and repose in those victories, he quickly recovered by a new appeal to his own judgment; so that, in all his sallies and retreats, he was in fact *his own convert.*"

Sometimes, however, the vertigo seizes the public, a whole community, a whole sect or party, only here and there an individual being spared. What shall these individuals do? Then, too, there are great interests and questions, in respect to which the legitimate condition of the human mind is one of progress, and the natural order of this progress is that the few should be in advance of the many. Shall the few, from fear of the many, or from a slavish regard to public opinion, be unfaithful to this trust? Foreigners contend, and I am afraid not entirely without reason, that, owing to political and social peculiarities, there is no country on the face of the earth where a selfish or timid subserviency to public opinion is carried so far as it is here; in short, that, with all our boast of independence, there is no people among whom so little *real* independence is to be found, especially among those who ought to lead and not merely to follow public sentiment. "Ye have not so learned Christ; if so be that ye have heard him, and have been taught by him, as the truth is in Jesus." To allow the individual to be merged and lost in the mass, to be turned into a mere tool, copy, echo of the public will and the public voice, would be to forget and frustrate the essential purpose, the very genius, the distinctive peculiarity of Christianity. Every man, we are told, is to bear his own burden; every man is to have his rejoicing in himself, and not in another: to his own Master he is to stand or fall. Moreover, the whole doctrine of Divine influences supposes a man to act from his own spirit, as the same has been touched and regenerated by the Spirit of God. We may still think with others; on most subjects we probably shall, and it is natural and right that we should; but it must be because we really think with them, and not because we allow them to think for us, turning us this way or that as they will. Under all circumstances, at any risk, we must have a mind of our own, as the condition of having a soul of our own; "that we henceforth be no more children, tossed to and fro and carried about with every wind of doctrine, by the slight of men and cunning craftiness whereby they lie in wait to deceive; but speaking the truth in love, may grow up into him in all things which is the head, even Christ."

1856.

XIV.

AM I NOT IN SPORT?

"*As a madman who casteth firebrands, arrows, and death, so is the man who deceiveth his neighbor, and saith, Am not I in sport?*" — PROVERBS xxvi. 18, 19.

IT is incalculable how much pain is inflicted, and how much injury is done, without any thing which can properly be called malicious intent, or deliberate wrong. Thus there are those who, like the madman mentioned in Scripture, will cast firebrands, arrows, and death, and then think it a sufficient excuse to say, "Are we not in sport?" Let it be that they *are*, I think it will not be difficult to show that this will not excuse, or do much to palliate, the conduct in question. I think it will not be difficult to show that men are answerable for the mischiefs they do from mere wantonness or in sport, and that it is wrong-doing of this description which makes up no inconsiderable part of every one's guilt.

It is to little or no purpose to be able to say that such offences do not originate in conscious malice, for, as has just been intimated, the same is true of a large proportion of acknowledged crimes. It is seldom, very seldom, that men injure one another from hatred, or for the sake of revenge, — because they find, or expect to find, any pleasure in the mere consciousness of inflicting pain. Men injure one another from wantonness, or want of consideration; or, more commonly still, because the carrying out of their policy, or their prejudices, or their sport happens to interfere with the interests and comfort of others, and, though really sorry for this, they are not prepared to give up either their policy, or their prejudices, or their sport to spare another's feelings. Wars are waged and conquests made, and mourning and desolation spread through a whole country, in the wantonness of honor, or to gratify an insatiable ambition; but without any thing which can properly be called malice, either in the first movers or immediate agents. Men opposed to each other in politics or religion will allow this opposition to go to very unjustifiable lengths, even to the disturbing of the peace of neighborhoods, and the breaking of friendships and family connections; and all this, to be sure, must give rise to a great deal of ill-will and hot blood; but it does not originate in malice, properly so called, — in positive malice towards any body. So likewise a rash and improvident man may bring incalculable mischiefs on all connected with him, involving them in pecuniary difficulties, or committing and paining them in other ways, and yet be able to allege with perfect truth that he did not mean to do them any harm; that, so far from being actuated by malice, he feels nothing and has felt nothing but the sincerest affection for the very persons whom he has injured, and most affection, perhaps, for those whom he has most injured. But why multiply illustrations? The whole catalogue of the vices of self-indulgence and excess, — black and comprehensive as it is, — has nothing to do with malicious intent; that is to say, these vices do not find any part of their temptation or gratification in ill-will to others, or in the consciousness of causing misery to others. And yet who, on this account, denies that they are vices, or that they are among the worst of vices?

Hence, the moral perplexity existing in some minds on this subject may be traced to two errors: making malice to be the *only* bad motive by which we can be actuated; and confounding the mere *absence of malice* with that active principle of benevolence, or love of our neighbor, which Christianity makes to be the foundation and substance of all true social virtue.

How unfounded the first of these assumptions

is, appears generally from what has been said; but the same may also be shown on strictly ethical grounds. We must distinguish between what is simply *odious*, and what is immoral: the malignant passions when acted out by animals are odious, but they are not immoral, because they are not comprehended in that light by the agent. The reason why the malignant passions are immoral in man is that he knows them to be immoral; and accordingly any other passion, which he knows to be immoral, becomes for the same reason alike immoral to him as a principle of conduct. Hence it follows that, though not actuated by malice, we may be by some other motive equally reprehensible in a moral point of view, though not perhaps as odious, — by the love of ease, by vanity or pride, by unjust partialities, by inordinate ambition, by avarice or lust, — dispositions which have nothing to do with malice, but yet are felt and acknowledged by all to be bad and immoral. Moreover, the tendencies of modern civilization are to be considered in this connection. Times of violence are gradually giving place to times of self-indulgence and fraud; and the consequence is that now, where one man is betrayed into vices of malevolence and outrage, twenty are betrayed into those of frivolity, licentiousness, or overreaching. I go further still.

Suppose a man actuated by none of these positively bad motives; nay, suppose the injury done to be accidental and wholly unintentional, this will not in all cases justify the deed. The question still arises whether the injury done, supposing it to be wholly unintentional, might not have been foreseen and ought not to have been foreseen; for, where the well-being of others is concerned, we are bound not only to mean no harm, but to take care to avoid every thing which is likely to do harm: and negligence in this respect is itself a crime. So obviously just is this principle, so entirely does it approve itself to the reason and common sense of mankind, that we find it everywhere recognized, in some form or other, in the jurisprudence of civilized countries. "When a workman flings down a stone or piece of timber into the street, and kills a man, this may be either misadventure, manslaughter, or murder, according to the circumstances under which the original act is done. If it were in a country village, where a few passengers are, and he calls out to all people to have a care, it is misadventure only; but if it were in London, or other populous town, where people are continually passing, it is manslaughter, though he gives loud warning; and murder, if he knows of their passing and gives no warning at all, for then it is malice against all mankind."[1]

[1] Blackstone.

Equally groundless is the second of the abovementioned assumptions, — to wit, that of confounding the mere *absence of malice* with the active principle of benevolence itself, or that love of our neighbor which Christianity makes to be the foundation and substance of all true social virtue. There is nothing, perhaps, which more essentially distinguishes worldly propriety and legal honesty from Christian virtue than this, that *they* stop with *negatives.* They are content with avoiding what is expressly forbidden, not reflecting that this, at the best, only makes men to be *not bad;* it does not make them to be *good.* Besides, if we take this ground, if we allege the absence of all anger and resentment, we bar the plea that we were hurried into the act by the impetuosity of our passions, — a plea which the experience of a common infirmity has always led men to regard as the strongest extenuating circumstance of wrong-doing. If we have given pain to a fellow-creature, it is stating an aggravation of the fault and not an excuse, to say that we did not do it in passion but in cold blood; and worse still, if we say that we did it in sport. What! find sport in giving pain to others? This may consist, I suppose, with the absence of what is commonly understood by malice; but I utterly deny its compatibility with active Christian benevolence, or with what indeed amounts to the same thing, a kind, generous, and magnanimous nature. Were I in quest of facts to prove the total depravity of man, I should eagerly seize on such as the following: — the shouts of heartless merriment sometimes heard to arise from a crowd of idlers collected round a miserable object in the streets; a propensity to turn into ridicule, not merely the faults and affectations of others, but their natural deformities or defects; jesting with sacred things, or practical jests, the consequences of which to one of the parties are of the most serious and painful character; and the pleasure with which men listen to sarcastic remarks though causeless and unprovoked, or to wit the whole point of which consists in its sting. Not that the doctrine of universal and total depravity is actually proved even by such conduct, for happily the conduct itself is not universal; to some it is repugnant from the beginning; and besides, even where it is fallen into, I suppose it is to be referred in a majority of cases to a love of excitement, rather than to a love of evil for its own sake. Still I maintain that the conduct in question, however explained, is incompatible, or at any rate utterly inconsistent, with thoughtful and generous natures.

Still, many who would not think entirely to excuse the conduct in question can find pallia-

UofM

tions for it and extenuating circumstances, some of which it will be well to examine.

In the first place it is said that the sport is not found in the sufferings of the victim, but in the awkward and ludicrous situations and embarrassments into which he is thrown. Now I admit, that, if these awkwardnesses and absurdities could be entirely disconnected with the idea of pain, they might amuse even a good mind: but as they cannot be thus disconnected, — as all this is known and seen to be the expression of anguish either of body or mind, or to be the consequence of some natural defect or misfortune, or some cruel imposition on weakness or good nature, — I affirm as before, that he whose mirth is not checked by this single consideration betrays a want of true benevolence, and even of common humanity. Neither will it help the matter much to say that the pain and mortification are not known, are not seen, or at least *are not attended to;* that this view of the subject is entirely overlooked, the mind being wholly taken up with its ludicrous aspects. For how comes it that we have so quick a sense to every thing ludicrous in the situation and conduct of others, but no sense at all to their sufferings? Our hearts, it would seem, are not as yet steeled against all sympathy in the sufferings and misfortunes of our neighbors, provided we can be made to apprehend and realize them; and this is well: but why *so slow* to apprehend and realize them? If, though directly before our eyes, the thought of them never occurs to our minds; if we can say, and say with truth, that while we enjoyed the sport it never once occurred to us that it was at the expense of another's feelings, though this fact was all the time staring us in the face, — does it not at least betray a degree of indifference or carelessness about the feelings of others, which is only compatible with a cold and selfish temper? Put whatever construction you will, therefore, on this kind of sport, it argues a bad state of the affections: for either its connection with the pain and mortification of others is perceived, and then it is downright cruelty; or it is not perceived, and then it is downright insensibility.

Another ground is sometimes taken. There are those who will say, "We cannot help it. Persons of a constitution less susceptible to the ludicrous, or less quick to observe it, may do differently, but we cannot." Obviously, however, reasonings of this sort, if intended as a valid excuse, betray a singular and almost hopeless confusion of moral ideas. They cannot help it? Of course they do not mean that they would be affected in the same way by the same thing, under all circumstances and in all states of feeling. Let the coarse jest be at the expense of a parent, or of a sister; or let its tendency be to bring derision on an office, a cause, or a doctrine which we have much at heart; or let it offend beyond a certain point against the conventional usages of what is called good society,—and, instead of provoking mirth, it provokes indignation or contempt. All they can mean, therefore, is simply this: their sense of the ludicrous is so keen, that, when not restrained by some present feeling of justice, humanity, or decorum, it becomes irrepressible. Undoubtedly it does; but this is no more than what might be said of the worst crimes of sensuality and excess. What would you think if a sordid man should plead, that being sordid by nature, and not having any high principle or feeling to restrain him, he cannot help acting sordidly? Does he not know that it is this want of high principle and feeling which constitutes the very essence of his sin? We have shown that to find sport in what gives pain, argues a bad state of the principles and affections. Manifestly, therefore, it is to no purpose to urge as an excuse, that *in the existing state of our principles and affections* we cannot help it; for the existing state of our principles and affections is the very thing which is complained of and condemned.

It may be contended, as a last resort, that this state of mind is consistent, to say the least, with amiable manners, companionable qualities, and good nature. But if herein is meant to be included real kindness of heart, or the highest forms of generosity and nobleness of soul, I deny that it can be. There is no necessity of trying to make it out that men of this stamp are worse than they really are. Unquestionably they can and often do make themselves agreeable and entertaining, especially to those who are not very scrupulous about the occasions of their mirth, and feel no repugnance to *join* in a laugh which perhaps they would hesitate to *raise*. Good-natured also they may be, if nothing more is meant by this than the absence of an unaccommodating, morose, and churlish disposition: for there are two sorts of good nature; the good nature of benevolence, and the good nature of ease and indifference. The first will not consist, as we have seen, with wrong-doing from wantonness or in sport; but the last may; yet even when it does, not much credit can accrue from this circumstance. Worthy of all honor is that good nature which springs from genuine kindness and sympathy, or a desire to make and to see everybody happy; but the same can hardly be said of what often passes for good nature in the world, though it is nothing but the result of an easy temper and loose principles.

Still, I cannot but think that a large majority of those who sometimes look for sport in wrong-doing have enough of humanity and of justice to restrain them, if they could only be made to understand and feel the extent of the injury thus occasioned. Take, for example, jesting with *sacred* things. Its influence on those who indulge in it is worse than that of infidelity; for it destroys our reverence, and it is harder to recover our reverence, after it has been lost, than our convictions. Nay, it is often worse than that of daring crime: the latter puts us in opposition to religion; but it does not necessarily undermine our respect for it, or the sentiment on which the whole rests. Consider, too, its effects on others. The multitude are apt to mistake what is laughed at by their superiors for what is ridiculous in itself. In France it was not the sober arguments of a knot of misguided atheists, but the scoffs and mockeries and ill-timed pleasantries in which the higher classes generally shared, which destroyed the popular sense of the sanctity of religion; and when this great regulative principle of society was gone, it was not long before the mischief came back, amidst scenes of popular license and desperation, "to plague the inventors." And so of *cruel* sports. In reading the Sermon on the Mount, you must have been struck with the fact, that, while he who is angry with his brother is only said to be in danger of the judgment, "whosoever shall say, Thou fool, shall be in danger of hell fire." But, on second thoughts, is this any thing more than a simple recognition of what we all know to be true ; that hatred does not inflict half so deep or bitter a feeling of wrong as scorn? Much is said about the disorganizing doctrines and theories of the day; but, bad as these are, they are not likely to do so much to exasperate the poor against the rich, and break down the bulwarks of order and law, as the conduct of some among the rich themselves. The time was when the few could trample with indifference on the interests and feelings of the many, and make sport of their complaints with impunity; but that time has passed away.

One word also on those cruel sports where animals, and not men, are the sufferers. Cruelty to animals is essentially the same feeling with cruelty to a fellow-creature, and in some respects it is even more unbecoming. Man is as a god to the inferior races. To abuse the power which this gives us over the helpless beings that Providence has placed at our mercy, is as mean as it is inhuman. If we would listen to the pleadings of what is noble and generous in our natures, it would be as impossible for us needlessly to harm an unoffending animal, as it would be to strike an infant or an idiot. Shame on the craven who quails before his equals, and then goes away and wreaks his unmanly resentments on a creature which he knows can neither retaliate nor speak! Besides, we may suppose that there are orders of beings above us, as well as below us. Look then at our treatment of the lower animals, and then ask yourselves what we should think, if a superior order of beings should mete out to us the same measure. What if in mere wantonness, or to pamper unnatural tastes, they should subject us to every imaginable hardship and wrong? What if they should make a show, a public recreation, of our foolish contests and dying agonies? Nay, more; what if it should come to this, that in their language a man-killer should be called *a sportsman* by way of distinction?

But I must close. I wage no idle and bootless war against innocent mirth. We have it on the authority of the Bible, and we read it in the constitution of man, that there is "a time to weep and a time to laugh." There will also be ample scope for the legitimate action of caustic wit, so long as there are follies to be shown up, pretenders to be unmasked, and conceit and affectation to be taught to know themselves. But, in the serious strifes of the world, the ultimate advantages of this weapon, though wielded on the right side, are more than dubious. "The Spaniards have lamented," it has been said, "and I believe truly, that Cervantes' just and inimitable ridicule of knight-errantry rooted up, with that folly, a great deal of their real honor. And it was apparent that Butler's fine satire on fanaticism contributed not a little, during the licentious times of Charles II., to bring sober piety into disrepute. The reason is evident: there are many lines of resemblance between truth and its counterfeits; and it is the province of wit only to find out the likenesses in things, and not the talent of the common admirers of it to discover the differences." At any rate we can shun the rock of small wits, who think to make up for poverty of invention by scurrility and grimace, who think to gain from the venom of the shaft what is wanting in the vigor of the bow. We can imitate the example of those among the great masters of wit in all ages, who have ennobled it by purity of expression and a moral aim; so that, in the end, virtue may not have occasion to blush, or humanity to mourn, for any thing we have said or done. Take any other course, and we are reminded of the confession which experience wrung from the lips of the Wise Man: "I said in my heart, Go to now, I will prove thee with mirth ; therefore enjoy pleasure : and behold this also is vanity. I said of laughter, It is mad ; and of mirth, What doeth it ? " "Even in laughter the heart is sorrowful, and the end of that mirth is heaviness."

1827–1857.

XV.

HONESTY.

"*In all things willing to live honestly.*" — HEBREWS xiii. 18.

WHEN a man's honesty is questioned, it is common to refer the charge to some business transaction. But this is taking a narrow and false view of the subject. A partisan who knowingly avails himself of sophistical arguments in recommending a cause however sacred, is a dishonest man. A demagogue who makes use of popular prejudices which he secretly despises, in order to compass ambitious schemes, is a dishonest man. The hypocrite, the sycophant, the charlatan, — these are all dishonest men. Thus there are a multitude of ways in which a man can show himself honest or dishonest, — ways which have nothing to do with buying or selling.

Honesty includes all those qualities which go to make up that sort of character which inspires confidence. By an honest man we mean a *true* man, — a man who can be depended on in all changes of circumstances, in all vicissitudes of fortune. He is one who feels what he professes, thinks and means what he says, *is* what he *seems*. He is not one man to-day, and another man to-morrow; one man in one company, and another man in another company; one man to me and another man to you. You always know where to find him. An honest man may have his failings; nay, more, he may have great faults, — faults of manner and faults of temper. Honest men are not necessarily perfect men. They may be wrong-headed to almost any extent, — ignorant, prejudiced, overbearing, irritable, malicious even; but it is contrary to their nature to be *false*. Honesty of character is another name for directness and transparency of character; what is *without* corresponds to and indicates what is *within;* in one word, the life is an acted truth, and not an acted lie.

But who is likely to listen to a sermon on honesty, as being personally interested in the appeal? Men are not slow to acknowledge themselves guilty of other sins, or at least extremely liable to them, — the sins of ignorance or weakness, of passion or inconsideration; but who will confess that he is dishonest? Who feels that he is in much danger of becoming so?

What does more perhaps than any thing else to create and foster this delusion is the verbal paradox, that a man may be honest and yet not be honest at the same time. That is to say, he may be honest in one sense of the word and not honest in another; for honesty is a word which is used in different senses. Sometimes it stands for what is called *legal honesty*, meaning thereby that sort of honesty which is determined and enforced by human laws. Sometimes it stands for what is called *worldly honesty*, meaning thereby that sort of honesty which recognizes nothing higher than public opinion as its motive, measure, and end. And sometimes it stands for what alone should be called *Christian honesty*, meaning thereby that sort of honesty which consists in being honest according to the gospel standard of honesty, for its own sake, and in the fear of God.

Now I am willing to admit that most persons moving about in respectable society are honest in one or another of these ways. We hear a great deal about "*common* honesty," and doubtless there is a kind or degree of honesty which is common enough. But who will say that this is true of Christian honesty? And here it becomes us to consider whether any of the other forms of honesty are not essentially defective *even as honesty*. In other words, must we not make a distinction between real and nominal honesty, just as we make a distinction between real and nominal Christianity?

Consider, in the first place, how little claim a man has to be regarded as really honest, who can pretend to nothing better than *legal honesty*, the honesty that never looks beyond or above human laws for its rule or its sanction. Human laws, as everybody knows, do not even so much as aim or profess to determine and enforce *all* right as such, but only so much of right as is necessary to the order and well-being of society. Beyond this, they very properly leave men to the restraints of conscience, and public opinion, and the fear of a future retribution. Even, therefore, if human laws were perfect as far as they go, it would by no means follow that it is enough to be honest *according to law.* There are a multitude of questions of right and wrong daily arising in the intercourse of society, which the laws do not touch; and if in respect to these a man shows himself regardless of moral principle, he shows himself to be at bottom a dishonest man. I say this advisedly. If when the laws, for good reasons, refuse to interfere, and devolve the whole matter on conscience alone, a man's conscience also fails to act, it shows that he has no conscience. It is an abuse of language to say of such a man that he is *honest according to law*, inasmuch as his obedience to law does not spring from a sense of right. Unless a man acts from a principle of honesty, he is not, properly speaking, honest at all. A man does not show himself to be really honest, in any form or degree, by being honest as long as the laws compel him to be so, but by being honest when he is free to be so, or not, as he pleases.

Besides, it is conceding too much in favor of what is called legal honesty, to allow it to be assumed that the laws themselves are always what they should be. There are such things as bad laws; and, though these can *legalize* wrong, they can hardly make wrong to be right. Indeed, now that laws are made and unmade with so much facility, and often under the disturbing influences of popular or party excitement, have we not almost as much to apprehend from wrong-doing under color and sanction of law, as from wrong-doing in open violation of law? Yet I suppose all will agree, that wrong-doing in either case is wrong-doing. If there is such a thing as being honest according to law, there is also such a thing as being dishonest according to law. Certainly I cannot be mistaken here. If I do what I know and feel to be unfair or overreaching, an iniquitous law may be found to screen me; but what of that? It may keep me from being actually treated as a dishonest man; but will it keep me from *de-*

serving to be so treated? I do not say but that, under a free government like ours, a bad law is to be submitted to, until it is repealed by the proper authorities, merely because it is the law. It is one thing, however, to submit to a bad law, — that is, to *suffer* under it, — and quite another *to take advantage* of it; the latter being in all cases, as it seems to me, neither more nor less than making use of one wrong to justify or excuse another.

Thus does it appear that legal honesty, meaning thereby that sort of honesty that can be, and is, enforced by human laws, is radically and essentially defective, even as honesty. It is so, in the first place, because human laws are sometimes bad and iniquitous in themselves; in the second place, because these laws however good in themselves are sometimes made, through the imperfection of human foresight and human language, to cover cases of substantial injustice; and in the third and last place, because human laws even when right in themselves, and rightly executed and applied as far as they go, do not even so much as aim or profess to determine and enforce all right as such, but only so much of right as is necessary to the public welfare. I do not mean that there is no honesty in obedience to the laws, or that any man can be honest, in a community like ours, without such obedience; but this I say: the *proof* of his honesty, instead of beginning where this obedience begins, begins rather where this obedience ends. *To prove* that we are honest, we must persist in doing what is right, not only as long as the laws stand ready to coerce it, but also when, from any cause, they leave us free to do otherwise.

Let us next inquire how it is with *worldly honesty*,—the honesty, I mean, which has no better foundation than a regard for public opinion and worldly success. This, I hardly need say, is sometimes better, and sometimes worse, than a strictly legal honesty. It is sometimes better, because public opinion for the time being may be in advance of the laws, and require more; on the other hand, it is sometimes worse, because public opinion, for the time being, may fall behind the laws, and require less. In the latter case, the best of laws, though unrepealed, are apt to become either wholly or in part a dead letter. Making the most of worldly honesty, it is but another name for what may be called the average virtue in the community, for the time being, with this distinction, that it supposes some degree of reflection and forethought. It is the virtue of men who are wise in their generation, and think to find in worldly wisdom alone a sufficient foundation and guarantee of upright conduct. It is the virtue of men who are for ever recurring to the maxim that "honesty is the best policy;" who think it is only necessary for men to know what their interest is, and they will do what is right; who would fain resolve all crime into ignorance or mistake, and cannot find it in their hearts to say any thing worse of sin, than that it is a great blunder.

Now unquestionably there is much truth in these assumptions; it is not however the whole truth, and nothing but the truth. A Christian should be the last person in the world to deny that "honesty is the best policy." God has made it to be so in all cases. It is not only the greatest rule, but there are no real or imaginable exceptions to the rule, so long as *all* a man's interests are taken into the account. In no case whatsoever is it consistent with a man's interests to deviate, though but for a hair's breadth, from strict right, if by "a man's interests" are meant *all* his interests. But if we are going to restrict our view to *a part* of his interests, and to the lowest and most inconsiderable part, that alters the case. It is by no means so clear but that some deviations from strict right may be consistent with a part of a man's interests, — with those, for example, which pertain to this world. It may still be true, as doubtless it is, even if we look not beyond this life, that honesty is the best policy *as a general rule;* but who will say that it is a rule which admits absolutely of *no exceptions?* And the mischief of these exceptions does not end with leaving virtue unsupported, when they actually occur. The idea that there *are* exceptions will tempt every person, who is sorely tried, to believe or to assume that the case in hand is one of them; and he will act accordingly.

I come, therefore, to this conclusion: even if policy of any kind were sufficient of itself to make a man honest, it would not be *worldly* policy. It must be a policy which comprehends *all* a man's interests, — the interests of his soul as well as those of his body, the interests of eternity as well as those of time; in short, it must be Christian policy: otherwise it would be essentially defective *even as policy.*

But I am far from believing that *policy*, of any name or nature, is to be regarded as the legitimate ground, or as a sufficient safeguard of strict honesty. Those who think it enough to demonstrate that "honesty is the best policy" would seem to proceed on the assumption, that every man takes that course which he is convinced will be for his interest in the long run. But is it so? Dismiss, for a moment, all theories on the subject, and look at facts. Take that vast catalogue of vices and crimes which originate in disordered appetite or unbridled passion. Do you suppose that the men who give way to these temptations really think they are consulting their *interests* here or hereafter; that they are doing what it is good policy to do? No! a thousand times, no! If you still entertain any doubts on the subject, go and ask them in moments when thought returns, and they will answer you just as I have done, mingling the confession with bitter imprecations on their own weakness and folly.

On this point we must guard against a mistaken inference from men's acknowledged selfishness. Men are selfish; but it is a selfishness which, when left to itself, looks not to *self-advantage* but to *self-indulgence*, and to self-indulgence at any cost. You may think to find an exception to this remark in the griping and pinching habits of the miser; but it is an exception in appearance only. Even he is not counting on any real and substantial benefits as the reward of his labors and sacrifices; he does but yield to the blind impulse of a present passion, the greed of gain.

No: what we chiefly need is not more selfishness, Heaven knows; but more principle, — a reverence for what is right, fidelity and devotion to duty. And this is precisely that state of mind which Christianity aims to induce. It is taking a most unworthy view of the gospel, to suppose it contents itself with setting before us life and death, heaven and hell, and leaving them to act as they may on the selfishness of our nature. The aim of our Saviour's teachings, I might almost say their whole purport and end, is to excite, develop, and enlighten our moral and spiritual faculties; to create within us a spontaneous aversion and disgust for what is mean and base; to awaken and call out disinterested and inextinguishable aspirations for what is pure and noble, and a living and all-sustaining sense of the Divine presence and agency. When this change is wrought upon us, and not before, we may hope to comprehend the full import of that dark Scripture, "Whosoever is born of God doth not commit sin; for his seed remaineth in him, and he cannot sin, because he is born of God."

Taking this view of honesty, who will say that the subject is not a proper one for the Christian pulpit at all times? If I went no further than to recommend legal honesty, or worldly honesty, or even a pagan or deistic honesty, it might be otherwise. The old cry might be raised, "You are preaching no more than what Socrates and Seneca preached." But certainly neither Socrates nor Seneca ever preached Christian honesty; the honesty that finds its law, its spirit, and its tests in the New Testament. The indiscriminate offence taken by some, at what they call "moral preaching," grows out of confounding together two propositions which are very far from being identical. They say that religion is one thing, and morality another; and this is true. They go on to say, as if it were to repeat the same doctrine in other words, that Christianity is one thing, and morality another; but this is not true. The reason is that the gospel everywhere inculcates a peculiar morality as well as a peculiar religion; so that the former is just as much Christianity as the latter. Do not understand me to say one word against evangelical faith, or evangelical piety: all I ask for is that to these may be added more and more of evangelical honesty.

There is call for this exhortation in all sects, and especially in those which make the greatest pretensions to sanctity and zeal. Whose fault is it, that men of business are put on their guard when they find themselves dealing with one who assumes to be more than usually religious? Is it not because long experience has taught them that the honesty of professed Christians is often a very different thing from Christian honesty? Is this scandal to last for ever? Christianity will never stand before the world on the vantage-ground it ought to hold, until those who claim to represent it are known, not by the badges of this or that sect, but by the singular purity and rectitude of their conduct. And this suggests the best criterion by which to determine the comparative merits of rival creeds. One is best for one thing, and another for another. One induces reverence for authority; another stirs the religious emotions; a third makes missionaries and martyrs. All this is well as far as it goes; but the result is not a complete and well-balanced Christian character. The best form of religion is that which assigns a proper place to reverence, to the emotions, and to zeal, but lays its principal stress on the doctrine that, to be accepted of God, a man must be good,—thoroughly good, honest, trustworthy, in all the relations of life. The best form of religion is that which leads men to respect one another, and deal fairly with one another; the worst form of religion is that which leads men to hate or despise one another.

Let me add that the inculcation of strict probity and incorruptibleness is doubly necessary in seasons of great social and political disturbance. It is sometimes said that war, even a civil war, is favorable to the higher virtues; and so in a certain sense it is. It offers frequent occasions for heroic deeds; it calls for self-denial and self-sacrifice in tones of unwonted power; it is also a school for the manly qualities of courage and endurance, of a generous patriotism and a lofty ambition. All this I freely admit; but I must qualify it by observing, that opportunities are afforded, at the same time, for giant frauds; that the restraining power of public opinion is disordered, and on some subjects wholly perverted; in fine, that minds, and good minds too, become so intent on success as to be more or less unscrupulous about the means. In this state of things, why wonder that measures should be sometimes advocated, and men upheld, on principles to which nothing but the blinding and corrupting influences of the terrible struggle could reconcile a people of any pretensions to justice and honor.

To counteract such tendencies let the pulpit be faithful to its high function, and amidst the din of conflicting interests and passions hold up the Christian standard of a perfect righteousness. Woe to those who traffic in the public distresses and perplexities with a view to dishonest gains! Woe to those who palter with the public conscience, even though it is with a mistaken view to the public good! Our country, in this hour of her extreme peril, expects great sacrifices from us, but not the sacrifice of integrity and honor. We believe that the right is on our side: let us stand on that right, and glorify it by a conduct worthy of the great and solemn issue! Not only the future of our own country, but that of freedom and human rights everywhere, is at stake: the battle is fought in the face of a world from which we look for little sympathy; still the danger is not that we shall be slain by the sword, but that we shall fail to exhibit a degree of private and public virtue equal to the exigency, — that we shall not have union enough, or magnanimity enough, or Christian principle enough to save us from a general demoralization, in which our own honor and the best hopes of mankind will go down together. Whatever calamities befall us, may God in his infinite mercy vouchsafe that righteousness which is the glory and the strength of a Christian nation, and avert that sin which is the reproach and ruin of any people!

1861.

XVI.

THE DANGERS OF COLLEGE LIFE.

"*Ye, therefore, beloved, seeing ye know these things before, beware lest ye also, being led away with the error of the wicked, fall from your own steadfastness.* — 2 PETER iii. 17.

IN speaking of his early days, Mr. Gibbon observes: "Every time I have since passed over Putney Common, I have always noticed the spot where my mother, as we drove along in the coach, admonished me that I was now going into the world, and must learn to think and act for myself." I am not surprised at the deep and indelible impression which this simple fact, on account of its connections, appears to have left on the mind of the great historian. He had arrived at one of those critical periods in the life of man, where much would depend on the way in which he should begin. He had just left, perhaps for the first time, the constant and countless restraints of home; he would soon find himself in a new situation, in the midst of strange faces, beset by unaccustomed difficulties and temptations, and would there be called upon, with the scanty stock of experience he must be supposed already to have acquired, to shape his course by his own unassisted discretion as he best could.

Thus it is, that, under the same or like circumstances, the entrance of any young man into the little world of a large public school or college, where by necessity he must be left, for the most part, to think and act for himself, constitutes no ordinary trial of character. But it is a satisfaction to know that whoever sees fit to meet it with upright intentions, and a good share of forethought, self-distrust, and self-control, will find himself equal to this trial. And, if he succeeds here, it is the best earnest he can possibly give of success in after-life; for the foundation of human trial, and the foundation of our superiority to it, are everywhere substantially the same. All turns on the single question, whether we can safely be trusted with the liberty to think and act for ourselves. To do right under constraint, when we are not free to do otherwise, is nothing: one man will do it as well as another. It is only when this constraint is relaxed, and men are put to a considerable extent under their own keeping, and called upon to think for themselves and act for themselves, that the great distinctions among them arise. He only who knows how to use his liberty without abusing it, succeeds; and he who knows how to do this in one place will be likely to know how to do it in another.

As I have said, there is nothing in the trials of a college life to deter or dishearten a person of good and strong purposes. Still it would be treachery of the worst kind to hold out the lure of safety and ease, — to affirm, or to imply, or to allow it to be presumed, that the failures are not frequent, or that the dangers are not many and great. And what makes it worse in respect to many of these dangers is, that often they are not suspected, or, which amounts to the same thing in practice, not sufficiently considered until it is too late. For this reason I have thought it would be well to begin the religious instructions of the academic year by calling your attention to some of the dangers peculiarly incident to an academic life: so that, knowing these things before, you may be less likely to be led away with the error of the wicked, and fall from your own steadfastness.

One of these dangers, though occurring here, is to be referred to causes which the student brings along with him; I mean his *constitutional predispositions.* It was a favorite notion of some of the French philosophers, in which they were followed but too closely by our Franklin, that mankind in general come into the world with precisely the same rational endowments, all the differences which afterwards arise originating in differences of education. Few, if any, will be found to entertain this doctrine now, the tendency of common opinion and of the popular philosophy being to the opposite extreme. Great stress is now laid on distinctions of race and blood; innate and often hereditary biasses are thought to influence, and for the most part to determine, the whole life; and men are found who are fain to read in the organization of the child his future destiny. This, as I have said, is the other extreme; it supposes us to be born with propensities which it is the work of life to manifest, and not to govern and control. Obviously however it is so far founded in truth as this, that some men have strong constitutional predispositions to excess or defect in one direction, whilst others have equally strong constitutional predispositions to excess or defect in another: and hence their principal danger.

And the danger in this case is made tenfold greater, if the individual does not know himself; if he will not consider the errors to which, from his constitution and temperament, he is peculiarly exposed; in short, if from any cause he will not acknowledge even to himself his besetting sins. Some there are who are slow to confess to besetting sins of any kind, because they are not conscious of desiring any evil for its own sake; but such persons entirely mistake what is meant by a besetting sin. A besetting sin, as here understood, does not suppose a man to desire evil for its own sake, but only that he desires something else so inordinately, that he is always in danger of doing evil in order to gratify this desire. For example; it may be the love of ease, or the love of company, or the love of pleasure, or the love of display. Now it is not pretended that ease, or company, or pleasure, or display is bad in itself, that is to say, in its proper place and degree. But if all a man's constitutional leanings incline him to one of these forms of gratification, the danger is that, in order to gain it, he will not scruple to sacrifice or neglect more important objects, and so fall into transgression. We are not to blame for our constitutional predispositions; we cannot help them if we would: but we can know them if we would, and we can consider them in every thing we do; always remembering that the great question is not what is safe for *others*, but what is safe for *us;* always remembering, also, that the price of safety is perpetual vigilance.

Another form of danger incident to college life grows out of *hastily-formed and ill-assorted friendships and intimacies.* One of the most perplexing facts in Divine Providence is, that we should be responsible for our characters, and yet that our characters should depend so much on the conduct of others. A young man, probably without confirmed principles, for these generally suppose long experience and a confirmed faith, but with upright intentions and good impulses, comes under the influence of a stronger mind than his own, and how apt he is to become but little more than a reflection of that stronger mind! Thus it is that the ascendancy, and the social and winning qualities, of a single bad man will blight the prospects and sometimes utterly ruin the hopes of many, not only for this world but also for the world to come. Nevertheless, it is proper to observe that in all such cases the victims are, to a certain extent, *willing* victims: they cannot be thus used until they consent to be thus used. Hence their fall, considered as a difficulty in Providence and a moral anomaly, is, in some measure at least, cleared up; for, by allowing others to destroy them, they may be said, in some sense, to destroy themselves.

But these are not the only ill-assorted friendships and intimacies to which a community like this may be expected to give birth. As has been intimated before, there are few persons so happily constituted by nature as not to be troubled by a constant leaning to one side or the other, which must be resisted, or they would fall. These leanings, however, are different in different persons; and where, as sometimes happens, this is the case with intimate friends, it may even be said that the faults of one help to balance and correct the faults of the other; so that both are made better by the intercourse. But I hardly need say, that the contrary is more likely to happen; especially with persons of but little reflection, who are drawn together unconsciously by the very fact that they have so many tastes, or, it may be, so many failings, or so many dangerous propensities, in common. Because they like to do the same things, they are likely to go together, — the indolent with the indolent, the reckless with the reckless, the pleasure-loving with the pleasure-loving. And what is likely to be the consequence? Plainly this, that they will encourage and stimulate each other to act out, and to act out with less and less reserve, inclinations which it should be the labor of their lives to restrain and repress. Thus, without pretensions to much power of any kind, without any bad purpose or disposition, nay, under strong and perhaps sincere professions of love and regard, they contrive to do each other precisely the greatest harm of which they are susceptible, that is, break each other down at the very point where they are least likely to recover.

Of the same general description is another

danger almost sure to grow up in a community, the members of which think and act by themselves, being isolated to a considerable extent from the rest of the world. I mean the danger resulting from an *artificial state of public opinion, and an artificial, and consequently more or less unsound, standard of manners and morals.* It is a mistake to suppose that friendships and intimacies are *forced* upon us by the single circumstance that we are constrained to live together, as in a ship, a camp, or a college. Each one is still at liberty, and is generally found, in point of fact, to exercise the liberty, to choose his intimates according to his own inclinations and tastes. Over all, however, by common though it may be tacit consent, certain rules and maxims gradually acquire the authority of law, which persons possessing no more than ordinary strength and independence of character can hardly be expected to disown, or even so much as call in question. On these points, therefore, their conduct, instead of being as it ought to be a manly expression of their own individual convictions of duty, is always in danger of degenerating into a mere echo of the general voice, a timid and servile acting out of the general will.

I am not disposed to speak disparagingly, on the whole, of the sort of public opinion which is apt to be generated in a community of young men, whose bond of union is the common pursuit of liberal studies. As a general rule, I believe it is singularly free from the alloy of meanness, selfishness, and untruthfulness of every kind, and that its very errors may be traced for the most part either to an excess, or to a misapplication, of principles which are in themselves eminently good. Still, it can hardly be without permanent injury to a man's moral nature, that he should subscribe himself slave to any artificial and arbitrary rule; and besides, we must not shut our eyes on the fact that no principles have done so much harm in the world as perversions of the best principles. Some may think that there is no real danger in this case, because every student on leaving college, if not before, is found to disclaim and ridicule the rules and maxims here complained of, as a matter of course. But why disclaim and ridicule them as a matter of course, if they are felt to be just and safe? Moreover, is there no danger that the habit once formed of submitting to a factitious standard of right in the place of conscience, will be continued, the only change being in the factitious standard itself, and this, too, probably a change for the worse? Is there no danger that the habit of a weak or timid conformity here may turn out to be a training for that conformity to the world, which the gospel takes occasion to condemn more frequently and more strenuously, perhaps, than any other error or sin?

The other dangers peculiarly incident to a college life originate in mistaken notions of the nature and extent of education, and of the proper motives to study.

Let me begin what I have to say on this topic by disclaiming all sympathy with those who condemn altogether a regard for distinction as expressed in the approbation of wise and good men. In the first place, I cannot bring myself to look on such condemnation as just to human nature, or as being, in most instances at least, sincere. Furthermore, we need, we imperiously need, the good opinion of others to encourage and assure us in the course we have begun. Certainly we must not study for distinction in itself considered, but for distinction as evidence that we deserve it, — an evidence peculiarly necessary and therefore peculiarly welcome to humble, distrustful, and ingenuous minds. At the same time there is evident danger that, in the rivalries among students, they may look exclusively or mainly to *immediate* distinction; that they may strive for the premature; that they may not be willing to labor patiently and untiringly for a distant good; that they may think that the love of distinction may be substituted for the love of excellence. There is no such thing. An aphorism, which a truly distinguished son of this college inscribed on the walls of his studio, is applicable to every form of mental effort. "No genuine work of art ever was, or ever can be, produced but for its own sake; if the painter does not conceive to please himself, he will not finish to please the world."

Again, the student is always in danger of not sufficiently considering that the paramount object of education, and especially of a general and preliminary education, is not to *fill* the mind, but to *strengthen* and *enlarge* it. It has sometimes been said that the training of animals is better understood than the training of men; for in the former case the whole aim is to form the animal to the *qualities* required. Perhaps it will be objected that *qualities* cannot be *taught;* and this is true; but they can be *developed*, which amounts to the same thing in effect, the result being that those have them, who otherwise would not. Therefore it is, that, in regard to any study pursued at school, or in college, the great question is not, of what use will be the knowledge it will impart, but of what use will it be, considered as a means of exercising and disciplining the mind itself. Look at the persons who have succeeded best in the various departments of human industry; inquire into their history, and you will find them to owe their success much less to the stock of knowledge which they brought with them into active life than to their *personal qualities*, — that is, to previously formed habits of attention and observation, of activity, presence of mind, self-control, and the power of concentrating their entire and utmost energies on the business in hand.

But if there is danger in neglecting the cultivation of the mental qualities mentioned above, how much greater that which consists in neglecting the cultivation of the conscience and the heart! I have spoken of success in life; but a moment's reflection must convince every one that this is not the ultimate object of education. The ultimate object of education is happiness considered as the fruit of duty and usefulness. Success in life may be looked to, I grant, as one of the means of usefulness and happiness, and as such be provided for in a judicious education; but, viewed under this relation, it is not worthy to be compared with the unavoidable influences, either for good or for evil, of temper and character. The world is full of examples of what is called success in life, without any thing which deserves the name of happiness, content, or self-respect. Nay, should you have any doubts on this subject, let me ask you to bring the question to the test of your own experience. Put all you have suffered from outward adversities into one scale, and all you have suffered from a mortified vanity and pride, from a disappointed ambition, from hasty or ill-governed passions, and from a guilty conscience into the other, and see which preponderates. In short, when education, from any cause, is divorced from morals, when it is sought after and obtained as a mere *power*, with no security that this power will not be abused, its principal recommendation is gone, and the old question returns, not without reason, whether after all it is a blessing or a curse.

Let me conclude by adverting to a danger in education more fundamental still; I mean the danger of thinking to find any other basis for character but religious principle and the Christian faith. I speak not here of religious dogmas; but of a religious spirit, of the religious sentiment, of religion considered as an element, or rather as the foundation, of character, which is found to subsist in almost equal perfection under the greatest diversity of religious dogmas. What we need is to be trained from the beginning in the habitual recognition of the constant presence, agency, and government of Almighty God. What we need is, that our hearts, before they have become fixed and hardened by worldly influences, may be touched to higher issues, may learn to respond to higher relations and a higher destiny; in one word, that what is divine in our own souls may be so quickened and developed as to bring us into communication with what is divine in nature, in Scripture, and in life. Let this be neglected, let the neglect become general, and I do not believe that a high and pure virtue could be maintained; above all, I do not believe that civil liberty would be either practicable or desirable. There never has been but one experiment on a large scale, to see whether men can live together in society without religion, and you know the result. Robespierre himself, "in his remarkable discourse on the restoration of public worship, denounced atheism as inconsistent with equality, and a crime of the aristocracy; and asserted the existence of a Supreme Being, who protects the poor and rewards the poor, as a popular consolation, without which the people would despair."

I have discoursed of the dangers and difficulties which encompass the student from the beginning. But I am unwilling to quit the subject without repeating what I have said before; it is a pleasure and satisfaction to know that to many these dangers and difficulties exist only to be overcome, and so to be turned into occasions of triumph. To persons of good and strong purposes the promise of the gospel is fulfilled: "Behold I give unto you power to tread on serpents and scorpions, and over all the power of the enemy; and nothing shall by any means hurt you."

Preëminently among such was the young member of this society, the intelligence of whose recent, sudden, and, as we in our shortsightedness are tempted to say, untimely death has filled all our hearts with sadness.[1] So happily was he constituted by nature, that all *his* prevailing tastes and inclinations seemed to be to good. Again, he could suffer but little from ill-assorted friendships and intimacies, as he was led to seek companionship only as a means of self-improvement, of generous ambition, or of innocent pastime. He also knew how to conform to the conventionalities of the place as far as a genial temper and an unselfish prudence required, without the sacrifice of that moral independence which he taught others to respect by respecting it himself. Finally, we have reason to believe that he never essentially mistook the motive or the end of a truly Christian education; which is to fit man for the performance of the highest duties from the highest principles. For ever blessed be the memory of one who has recommended goodness, by

[1] The allusion is to JOHN N. MEAD, of Brattleboro', Vt., a member of the Class of 1851.

combining with the qualities which command our reverence, the qualities which win our love.

His work is accomplished. Much of ours remains to be done ; and this too, as we have seen, in the face of formidable dangers and difficulties: so much so, that it would be with a heavy heart that I should bid you go on, if I could not bid you at the same time, " God speed." " As an eagle stirreth up her nest, fluttereth over her young, spreadeth abroad her wings, taketh them, beareth them on her wings, — so the Lord alone will lead you. Even the youths shall faint and be weary, and the young men shall utterly fall. But they that wait upon the Lord shall renew their strength ; they shall mount up with wings as eagles ; they shall run and not be weary, and they shall walk and not faint."

1850.

XVII.

WHITE LIES.

"*For if the truth of God hath more abounded through my lie unto his glory, why yet am I also judged as a sinner?*" — ROMANS iii. 7.

SOME confusion has been introduced into our reasonings on moral subjects by not marking carefully the distinction between *truth* and *veracity*. Truth, in its primary acceptation, is not a quality of character, but a quality of statements. A statement is either true or false; that is, it does or does not accord with the facts in the case. But even if it be false, a man may utter it and yet not be guilty of lying; because he may utter it, believing it to be true. Such a man may be said to want the truth; that is to say he is in error, he is mistaken: but he cannot be said to want veracity; he tells the truth as he understands it. Accordingly we have no right to blame a man merely because his statements are not true. This is an objection to the *statements*, but it is no objection to the *man*, if he really thinks them to be true, and has taken proper pains to inform himself.

What we have a right to blame a man for is the want of veracity, the want of a disposition and intention to speak the truth. Here the imputation extends, as you will observe, to the man himself. It supposes something to be wrong not only in the statement, but in the man who makes the statement.

Hence it by no means follows that every false statement is a lying statement; for to make it such it must be uttered by one who believes it to be false.

A candid and generous application of this obvious distinction, in the every-day intercourse of society, would make men slower than they commonly are to impeach each other's veracity, how much soever they might still distrust each other's information or judgment. They would see that a large proportion of the popular delusions, unfounded calumnies, and idle rumors in circulation in the community, can be satisfactorily accounted for and explained, without ascribing them to intentional and deliberate perversion of the truth. I do not mean that a man who is always ready, on slight grounds, to take up with a report injuriously affecting his neighbor, and assist in spreading it, is innocent. Neither do I mean that the dealers in crude and disorganizing theories in philosophy, politics, or religion are innocent. Such men are not innocent.

Far from it. But, generally speaking, their fault does not consist in lying; that is, in a conscious purpose to deceive or mislead. Their fault consists, rather, in hasty and rash judgment, in an overweening conceit in their own abilities, in mistaking a love of novelty and paradox for a love of truth, or in not taking sufficient care to guard against a credulous turn of mind. And it is absolutely essential that he who undertakes to expose and correct their fault should consider this. How can you expect to cure a man of a fault of which he is really guilty, by accusing him of another fault of which he knows he is not guilty? These men believe what they say, just as much as you believe what you say. Their fault does not consist in saying what they do not believe; but in believing on insufficient grounds and under wrong biasses, in over-confidence in what they believe, and in the presumption and injustice to which this over-confidence leads. The weakest of all weaknesses is, to suspect everybody who differs from us of insincerity.

Most persons, perhaps, will be willing to concede this in favor of the ignorant multitude, the deluded masses, the blind followers, as they are called; but not so as regards the leaders. Such a man, we often hear it said, *must know better.* But he may not after all. The ways of self-mystification, the artifices of self-deceit, transcend by far, both in number and in subtilty, what is commonly supposed. And besides, credulity is an inborn propensity of some minds, so thoroughly ingrained that no kind or degree of teaching or experience can effectually work it out of their constitution. Hence we often meet with very learned and very ingenious men who are among the easiest to be imposed upon; especially if the folly or the cheat can be made to wear a learned and ingenious look. If I were bent on propagating a new extravagance, I would rather take my chance, at least in most cases, with thinking and speculative men than with plain, practical men; and for this reason. I should expect to find less difficulty in persuading the former than the latter to drop the substance and catch at the shadow, — that is to say, at a theory.

History, rightly read, confirms what has been said. If the truth were known, I suspect it would be found that, in most instances, the authors and principal instigators of the great popular delusions have differed from their followers chiefly in this, that they were among the first to be entirely carried away by the delusion. Who doubts, at the present day, that Mohammed and Cromwell entered on their career in good faith, and that, but for this, nothing but defeat and disgrace would have waited on their imbecile presumption?

I do not mean that such persons are never guilty of prevarication and insincerity in particular things, in order to help the delusion over a difficulty or round a corner; but I do mean that in regard to the delusion itself they are generally, — not always, but *generally*, at least at the beginning, — honest. There is more or less of lying mingled, I am afraid, with almost every life; but I do not believe that it is common to find a life which is *built on a lie.*

You will perceive how slow I am to give credit to charges of wholesale lying, which malice, jealousy, or narrow-mindedness is so ready to bring against individuals, and even against whole sects or parties. This, however, does not hinder me from suspecting and believing that there is a vast deal of lying *in a small way;* and, what is more and worse, a disposition everywhere to justify or excuse it, on the ground that though these are lies, they are *white lies.* I have no faith in this distinction. I do not believe it has any proper foundation in reason or Scripture. Let us not be misled by names. Show that the error is not a lie; resolve it into ignorance, misunderstanding, illusion of any kind, and all is well; at any rate, it is not a lie: but admit it to be a lie, and I do not believe that it is in the power of any ingenuity of construction or explanation to wash it entirely white.

On this hint I am going to speak. I am not

going to speak of gross lying, the baseness and turpitude of which all the world is loud enough to condemn, but of these so-called *white lies*, which partake as it seems to me, in different degrees, of the same baseness and turpitude, and from which in point of fact the bulk of the community have much the most to fear, both in themselves and in others.

The principal reason why so many are ready to acquiesce in the distinction in favor of white lies, is to be found in their superficial and inadequate views of what constitutes the sin of lying. They make it to consist wholly or chiefly in the harm done the individual to whom the lie is told, or, at most, in the social evils or inconveniences occasioned, directly or indirectly, thereby. Without doubt these are important considerations as far as they go, and are to be taken into account in estimating the aggravations of the offence, and the motives which should deter us from committing it; but they do not constitute the essence of the sin. The essence of the sin of lying, as such, does not consist in the injury done to others, but in the wrong done to our own souls, through the violation of that eternal law of truth which God has wrought into our moral constitution, through the stifling or overruling of the instinct or sentiment of veracity, which no man whose heart is right can do, without being self-condemned. If I purposely injure my neighbor by lying, I commit a *double* crime, the crime of malice and the crime of falsehood, the crime of malice *in addition to* the crime of falsehood. In other words, I commit one crime by means of another. And in this case, the criminality of the means does not depend on the criminality of the end; the malice does not make the lying to be criminal, any more than the lying makes the malice to be criminal: both are criminal, each in its own essential and unalterable nature. For this reason, the great question is, as it seems to me, not whether other men under certain circumstances have, or have not, a right to the truth, but whether we, under any circumstances, have a right knowingly to utter an untruth; not whether duplicity and deception will be good or evil in particular instances or in view of general consequences, but whether duplicity and deception are not evils in themselves; and if so, whether we have a right to do evil that good may come; or, for it comes to this at last, whether the end sanctifies the means.

And what say the Scriptures? "Lying lips are an abomination to the Lord." "Putting away lying, speak every man truth with his neighbor." "Ye shall not steal, neither deal falsely, neither lie one to another." "Knowing this, that the law is not made for a righteous man, but for the lawless and disobedient, for the ungodly and sinners, for the unholy and profane, for murderers of fathers and murderers of mothers, for man-slayers, for man-stealers, for liars, for perjured persons, and if there be any other thing that is contrary to sound doctrine." I quote these passages, because to Christians they are, as it seems to me, decisive. Besides, they are full of instruction, because, in the first place, they show with what crimes lying is associated and classed in the Word of God, — with perjury and man-stealing and parricide. Not that the heinousness and turpitude of the crimes thus brought together are necessarily *equal*; but I think that we have a right to infer that their guilt, whatever may be its degree, is equally *essential* and unalterable. Again, it is still more in point to notice that, with respect to lying, there is no trace in these passages that its guilt depends on the circumstances, or the end aimed at. Nothing is said about *white* lies; we are not told never to lie except when we think it will be harmless, or do more good than harm; but the prohibition, according to any fair construction which I can put upon the language, is as unconditional and unqualified as that against murder, man-stealing, or theft.

If there are any on whom this appeal to Scripture is thrown away, on the ground that the Scriptures are nothing to them, let them at least consider what is universally regarded as *the point of honor* among men of the world. There is nothing which men, who think at all of reputation, resent so promptly and so indignantly as a questioning of their word, as a direct impeachment of their veracity. Now if the mere imputation of this crime gives such mortal affront, it must be because the crime itself is accounted one of the basest; otherwise we must conclude that the objection of a man of honor is not to *being* a liar, but only to being *called* one. Neither can we, in consistency with what is said about the disgrace of lying, make distinctions in this vice. The disgrace of lying, even in the opinion of the world, does not depend on the uses to which it is put, or on the mischief it does, but on the fact that under any and all circumstances it betrays a want of courage, manliness, and sincerity. I come, therefore, to this conclusion. Even if we lay the Bible out of the account, and look only to the standard of the world, either the exceeding sensitiveness everywhere manifested by gentlemen to the doubting of their word is mere cant and hypocrisy, or they do really feel that lying of itself, in every form and degree, leaves an indelible stain on the character.

But on a purely practical subject like the present, it is not well to stop with generalities, which nobody perhaps will dispute, and at the same time nobody will apply. Let us, therefore, descend to particulars, and, taking up some of these pretended white lies, look a little into their title to be so regarded as innocent or venial.

I shall begin with *lies of custom.* Here we must take care not to mix up questions which have nothing to do with each other. Custom or usage, I hardly need say, determines the meaning of language in all cases; and sometimes it gives to a whole phrase, as in the instance of the common subscription to a letter, a peculiar significance different from the one it had originally, and different from the one which grammatical construction would give. But this has nothing to do with the subject. It is enough if a man uses these phrases truly; that is to say in their customary import, so that he really means all he is understood to mean. In such a case his language stands in no need of indulgence on the plea of being a white lie. It is no lie at all; no mutual understanding is violated; no confidence is abused; nobody is deceived or misled. But if by lies of custom is meant that degree of real deception which may happen to be customary in the community, and if the doctrine is, that deception to this degree is allowable or venial, nothing can be more false and dangerous. You might just as well extend the same doctrine to other vices. You might just as well say that, where a certain degree of intemperance or knavery is customary, intemperance and knavery to that degree are innocent. Accordingly when it is said that in some professions, and in some kinds of business, a strict adherence to truth is *not expected*, it is not meant that it is not required, or that it is not necessary, there as elsewhere, to integrity and honor. What is meant is simply this, that, in the situations referred to, the temptation to swerve from integrity and honor is found to be too strong for the principles of most men, so that it is hardly to be expected in most men.

I turn next to *lies of courtesy*. Here, again, there is occasion for discrimination. There are splenetic and churlish men who condemn, without distinction or reserve, what is termed politeness in refined society, as being no better than an acted lie. But is it so, — always, I mean? What does a man profess or imply by politeness, rightly understood? Simply that he is actuated by a benevolent wish to make his presence agreeable to the company. If, therefore, he is really actuated as he *ought to be*, and as men sometimes certainly *are*, by a benevolent wish to make his presence agreeable to the company, his politeness does not *lie;* it speaks the truth. Genuine Christian politeness is consistent with the utmost sincerity and transparency of character. It is only when we begin to resort to falsehood and deception as a means of pleasing, and encumber those whom we meet with protestations of regard which we do not feel, and feed their vanity with flattering speeches, that our politeness begins to lie; and then it begins to be a sin, and a sin without excuse. In such cases, it is to no purpose to say that fools only are deceived; for in the first place it is not true; and in the second place, even if it were true, we have no right to deceive fools. And besides, the great mischief of such politeness is not that here and there an individual is deceived, but that, in proportion as it prevails, a general suspicion and distrust is awakened, and everybody's confidence in the openness and sincerity of social intercourse is disturbed.

From lies of courtesy I pass to *lies of humanity*, meaning thereby such as are told not to injure, but to benefit others, from feelings of real tenderness and concern, and not of malice. Paley includes among white lies of this description those which it is allowable to tell madmen for their own advantage. But is such conduct, speaking generally, within the strict interpretation of Christian duty? Even as regards the policy of the proceeding, those only should speak who are best qualified by their experience and observation to pronounce judgment in the case. A traveller in France, in his account of one of the principal hospitals for the insane in Paris, says that the great object aimed at by the officers is, "to gain the confidence of the patients; and this object is generally attained by gentleness, by appearing to take an interest in their affairs, by a decision of character equally remote from the extremes of indulgence and severity, and *by the most scrupulous observance of good faith.* Upon the last condition, particular stress seems to be laid by the head of the institution, who remarks, 'that insane persons, like children, lose all confidence and all respect, if you fail in your word to them, and they immediately set their ingenuity to work to deceive and circumvent you.'" Here we have, I doubt not, but a single illustration of what is universally true. The laws of God act together in perfect harmony; there is never any clashing between what is really expedient and what is really right; if we could see to the bottom and to the end of things, we should see that, in every case, what prudence suggests as the wisest course, and reason approves as the fittest course, conscience also enjoins as the only right course. But it is given to but few to see to the bottom and to the end of things. Hence I do not believe that it is ever safe or justifiable to let our views of expediency, always uncertain and short-sighted, and liable to be perverted unconsciously by our personal leanings, smother the moral instincts of our nature, or turn aside the acknowledged inculcations of the Divine Word, which require that the law of truth should always be in our mouth. The moment we begin to allow our notions of policy, or even of humanity, to modify or overrule our notions of right and wrong, of sincerity and deceit, we open a door to abuses which no man can shut.

On the same bad plea some think to defend a system of studied concealment, and at times even of downright prevarication and falsehood, in intercourse with the sick and dying. It is all done, we are told, from real kindness of heart; and so perhaps it is; but it does not follow that it is done wisely or innocently. The reason commonly assigned is, that to know the truth will discompose the sick, aggravate their disease, perhaps shorten their days. I do not believe that, in ordinary cases, there is any ground whatever for this apprehension. On the contrary, I believe that entire openness and unreservedness of communication with the sick will help, in nine cases out of ten, to brace up their energies; in one word, that manly treatment will inspire manly feelings. Besides, as it has been justly said, "there is a peculiar inconsistency sometimes exhibited on such occasions. The persons who will not discompose a sick man for the sake of his interests in futurity, will discompose him without scruple if he has not made his will. Is a bequest of more consequence to the survivor than a hope full of immortality to the dying man?" You may allege that it is too late now for the dying man to do any thing to prepare for eternity; but this is more than you know. You do not know what, in the secrecy of his soul, he has to do, nor how long it will take him to do it, in order that he may die in peace. You do not know how much the penitence of a day, of an hour, of a minute, may serve to reconcile him to God. But to this you may reply that you are not afraid to take the risk. If you could take the risk, the answer would be pertinent, however presumptuous and unsatisfactory: but you cannot take it; for this plain reason, that it is not yours to take, but the dying man's. As, therefore, you cannot stand between him and a peril, the magnitude of which, whatever you may think about it, you do not and cannot know, there is unspeakable presumption in thus devolving it deliberately and purposely on his undying soul. The *motive*, I grant, may be good, so far as a mistaken tenderness and humanity may deserve this appellation: but who that knows any thing about human nature, or has turned over the pages of history, or has moved about in society with his eyes open, has yet to learn that some of the worst evils and worst crimes to which we are liable, spring from perversion and abuse of the best feelings?

It only remains for me to say one word of what are often regarded *as lies of high expediency and necessity.* We have nothing to do here with stratagems in war, which are not so much lies as surprises; no confidence is violated. But where confidence is violated, it is by no means clear that any degree of expediency, even of moral expediency, or that any pressure of necessity, will authorize or excuse a conscious departure from the law of truth. Undoubtedly it is perfectly natural that a good man should desire to keep up the spirits of those who are acting with him in what he holds to be a righteous cause; but if this cannot be done except by means of false pretences, it is better that their spirits should flag. Viewed in the light of expediency alone, he will find, I suspect, in the long run, not only that truth is better than boasting, but that truth is better than immediate or apparent success. Again, it is perfectly natural that a man should wish to preserve his life, nay, that he should think it expedient to do so, even though at some expense of sincerity; and this, too, not from private but from public considerations, out of regard to the important services he may in that event be able to render the cause of truth and humanity. Is it certain, however, that he cannot do more to build up that cause by dying for it in good faith, without any stain on his honor or purity, than by living for it and laboring for it under the reproach of a tarnished name? Who does not know that the Church, for one example, actually gained more in influence and power from the blood of the holy martyrs, than from the more wily policy and the more protracted services of her temporizing friends? Nor is it to be forgotten that the threatened evils, to be averted by the lie, ought never to be set down as certain. The open and fearless avowal of the truth commands respect, inspires awe, even among bad men; and the intrepidity of one's behavior in making this avowal, the sobriety and dignified moderation of his courage, and the reasonableness of his expostulations may be such as to disarm a fiend.

But it is not given to all men to be heroes; hence we should be slow to judge one another in these high requisitions. It is enough to say that the general plea for lies of expediency and lies of necessity should be questioned at every step. It is to dishonor the character and government of

God, to suppose that he has made it expedient or necessary in the constitution of the universe, that men should lie, thus requiring in his works what he has forbidden in his Word. It is possible that good men may occasionally fall into this error, and still be entitled to be regarded as good men; but they are *not perfect* men. To prove this, take the perfect character of Jesus, — suppose *him*, in any case whatever, to have resorted to falsehood or artifice, either to save his own life or that of his friends, to avert any calamity however formidable, or to hasten the triumph of his cause, though that cause was the salvation of the world: who does not perceive that it would sink immeasurably the veneration now inspired by his spotless and peerless virtue?

We may be unable effectually to promote a worthy object except by some sacrifice of truth and sincerity. If so, then it is certain that God does not call on us to aid in that work, and we should leave it to other and more suitable agents whom God will raise up in his own time. Omnipotence can accomplish its eternal purposes without our help; certainly without the help of our sins. Let us put more trust in God. If we would put more trust in God, we should find occasion to put less trust in ourselves, and less still in the world, and none at all in *lies*.

T 1851–1857.

XVIII.

HOW TO MAKE THE SUN STAND STILL.

A NEW YEAR'S SERMON.

"*So the sun stood still in the midst of heaven, and hasted not to go down about a whole day.*" — JOSHUA x. 13.

SEVERAL Hebrew books are referred to by the sacred writers, which are now lost. Among these is the book of Jasher, being, as the name would seem to import, a collection of odes or ballads in which the exploits of the great men of antiquity were celebrated. One of them appears to have contained a highly poetical description of the victory which Joshua gained over the five confederate kings; in the course of which he is represented as commanding the sun to stand still: and it obeyed him.

Many of the best scholars, Catholic as well as Protestant, agree in making this passage signify that the defeat which the Hebrews inflicted on the Canaanites was as great *as if* the sun had stopped in the midst of heaven, and had thus prolonged the day to twice its usual length. This construction of the narrative may be correct, or not; at any rate it suggests, as a fit topic for discourse at the commencement of another year, the only way in which *we* can make the sun stand still. The amount of work accomplished by us must be as great as if it had stood still. Our days on earth were numbered from the beginning: many of them are finished; if, however, from this time we double our diligence in what we have to do, it will have the effect to make each remaining day twice as long. In other words, it will be the same in effect as if Joshua's miracle were repeated, in respect to us, every day.

To enter into the truth and full significancy of this statement, it will be necessary to consider for a moment the nature of time itself, and the customary modes of measuring time.

You remember the old reply to the question, What is time? "If you do not ask me, I know." The same might be said of many other things, and for the same reason. It is because the common occasions of life make us familiar with them under some of their aspects, and we mistake this familiarity for knowledge until called upon to state what we know. Thus everybody is familiar with time under some of its aspects, and this familiarity with it is mistaken for a proper and full understanding of it. We think we know it already, and this conceit hinders us from even so much as trying to obtain profounder views. In saying this, I do not mean that men are bound to trouble themselves with metaphysical subtilties on this subject or on any other; but it will not do, under color of the common prejudice against metaphysics, to reject and disown all serious and profound thought. There is, I believe, a great deal of superficial *living*, which has its origin in superficial *thinking*. Thus much at least is plain, that we should seek to extend our knowledge of the nature of time if it can be shown to be of importance in any way to faith or morals, and especially if we find aid and encouragement in doing so, in the Word of God.

The first general remark which I have to make respecting time is, that, according to Scripture as well as reason, it is not the same to God as it is to men: he is not *subject* to it, as we are. "But, beloved, be not ignorant of this one thing, that one day is with the Lord as a thousand years, and a thousand years as one day." By reason of the limitations of the human mind we are unable to consider more than one thing at once; so that, if many things are to be considered, they must be considered one after another; that is, *successively:* and succession supposes what we call time. All events exist therefore to the human mind subject to the conditions and laws of time; but we have no right to conclude that this holds true of a being who has none of our limitations, — of an absolute and infinite being like God. What we apprehend successively, he grasps at once, — the past, the present, and the future; for it is no more certain that he exists at once, in every point of space, than it is that he exists at once in every instant of duration: and therefore it is said of him that he inhabiteth eternity.

Of course we cannot conceive *how* this can be, because we, in our modes of immediate existence and knowledge, are limited to the present, to the *here* and the *now;* but we must not presume to impose our limitations on God, or make our necessities the standard of his. The fact itself which this doctrine teaches, we *can* understand, and this is all we are called upon to believe; and so much it is of great practical moment that we should believe. For it shows the vanity of the sinner's hope, who counts on the long delays of the divine justice as a ground of immunity or escape. "Because sentence against an evil work is not executed speedily, therefore the heart of the sons of men is fully set in them to do evil." This could hardly be if they remembered that what is a long time to us is not so to God; or, in other words, that his measures of time are not like ours. We measure one time by another; he measures all times by eternity. With him therefore one day *must be* as a thousand years, and a thousand years as one day; so that what seems to us to be separated by long intervals, by long delays, is to him but the constant, eternal, ever-present unfolding of his immutable purpose.

The second general remark which I have to make in this connection is, that, *even for us*, there are no absolute measures of time; that is to say, no time which is absolutely short or absolutely long. Here, again, it is the same with time as it is with space; there being no absolutely great, no absolutely small, space. "If"—to borrow a familiar illustration—"any one were to affirm that the universe was continually growing less and less, all the parts altering in the same proportion, and the dimensions of the human race with the rest, in such manner that the whole solar system would now go into a nut-shell, such as nut-shells were a thousand years ago,—it would be impossible either for him to prove it, if true, or for any one else to prove the contradiction, if false. In like manner, if any one were to say that the revolutions of all the heavenly bodies were continually accelerating, but that the properties of matter were also continually altering, and the speed with which ideas are formed and communicated, and muscular efforts made, continually increasing, —it would be impossible to prove a contradiction." It would seem, therefore, that there is no absolute standard to which we can appeal, in our measurements of time. We sometimes say that a day is a day, or that a year is a year, whether much or little takes place in it, whether we can give any account of it or not; but this does not follow. After all, a day or a year is not a measure of time, properly so called, but of a series of events, of a definite series of events, which might be quickened or retarded to any extent without our knowing or suspecting it, provided only that all other events were quickened or retarded in the same proportion. We sometimes pass whole days and years in a dream, yet find on waking, that we have been asleep but a few minutes, as measured by the clock. This is commonly accounted for, I know, by saying that in the dream we mistake thoughts for events; but who will assure us that the events themselves might not be crowded into the same space, supposing all other things to be adjusted to this new ratio of speed.

But it is not necessary to dwell in these transcendental regions. It is enough if we have seen that the common divisions of time are "*as nothing*" in the sight of God, and that they have *no absolute value* even with men.

My next general remark is, that in our practical estimates of time, and in common conversation, we call the same period long or short according to the subject with which it is connected or compared. Thus, to live fourscore years is a long life now, but it would have been a short one, mere childhood, among the antediluvians. Fifty years make a large portion of the life of a man, but would not be accounted much in the life of a nation ; so the history of a dynasty or an empire. A thousand years are a long period even in the history of nations and empires, but would be regarded as a short one, as a mere day, in the history of the earth itself, or of the solar system, or of the stellar universe. Accordingly in the Mosaic account of the creation, the "*days*" are thought by some to stand for geological eras, each one of which is supposed to have consisted of countless myriads of centuries.

But I need not multiply arguments and illustrations to prove, that, whenever we speak of a long time or a short time, it is *comparatively*, and not *absolutely*. One thing, however, in this connection, is particularly worthy of note. The period of discipline and preparation is always short in comparison with the period of maturity and enjoyment. Speaking generally and practically, our whole success in this life depends on fidelity during the half-a-dozen years in which we are fitting ourselves for it. I do not mean that there are no labors and trials afterwards, but fidelity during these few years will prepare us to meet such labors and trials; for it is the business of education to determine, not only what a man will *be*, but what he will *do*. Still more obvious and impressive is this difference, when we consider the present life as a preparation for the life to come. Has it never crossed your mind, with what unspeakable agony the lost soul will see at last, that, by fidelity during *a few short years* of probation, it might have secured *a whole eternity* of holiness and bliss?

Thus far I have spoken of time and its common measurements in their relations to mankind. I pass, in the next place, to speak of them in their relations to the individual.

Whatever time may be in itself, or whatever it may be to others, it is nothing to me if unattended by conscious thought. Of this, considered strictly as a physiological fact, there is abundant evidence in cases of sound sleep, of swoons, and of injuries, occasioning a long-continued suspension of consciousness. Accordingly it is no objection to the doctrine of what is called "The Sleep of the Soul," whether that doctrine be well or ill founded in other respects, to say that it separates life by a vast interval from its retributions; for if a person were really to sleep, with a perfect suspension of all mental operations, from this time until a general resurrection of the dead, the whole of that period would appear to him, and would be to him, but an instant. Hence it would seem to follow, as regards the individual at least, that time is not the measure of life, but life is the measure of time; so that, if we would know *how long* he has lived, we must ascertain *how much he has done.*

To this it may be objected, that time never seems so short as when we are most busily engaged, and the succession of our thoughts is the quickest; as in exciting scenes, or in interesting company and conversation. Here the fallacy consists in confounding a sense of the rapid passage of time with a sense that not much is passing. In the circumstances just mentioned, the time seems to be shorter in passing; but when it is passed, and we are able to look back upon it, and see it altogether, and so can apply a measure to the whole, it seems to be longer. Thus on a journey, the mind being occupied by a constant succession of diverting objects, the time seems very short while passing, very long in retrospect; and the same is true of the whole of life when it resembles such a journey. A day filled with twenty good deeds *does not drag* like a day which has witnessed only one; but the amount of satisfaction actually enjoyed by us in the course of it, is twenty times as great, and it is felt in the retrospect to be twenty times as long. I repeat it, therefore; life, true life, is not measured by the motion of the heavenly bodies, nor by the motion of the index on the dial-plate of the clock, but by the aggregate of what we have thought and done. He who has lived *much*, has lived *long*. In the calendar of heaven, "honorable age is not that which standeth in length of time, nor that is measured by number of years; but wisdom is the gray hair unto men, and an unspotted life is old age."

Who is there whose life does not bear testimony to the truth of the doctrine here advanced? Who is there, who, in great emergencies, has never had a single day so crowded with useful and virtuous activity, that, when night came on, he felt that he had lived to some purpose, and looking back on it afterwards has been more than once disposed to exclaim, "Oh, that all my days were such"? Do you wish to know how this prayer may be fulfilled? Simply by doing for yourselves what, in the cases referred to, the emergency did for you. The emergency has revealed us to ourselves. It has awakened in us powers and capacities which we did not know before that we possessed; but we now know that we possess them, and that we can put them forth at will. What therefore a pressure from without has made us do once or twice, we should make ourselves do continually by pressure from within, — the untiring urgency of a quickened conscience, a lofty purpose, and an immortal hope. In this respect the children of light would do well to take a lesson from the children of this world. When ambition or avarice takes entire possession of the soul, it does not act like an occasional emergency; neither is the influence which it exerts of the nature of a pressure from without: it is a perpetual pressure from within, stimulating those who feel it to incessant effort. They rest not day and night, crowding the work of years into months, and so turning months into years. "Now they do it to obtain a corruptible crown;" might not, ought not we to do as much "to obtain an incorruptible"?

All the preceding observations tend therefore to this; that the common distinctions, and the common notation of time are of comparative unimportance to an earnest and determined mind. Holy thoughts and good deeds, and not the pendulum of the clock, determine the measure of a life approved and accepted of God.

> "He most lives,
> Who thinks most, feels the noblest, acts the best."

Tried by this standard, how is it with you and me? When the year which has just closed, began, we had so much to do, and but so much time in which to do it. The year has gone; has a year's work been done? or have we suffered the work to accumulate on our hands? Have we done as much as we thought we should do, or as we meant to do? I am afraid there is not one among us all who can answer this question to his own entire satisfaction; or, if he can, I am afraid that the satisfaction itself is evidence that he has made no progress. Have you entirely mastered and corrected a single bad habit, a single bad propensity, a single infirmity of temper? Can you remember many instances in which you have borne provocation without malice, generously forgiven the wrong-doer, and overcome evil with good? Have you been ready to assist the needy, not only when it was easy to do so, but also when it called for self-denial and sacrifice? Can you remember a single friend or associate, who, as you have reason to believe, owes a single virtue to your example or your counsels? Let an awakened and an enlightened conscience pursue these inquiries, and the best of us would soon be convinced — perhaps the best of us would soonest be convinced — of how small a portion of the past year we can give a good and perfectly satisfactory account. Are you sure that all the good you have done in the twelve months might not have been crowded into a single week, or a single day? If it might have been, then remember that, according to the only measure of time which we know in heaven, the twelve months shrivel up into that brief space. You have not lived a year; you have only lived a week, or, it may be, a day.

From the past let us now turn to the future, — from the year that has just closed to that which has just begun. If a large proportion of the great and solemn work of life still remains to be accomplished in the ever narrowing term allotted us on earth, we may be tempted to cry out with the Hebrew chieftain in the hot pursuit of a half-vanquished foe, "Sun! stand thou still!" Vain and presumptuous expectation, if we look for its literal fulfilment! The lights which God has set in the firmament of heaven, to "be for signs, and for seasons, and for days and years," will hold on their course. What then can we do? It is often said that the formation of character is a slow work. If so, this is not a reason for being slow to begin; it is a motive for despatch. It used to be a common supposition that, where thirteen persons met at a feast, one of the number might be expected to die within the year. How much more certain that, before another annual revolution is completed, more than one of the number here present, and those perhaps who least expect it, will be summoned to give account of themselves to God. On the great and awful themes here involved, — God, Christ, the soul, retribution, eternity, — I do not think that the speculations of the wisest uninspired man are worth much. I turn to the Scriptures; and here I think I find that the only probation expressly allotted to man is the probation of this life. Without necessarily implying that the future state is a fixed state either to the good or the bad, it seems to me that the doctrine nevertheless is, that we choose sides here, with no reason to expect that we shall have either the disposition or the opportunity to change sides hereafter. Under the pressure of this infinitely momentous alternative, I ask again, What shall we do?

Though we cannot make the sun stand still in the midst of heaven, we can do what, as we have seen, will be the same in effect. By putting the work of two days into one, we can make one day equal to two. By crowding the year that is before us with generous purposes, and virtuous efforts, and noble sacrifices, we can make it equal to twenty years of ordinary life. It is sometimes said that the repentance which is to save us, is not the repentance of a day; and this is true, if all the fruits of repentance are meant to be included. But the repentance which consists in a solemn and religious change of intention and of heart, which supposes an inward and radical change of one's whole plan of life, so as to take him out of the class of the bad, and put him into the class of the good, — this is, or at least may be, not only the repentance of a day, but of an hour: I had almost said of a moment, of any moment, — of this moment. Afterwards we have nothing to do but to go on. If we are living when this year expires, consider, I beseech you, what unspeakable satisfaction it will give us to be assured that we are in the right and only safe path; that the interval has been lengthened out to twice, to quadruple, to tenfold its usual dimensions, considered as a measure of real life, by the number and excellence of the deeds with which it has been filled; that every day has been a step towards heaven. Remember, also, that our enjoyment of this satisfaction at that time will depend, not on what we wish *then*, but on what we determine, and on what we do, *now*.

1848–1857.

XIX.

ON THE SIN OF BEING LED ASTRAY.

"*My son, if sinners entice thee, consent thou not.*" — PROVERBS i. 10.

WHEN a young man falls into evil courses, it is common for his friends to find such consolation as they can in the thought that he was *led astray*. His original purposes and dispositions were good; he would have done well enough if left to himself; but he fell into vicious companionships, and was *led astray*. And this is often said in a tone which would seem to imply that the victims, in such cases, are objects of pity, rather than of blame.

But is it so? I do not forget that there are, as there always have been, "corrupters of youth," men who lie in wait for the innocent and inexperienced in order to entice them into sin. Neither do I forget that the strongest language of reprobation fails adequately to express the guilt of such persons. But, if there is sin in enticing, there is also sin in yielding to the enticement; nay, my object in this discourse will be to show, that the difference is by no means so great as is commonly supposed.

Those who think to excuse men's delinquencies, on the ground that they did not commit them of their own accord, but were led into them by others, should consider that on this ground *all* delinquencies might be excused, — even those of our first parents. Adam complained that he was led astray by Eve, and Eve, that she was led astray by the serpent; but we do not find that the plea was accepted, or listened to, in either case. And so it has been ever since. Men do not become sinners of their own accord, of their own motion, that is to say, without being tempted to become so; and in almost every instance, the temptation comes, directly or indirectly, through other men. We are led astray. Nevertheless, our sins are sins. Even those who now lead others astray, began by being led astray themselves; so that if this is an excuse for either, it is an excuse for both — for all. And besides, virtue does not grow up in the absence of all enticement to sin, but in the presence and in the resistance of such enticement; and it is this resistance which makes it to be virtue.

Look again at the nature of this excuse. "They would have done well enough if left to themselves, because they started in life with good purposes and dispositions." But when this is urged,

I am afraid that, in a vast majority of cases, their purposes and dispositions are called *good* merely because they are *not bad*; or rather, perhaps, because they have no *fixed* purposes and dispositions of any kind. And here there is no occasion to take the ground of high and unreasonable expectations. We do not expect men to start in life with a fixed *character;* for character is made up of habits, and the formation of habits is the work of time. All that we expect or have a right to insist upon is, that every one should start in life with fixed *purposes and dispositions;* that is to say, not merely with a willingness, but with a strong determination, to do well. But if a man is led astray by the common enticements incident to human trial, it proves that he was without this strong determination; so that the excuse fails. Good-natured, he may have been; but *good nature*, as that term is commonly understood, is much more frequently the sign of an easy than of a determined mind: and where this is the case, where good nature stands for nothing better than ease and pliancy of temper, instead of being an excuse for any thing else, it needs itself to be excused; at any rate, it is evidence of moral infirmity and danger.

Again; those who try to find an excuse for their delinquencies in the fact that they were led astray by others, are apt to *exaggerate* these enticements, as if to intimate that resistance under such circumstances was out of the question. In short, throughout the whole of the affair, they take a course perversely opposite to that which prudence and duty dictate. While the danger is in prospect, and they should be put on their guard against it, they make light of it; but after it has come, and done its work, they can then see it in all and more than all its magnitude, and find there a reason and an excuse for their fall.

In point of fact the danger, except to a comparatively small number, is neither so great, nor so imminent, as is generally thought. Let me not be misunderstood. We must make distinctions here. I do not forget that one of the greatest difficulties in Providence is found in the degree to which our conduct and characters are left to depend on others, while we ourselves are made to suffer the consequences in this world and the next. But the influence, and often the controlling influence, which other men have over our conduct and characters, is, for the most part, *general* and *indirect.* That is to say, it comes for the most part through a bad or neglected education, through a perverted or low state of public opinion, through the prevalence and perhaps the popularity of corrupting customs and institutions, and the like; and not through *a direct instigation to particular sins.*

When any one yields to such direct instigation, it proves, as it seems to me, one of two things; either that he is more than usually weak-minded, or that he has a strong natural proclivity in the same direction. Consider how it is where large numbers are thrown together, and are under the necessity of living together for a considerable time. They immediately fall into distinct associations and companionships, according to their several tastes and habits; the great majority, as we are willing to believe, to follow out plans of usefulness or pleasure which they have chosen for themselves; a few to be led about, and made fools of, by any one who will take the trouble to do it; and who these few are, can generally be determined before they have been together six weeks.

I might go farther, and say that bad men seldom *try* to lead astray any except those who show beforehand a willingness to be thus led. We are apt to make men of loose principles and dissipated habits worse than they really are. They are not monsters; they are still men, and have many, at least, of the feelings and sentiments natural to men. They may be, and probably are, unduly disposed to suspect appearances; they have no respect for hypocrisy, and exult in its exposure: but whenever they meet with an example of modest and consistent virtue, they do not, and they cannot, resist the instinctive tendency of their nature to admire it. When these men read history, the characters whom they most admire are the same whom good men most admire; — not the triflers and profligates of the day, that is, the men who most resemble themselves, but the heroes, and, high above all, the moral heroes. With such feelings it is hardly to be supposed that they would deliberately plot the ruin of the very persons, whom in common with the rest of the community, they sincerely respect and revere.

But, it may be said, there are worse men than these; and so there are, — fiends in human shape, who would take perhaps a satanic delight in the fall, if it were possible, "of the very elect." Few however, as I suppose all will agree, attain to this pitch of wickedness. They *are* monsters; and what have the well disposed to do with monsters, known as such, except to avoid them? "Surely in vain the net is spread in the sight of any bird." It is not by monsters in crime that the innocent and inexperienced are most in danger of being led astray, at least in the first instance, but by those who have as yet proceeded only a little way in crime; whose crime consists, for the most part, in an uncontrolled love of ease and pleasure, gilded over with companionable qualities, and sometimes by real kindness of heart. These are the dangerous men; but dangerous to whom? In the case of such tempters it is idle, as I have said, to talk about a satanic purpose to corrupt virtue, as virtue. What motive is therefore left to induce them to take the trouble to lead another astray, but this; that they see in him congenial propensities, — a strong natural tendency to the same pleasures and unlawful gratifications; and this tendency they may help to develop a little sooner, though it probably would have been developed sooner or later without their aid.

I come therefore to these three conclusions. In the first place, a large proportion of those who are led astray are led astray *by themselves*, by their own evil thoughts; in the language of Scripture, "they are drawn away of their own lust, and enticed." Sometimes the temptation does not take the form of a natural taste or inclination for the vice itself, but that of a morbid curiosity to know what the vice is; yet in the latter case, as well as in the former, they are led astray by themselves, by their own evil thoughts. In the second place, a large proportion of those who are led away *by others*, purposely put themselves in the way of it; the bad company do not seek them out, but they seek out the bad company. They know, as well as others, that the community consists of two sorts of persons, the safe and the dangerous, the industrious and the idle, the virtuous and the vicious; and, knowing this, they nevertheless voluntarily connect themselves with the obnoxious class. As a general rule, therefore, they can hardly be said to be led away by the wicked; they *join the wicked*, differing from older transgressors in this only, that they were the last to join, — not veterans, but recruits. And, in the third and last place, the very fact that an attempt is made to lead a man astray is strong evidence against him. Men of unquestionable probity and moral inflexibleness are never spoken to, are never thought of, in this connection. The emissaries of evil know what they are about: they seldom approach any but such as they are convinced, by almost infallible signs, will turn out easy and willing victims. Hence it is a bad sign, I do not say merely that a man should be led astray, but that he should be singled out for this purpose; that his virtue should be even so much as attempted, is proof that all is not right.

Still it cannot be denied that melancholy cases do occur from time to time, in which persons, merely through ignorance and inexperience, are led astray by artful and designing men, — persons, too, who, under other influences and in other companionships, might have succeeded in life, and become useful and perhaps distinguished members of society. Nothing should be left undone which will help to save such persons; above all, they should be conjured to consider, before it is too late, the weakness, the guilt, and the ruin which *consenting* to be led astray involves.

Consider, in the first place, the *weakness* which such conduct supposes and involves. Moral strength, that is, the strength which is the opposite to the weakness here intended, constitutes what is called *personality;* it makes the distinction between a *person* and a *thing*, between a self-active, self-determining being, and one who moves only as he is moved. Some there are who manifest so little of this strength, as almost to leave us in doubt under which head they ought to be classed; they are never among the leaders, but always among the led; they are not so much persons as things, that is, appendages to persons. And here it is to no purpose to object that only a few can lead; the rest must follow: that the great majority in every community, from the necessities of their condition, or from want of information or natural ability, must follow. Certainly they must; but what has that to do with the subject in hand? There is a world of difference between following a man because we choose to follow him, and being led by him because he chooses to lead us. There is also a world of difference between following others because we think they will lead us aright, our own judgment approving the course, and following others when we know or suspect they will lead us astray, our own judgment disapproving the course. The only independence I am contending for here, is *moral* independence; an independence which refuses to follow when reason and prudence and conscience say, No! And this independence may exist, and does exist, in all classes; nay, is quite as often found in the humblest classes as the highest, among the uneducated as among the educated.

What I insist upon is, that a want of this independence, wherever met with, betrays the worst form of weakness. We call a man morally weak, who is led astray by *his own* passions; and so he is, for it shows that, however strong he is in himself, his passions are stronger still: he is weak relatively to his own passions. But a man who is led astray by other men shows that he is weak in himself, absolutely weak. This distinction must be taken into account in making up our judgment respecting many of the leading characters in history. Such men as Cæsar and Cromwell and Napoleon were not strong in the sense of having the mastery over their own passions, but in that of having the mastery of every thing else. They owed their ascendancy, not more to the power they had over others, than to the fact that others had no power over them in return; this circumstance giving a unity and persistence to their purpose, which made success almost certain. And so in business, so in scholarship, so in every walk and pursuit of life; one of the great secrets of personal and successful efficiency is found in making ourselves inaccessible to the influence of others any farther than we choose. It is only in this condition that we are safe against being turned aside from our own plans, against being laughed out of our own seriousness, against losing our own courage in the general distrust or timidity. We must be true to ourselves, whatever others may do or say. Just so far as we fall from this moral independence, we fall into pitiable weakness, — a weakness which not only supposes frailty, the frailty common to all, but a loss of proper personality, the loss of proper manhood. We become the shadows, the echoes, the tools of other men, and so are liable at any moment to become their dupes and victims.

Consider, in the next place, *the guilt* which is involved in being led astray. Guilt, as I have intimated before, does not consist in sinning in the absence of all temptation. Probably no such sin was ever yet committed by man or fiend; it would be to act without a motive. Sin and guilt consist in yielding to temptation. "If sinners entice you," it will doubtless add to the temptation, and so make it more likely that you will commit the sin; but it does not make the sin any the less a sin, either in its nature or consequences. But some will ask, If another man inveigles me into crime, is not he in some sense responsible for the crime? Certainly he is. It is remarkable of a crime committed by one person at the instigation of another, that *two* persons are guilty of it, and *two* persons will have to answer for it. But the question will still be pressed, Is not the instigator in this case unspeakably the more guilty of the two? And here, too, I answer as before, Certainly he is, if guilt is to be measured by wickedness of purpose in the outset. But this is not the only or the best way of estimating the moral harm incurred by wrong-doing. The best and only legitimate gauge of the gravity of a transgression is found, not in the state of mind in which it is committed, but in the state of mind which it produces in those who commit it. What and how much effect does it have in retarding, arresting, or reversing our moral progress? Tried by this test, I suspect it will often appear that the *led* are more thoroughly demoralized than the *leaders*. The reason is that the leaders are generally men of some strength of mind, and can stop when they please in a course of self-indulgence; often also their ambition and better instincts help to hold their love of pleasure in check. But not so with their imbecile dupes and victims. Hence it not infrequently happens that the very person who was the first to lead another astray, who taught him his first lessons in crime, soon becomes ashamed of his follower, and disgusted with his excesses, and casts him off.

It only remains for me to speak of *the ruin* which men bring on themselves by yielding to the enticement of sinners. Here, unhappily, there can be but one opinion. We may differ as to the share of guilt incurred by those who are not the originators, but merely the instruments and tools, in the mischief; our pity for their weakness may also do much to blind us to their criminality; but we cannot shut our eyes on the reality of the distress they bring on their friends, or the final and utter ruin they bring on themselves. How often have we been told that our prisons are filled, not only by those who contrived the wrong and perhaps profited by it, but by those whom they used as instruments and tools to carry their purposes into effect! The leaders escape; the followers are disgraced and punished. And so in respect to the fashionable views of society. Who are they who suffer most from these in the loss of property, reputation, and health? Not the leaders, who commonly know how to keep themselves out of the worst dangers and the worst excesses, but their unwary and facile followers; — followers, too, who sometimes have no taste for a dissipated life and find no real pleasure in it, but yet are willing to plant unspeakable anguish in the hearts of all who love them, and bring a fatal blight on their own prospects, merely for the honor of being noticed and flattered by dangerous and profligate men.

Would to God that what I have said might have the effect to put a single unwary soul on its guard against this peril! As has been intimated before, in every place, in every community, the associations and companionships are of two kinds, — the safe and the dangerous. There are men whose presence is a blessing and a benediction; whose company and conversation have the effect to confirm our faith, to strengthen all our good purposes, and fill the future with bright visions of honor, success, and usefulness. Again, there are those in whose company you cannot be for half an hour without feeling that virtue has gone out of you; "their feet go down to death, their steps take hold on hell." You are to make your choice between them; and remember, it is for your life!

1855.

XX.

THE YOUNG MAN'S DREAM OF LIFE.

A BACCALAUREATE SERMON.

"*And he dreamed yet another dream, and told it his brethren, and said, Behold, I have dreamed a dream more; and, behold, the sun and the moon and the eleven stars made obeisance to me. And he told it to his father, and to his brethren: and his father rebuked him, and said unto him, What is this dream that thou hast dreamed? Shall I and thy mother and thy brethren indeed come to bow down ourselves to thee to the earth? And his brethren envied him; but his father observed the saying.*" — GENESIS xxxvii. 9, 10, 11.

HUMAN nature is substantially the same now as in the days of the Hebrew patriarch. What is related of Joseph, — his father's manifest partiality, the fine clothes, and, above all, the two vain-glorious dreams, as they must have seemed at the time, — would be too much for the patience of most elder brethren. The bowing of the sheaves was bad enough; but when he dreamed again, and made not only "the eleven stars," that is, all his brethren, who, with one exception, were considerably older than he, but also "the sun and moon," that is, his father and mother, do him obeisance, it was too much even for the doting fondness of Jacob himself. Accordingly we are told that "his father rebuked him, and said unto him, What is this dream that thou hast dreamed? Shall I and thy mother, and thy brethren, indeed come to bow down ourselves to thee to the earth?"

The bold and confident aspirations of the stripling, as he stood in the family group, and told his dreams with so much simplicity, and we are tempted to add with so much imprudence, must have offended against Oriental notions of propriety even more than they would against ours. In the East, to the present day, immobility reigns; the future is expected to be merely a repetition of the past: experience, therefore, is wisdom, is every thing; age is looked up to with reverence; *elders* is another name for *rulers*. But with us it is not so. Among the Western nations, and especially among those of the race to which we belong, there has grown up from small beginnings a spirit of progress. Truth and right are looked for, not in the past, but in the future; and under the influence of this habit of thought, popularized and made universal, we cannot wonder that what is called the spirit of progress should often degenerate into a passion for change and reform. Some writers are fond of charging the whole movement, with all its good and all its evil issues, on the Protestant Reformation; but they mistake one of the effects of the cause for the cause itself. The movement began long before, and the Protestant Reformation was neither more nor less than one of its important results. And it is still going on. Reactions there have been, and will be, *on the surface;* but the deep under-currents are the same as heretofore, betraying themselves, *when excessive*, in contempt for every thing that is old, in disdain for experience and for the wisdom derived from experience. Hence, there is but too much ground for the complaint of one of the most liberal and just thinkers of the present century, that "the young man of to-day measures himself with the man of many years; before his school-days are over, the boy thinks and declares himself equal to his sire. This notion of equality of minds is carried so far that the judgment of eighteen has as much authority as that of fifty; and the reasoning of a day-laborer, on a question of policy, is considered as decisive as that of a statesman whose whole life has been passed in the midst of public affairs, or of a student grown gray in thought."

But there are two important considerations which the persons who are fond of dwelling on this topic are apt to overlook. In the first place, they forget how differently young men are educated now than formerly. Education, meaning thereby artificial and systematic education, is not intended to supply the place of natural ability, or to train minds which otherwise would not be trained at all; but simply to facilitate and expedite this training, and make it more thorough and comprehensive. Thus understood, it may be said in a certain sense, and to a certain extent, to be a substitute for experience: the thoroughly educated man is, in some respects, as old at twenty-one, as the uneducated at thirty or thirty-five. Why wonder, then, that he should speak and act, as if he were as old? Why deliberately apply these forcing processes, and afterwards affect to wonder and complain at the obvious and necessary result? Why multiply the arts of bringing forward and pushing forward young men into society, and afterwards affect to wonder and complain at finding them where you have chosen to put them? Again, it is to be considered that, in this country at least, many of the objects and pursuits, which once took up and occupied the exuberant ambition and activity of young men, have failed almost entirely. Only a very few can go into the army: the well educated are not busily engaged here, as in some other countries, in making their way at court; neither is there demand here for that high refinement, for that elaborate though superficial culture, which is expected in an aristocratical constitution of society. What, then, are our young men to do? Failing other objects of interest, is it at all wonderful that they should turn to politics or reform? that they should mix with their elders in important social action, or undertake to act by themselves, though at the risk of sometimes intermeddling with matters beyond their years?

However this may be, it is certainly natural that those who are just entering on life, and those who are soon to quit it, should differ in their views of life itself. The reason is, that the latter *know* what life is; they know it through and through, from actual experience; they know its early promises, and how far these promises are likely to be fulfilled, and how far unfulfilled. On the contrary, those who are just entering on life see but a single phase of it; the rest is hearsay, theory, conjecture, imagination. Like Joseph, they *dream* what will happen to them: awake or asleep, it matters not, still it is a dream, — *the young man's dream of life.* And this is my subject; not inappropriate, as it seems to me, either to the occasion or the place. Be assured, however, in the outset, that I have not selected this subject with a view to treat it lightly, or satirically, or irreverently. I believe that the young man's dream of life may come to pass, as in the case of Joseph; nay, more, that the dream itself often works its own accomplishment. Neither is this all: I believe there is often more wisdom, and more dignity, and more humble trust, in the young man's dream of life, than in the old man's philosophy of life. What I am anxious to do is simply this: — to call your attention to a remarkable discrepancy in these dreams; to impress you with the fact, that, while some of these dreams are true to our nature and our destiny, and lead to nothing but good, there are others which are false to our nature and our destiny, and lead to nothing but evil.

To the last-mentioned class belongs the dream of a life of *ease and pleasure and self-indulgence.*

The great law which applies to other dreams holds good also here: every man's *dream of life* is shaped and determined, for the most part, by his constitutional tendencies, and his antecedent habits of thought and experience. For this reason, it is chiefly among such as are born to wealth, and brought up amidst luxury and abundance, that we look for the mistaken anticipations of life of which I now speak. Up to the present time, theirs has been a life of ease and pleasure and self-indulgence, and they are fain to believe that it will be so to the end. But they forget, in the first place, the rotatory nature of family fortunes, at least in this country. With us, the law of inheritance and the distribution of property are such, that a rich man's son can hardly expect any thing more than to have his way made easy in the beginning, and to be helped a little afterwards; with the danger, too, that this expectation will take just so much from his self-reliance, and from his earnest and determined preparation to help himself. Even here it is not impossible, I know, that a family should continue rich through several generations; but it is only on condition that they continue distinguished for habits of thrift and frugality, thus excluding the thought of a life of ease, pleasure, and self-indulgence. Moreover, this is not the rule, but the exception to the rule; the rule is vicissitude; while one goes up, another comes down, not requiring, as it has been found by experience, more than three, or at most four, generations for the wheel to effect an entire revolution. If a class of young men, anywhere collected together in this country, could look forward to what will be their relative social position thirty years from this time, it would lead them to attach much less importance to what their relative social position is now.

Assuming, however, that a young man were sure to retain *the means* of a life of ease, pleasure, and self-indulgence, he cannot learn too soon that this is not the way to happiness, — to true and lasting content. *Self-indulgence* is not *self-satisfaction.*

The unwary are misled by a term which does not mean what it purports to mean. In point of fact, self-indulgence is not the indulgence of self, understanding thereby a man's *whole* self, but only of a part of self: it is not the indulgence of his whole nature, but only of part of his nature, and that the lowest; often, also, to the damage, and sometimes to the ruin, of his higher nature. What we call *self-indulgence* is not indulgence of *self*, in any proper sense of that word, but rather of this or that low or sordid passion which threatens the degradation and perhaps the ruin of self; and it is probably the secret consciousness of this fact which constitutes that drop of bitterness and self-reproach which is always found at the bottom of the cup of pleasure.

Still, the best antidote to dreaming of a life of ease, pleasure, and self-indulgence is found in a serious and thoughtful glance at its actual results in other men. It is not merely that they wake up at length, and *know it to be a dream;* for this is no more than what sometimes happens in respect to worthy and generous aspirations; but with a most important difference: in the latter case we do not regret the dream; we feel we are the better for it. On the other hand, there is no weariness and disgust of life like that which gathers over the spirits of a broken-down man of pleasure, who has found out, when too late, that his is that laughter in which the heart is sorrowful, and his that mirth the end of which is heaviness. With no relish for vice, and no confidence in virtue, the best that can be expected from the old age of such a man is a decorous conformity to conventionalities, for which there is left to him neither faith nor heart. One thing, however, he will never do, — and what could better illustrate and enforce my present argument? — under no circumstances whatever will he recommend it to his children to follow in his steps.

I am not inculcating a new doctrine. You are familiar with it as set forth in one of the most impressive apologues for which we are indebted to pagan wisdom: I mean, the Choice of Hercules. It has also been confirmed and consecrated, and adopted into the higher relations of the Christian life, in the account which the gospel gives us of our Lord's Temptation in the Wilderness. Both belong to a large class of exhortations and examples, intended to kindle the imaginations of youth in favor of a life of labor for noble objects, and against a life of indulgence. But if this is right and wise for men in general, it is doubly so for us, —*for you.* In the old world, and under a widely different political and social constitution, an order of men is found, who are not only raised by birth and position above the necessities of labor, but surrounded by elegant and refined amusements and society, and other objects of interest, to fill up their time and supply the place of regular and serious occupation. By their numbers, and the prestige of rank, they are also able to give a sort of dignity to the life they lead, to make it an object of respect, or, at least, of desire or envy. But here another state of things prevails. It is doubtless premature to speak of what will be in a remote future, but this much is certain: neither our institutions, nor the general condition of the people, have provided as yet for such a class of men. Here, therefore, whoever dreams about a life of elegant leisure will soon find himself to be out of place; with but little to occupy or interest or grace his leisure; with no privileged order to keep him in countenance, indeed almost alone, for if he turns for companionship to others as idle as himself, he will often have to put up with very poor companionship. In short, who does not know that in this country it is hardly considered respectable to be a gentleman, *and nothing else?*

Not much better is the young man's dream of a life of *selfish ambition and worldly success.*

The error before described pertains for the most part, as I have intimated, to minds naturally irresolute, and enervated still more by easy and prosperous circumstances; that of which I am now to speak belongs to persons the very opposite in both character and condition. It belongs to men who are conscious of their strength; who chafe under the restraints and limitations imposed upon them by what they regard as their hard lot; who cannot bear to see others, every way their inferiors except in the gifts of fortune, stand higher than they do; who start, therefore, with a determination to reverse this state of things, come what may. And this tendency is not necessarily lessened — in some respects, indeed, it is stimulated and quickened — in an educated young man. The energies which before were latent have become apparent; experience and reflection have had the effect to make him more keenly alive to the unequal distribution of external facilities and advantages, and he is apt to say to himself, "I have not only the abilities, but also the education, necessary to the struggle. I am at the bottom of the ladder now; but I will be at the top before I die, or die in the attempt."

Now this is *a dream; here* as well as elsewhere. Nothing is more common than to exaggerate, if not entirely to misconceive, the advantages resulting in this respect from our free institutions. Liberty, in the largest and best sense of that word, is, at least in its essential nature, merely a *negative*, and not a positive, good. It takes off restraints; it removes obstacles; it makes it impossible for a single man, or a privileged order of men, to hinder the progress of society or of individuals, against their will. Still it must not be counted on as supplying the place of this progress, or of the knowledge, ability, and effort necessary thereto. Our free institutions do not and cannot work the miracle, or rather the contradiction, of making everybody to be *first:* there must still be gradations in society; so that when the boys in a common school are told, as they often are, that any one of them may become President of the United States, the appeal is not only made to a vulgar motive, but the whole is founded on a palpable fallacy. Because the way to the highest distinctions is open to all, it does not follow that the highest distinctions are within the reach of all. In the practical working of the freest institutions of government and society, the great popular advantage is not that the highest distinctions are within the reach of all, but that competency and respectability are within the reach of all. And this should satisfy all. To expect more is *to dream.*

Nevertheless, I do not condemn it merely because it is *a dream;* nor yet, because it is a dream *of ambition.* Ethical writers have raised the question whether ambition is a virtue or a vice; but simply considered, and strictly speaking, it is neither one nor the other; not even self-love. Simply considered, it is *the desire of power*, of the power which mind has over matter, and over other minds, and takes its character of virtue or vice, of selfishness or philanthropy, according to the purpose and spirit by which it is animated. Thus a lawyer, or physician, or clergyman may be ambitious of excellence in his profession, merely with a view to greater usefulness in his profession; in which case his ambition does but measure the intensity of his desire to do good. Indeed, I cannot see the consistency, and I am slow to believe in the entire sincerity, of those who talk about wishing to do good, and yet fail to manifest, and perhaps affect to disclaim, all wish to enlarge their means of doing good. Look at these men, and then deny, if you can, that much of what passes for aversion to ambition on moral grounds, is but an after-thought to excuse a real and culpable indifference or indolence. Neither the spirit of Christianity, nor the letter of Scripture, forbid ambition, considered merely as a desire to extend the means, and the sphere, of one's influence. We are told, it is true, that "whosoever exalteth himself shall be abased; and he that humbleth himself shall be exalted." This language, however, as the connection shows, is not intended to rebuke ambition simply considered, but *selfish* ambition, — anxiety for outward and worldly distinction and success; — precisely the position I have taken above. To dream of a life of selfish ambition, of outward and worldly distinction and success, is as unwise as it is unchristian; not, however, as I have said, because it is *a dream*, for every anticipation of coming life is of the nature of a dream, but because it is a *noxious* dream.

It is so, in the first place, because a young man, starting under this illusion, is almost sure to forget what constitutes true worth; which consists in *deserving*, and not in *obtaining*, success. Again, it makes success to depend, not upon what he does or can do himself, but upon what others think of what he does; thus putting it out of his own power, in any proper sense of that word, and looking for it to the uncertain and ever-shifting caprices of the multitude. I am not calling your attention to imaginary evils. Travellers assure us that the faults or defects in the people of this country, by which a foreigner is most struck, are these three: — an unmanly solicitude about what their neighbors will say; a spirit of unrest, tending to fill the best life with petty annoyances, and taking from the best character the grace of repose; and, above all, a disposition to estimate every thing, even their abilities and virtues, not according to their real, but according to their marketable, value. And it is in this community, and amidst these tendencies, that your lot is cast, that you are to live and act, with a moral certainty of falling into the national fault, if you begin by committing the national error; if you begin by looking forward to wealth and office, or to leadership in some clique, or in some new movement, as if life had nothing better or safer to promise. Notwithstanding the general, the almost universal, diffusion of the means of material comfort, notwithstanding the boasted and real benefits of popular education, and the actual prevalence of a higher standard of thought and character, it is alleged, and I am afraid with but too much reason, that there is less contentment, less real happiness here, than in most other countries. This does not happen, as some have supposed, because we aim too high, but because we do not aim aright. In laying down our plans of life we dream of incongruous things, of things which are as uncertain and inconstant as the winds, or can only be obtained by means which are destructive of peace and self-respect. Leave these things to others, who are willing to pay the price for them; who are willing to cringe and fawn and crawl. It is enough if you are able to say, and say with truth, "I have not these things because I sought them not, because I desire them not, because I have what is better."

And this leads me to consider dreams of life of another character; which, though dreams, are nevertheless true to our nature and destiny, and do us nothing but good, whether they ever come to pass or not.

First among these I would mention the young man's dream of *extensive usefulness, wrought out with unsullied honor, and crowned with a good name.*

It is highly creditable to human nature, that, when men begin to dream of what they are to be and do, they almost always picture their future course as a highly beneficent one. Call this *castle-building* or what you will, no matter whether it ever comes to any thing or not, it proves thus much at least: that the first preferences, the natural leanings of the bulk of mankind, are in favor of what is noble and good. But soon, under the experiences of life, at least in the case of many, a change is apt to come over the spirit of this dream: they begin to distrust it, to be ashamed of it, to turn it into a jest. When this is the result of repeated disappointment, and treachery on the part of others, it is more an occasion of pity than rebuke; but not so when it takes place in consequence of a decay of virtue in the individual himself. In a majority of cases, especially among the young, the change may be traced, I suspect, to the indurating effects which habits of frivolity and guilty pleasure have on the human heart: all the generous aspirations of the soul are swallowed up and lost in "the lust of the flesh, the lust of the eyes, and the pride of life." A multitude of discourses have been written on the bad effects of early dissipation; but the most mournful among them all, because the most radical among them all, is this moral scepticism, this tendency to destroy all interest and all faith in goodness, and in doing good.

There is no reason why any one should despair of being constantly and eminently useful, who has a disposition to be so. It is a vulgar error to suppose that wealth, or station, or genius are necessary; very different has been the condition of most of those whom mankind have hailed as their deliverers and benefactors. Even the Lord of Life took the form of a servant, and chose his disciples from among the humblest classes, though with the promise and clear foresight that he and they should soon sit on thrones, and give laws to the world. To realize the fondest dream of single-hearted, unostentatious beneficence, nothing more is required than to have it always uppermost in your thoughts to do the good thing, or say the good word, which the occasion suggests and invites: — to counsel a friend, when a word or a look may be sufficient to decide the question of his whole life;

to lift up your voice for the weak and the wronged; to have the courage to be consistent and moderate under the pressure of popular excitements; and in general to win men through the gentle and quiet influence of a good example. Even professional usefulness would seem to have but little to do with what is commonly understood by professional distinction. Who is the useful clergyman? Not necessarily he who preaches what are called "great sermons," but he who is looked up to by the young and the old as the father of his flock; the umpire in all differences; whose presence in seasons of distress is as that of an angel of mercy; whose influence is also felt in education, as manifested not only in the schools, but in the taste and manners of the people, and even in their roads and dwellings, so that a stranger cannot drive through the village without being impressed with the evidence that a wise and good man has been there. Nothing, I repeat it, is needed for all this, so far as it depends on man, but the disposition. The only quality of mind for which Oberlin, the Protestant pastor in the Ban de la Roche, can be said to have been distinguished, was an earnest, straightforward purpose to do good; and the memorial of what he did is immortal.

The eyes of Christians are open, at length, to the full significance of the teachings of the gospel on this subject. "Whosoever will be great among you, let him be your minister; and whosoever will be chief among you, let him be your servant." Hence the principle of genuine philanthropy was never so active in the community as at this moment. You see it everywhere; in the perilous and self-denying course of the foreign missionary, bearing the blessings of Christian civilization to the most benighted parts of the earth; in the outcry of indignation at the neglected condition of a mercenary soldiery, and in the unprecedented efforts to mitigate their sufferings. You see it also, nearer home, in the thousand forms of that sensitive and restless compassion which extends its regards to the humblest and most abject, — to children in factories, to the poor debtor, to the discharged prisoner, to the maniac pauper, to the squalid misery collected in large cities, — "which pries," as it has been said, "into the stores and water-casks of every emigrant ship, which winces at every lash laid on the back of a drunken sailor, which will not suffer the thief in the hulks to be ill-fed or over-worked." Men are beginning to feel, as they never did before, that there is an important sense in which every one is his brother's keeper. Moreover, this service, which men have been content to regard hitherto as a part of duty, is beginning to be regarded as a part of greatness. The military hero and the intellectual hero have long been worshipped; the claims of the moral hero are beginning to be recognized. A dream, do you call it? But the success, far beyond the most sanguine expectations, which has attended many philanthropic enterprises, and the glory which has crowned it, show that it is a dream which is every day coming to pass. Merely as a dream also it makes a man better and happier, for it raises him above himself; and, even if he falls a martyr to it, how much better to fall here, than on the field of battle; where, as the greatest captain of the age has said, the horrors of a victory are only exceeded by the horrors of a defeat.

One word, in conclusion, on the young man's dream of *progress in knowledge and virtue;* his dream of *self-perfection.*

There is a sect of Christians, who derive their name from holding the doctrine that every one can and ought to become morally perfect in the present life. I am disposed to regard this as an idle and a mischievous dream; but it is mischievous from the circumstance that they look upon perfection as an *acquisition*, and not as an *aim;* it is a *perfection* which belongs to here and there one, and not a *perfectibility* which belongs to all. Let no one reject or dismiss the dream of perfection in the last-mentioned sense, on the ground that it pertains to enthusiasts alone. If there ever was a person not to be classed with enthusiasts, it was Dr. Franklin ; yet he tells us in his autobiography that, when he was a young man, he conceived the arduous project of making himself morally perfect ; and, from the manner in which he insists on the details, it is plain how much importance he attached to the attempt. In its most general signification, this dream of self-perfection simply expresses the fact, that, not being satisfied with the *actual*, we hold up before us an *ideal* good. As the artist holds up before him an ideal beauty, which he strives to copy and make his own, so the Christian holds up before him an ideal self, which he strives to realize. A life without these *ideals* would be stagnation and moral death. And besides, what can be more explicit than the teachings of the New Testament on this point? "Be ye therefore perfect, even as your Father which is in heaven is perfect." "Till we all come in the unity of the faith, and of the knowledge of the Son of God, unto a perfect man, unto the measure of the fulness of Christ."

This, then, is the application of what I have said, which I would impress on those especially, who are worshipping with us for the last time. You have dreamed of many things, while you have been here. If you have dreamed of a life of ease and pleasure and self-indulgence, or of a life of selfish ambition and worldly success and display, I beseech you to dismiss the thought from this moment. All such dreams are false to your nature and destiny; they are utterly unsuitable and impracticable in this country; and under the most favorable circumstances they can only end in self-dissatisfaction or self-contempt. But you have dreamed of better things than these. You have dreamed of a life of usefulness, and of a just and honorable fame. Even in the midst of levities and indiscretions, which have filled the hearts of those who love you with inexpressible concern, you have yet dreamed of a future career that would satisfy the best expectations of your friends, reflect honor on the place of your education, and help to uphold the institutions and liberties of our common country. Some of you have marked out for yourselves a line of conduct which will lead to eminence in business or in the secular professions; some of you propose to devote yourselves more exclusively to scientific pursuits, in the hope, and with the purpose, to extend the bounds of human knowledge for human good; some of you have made up your minds to give yourselves, more immediately and more entirely, to the great ministry of humanity, and to the Church of the Living God. Reverence these dreams of your youth. Make your future lives the fulfilment of these dreams. Remember, you are not to live for the past, for that is gone ; nor for the present, for while I am yet speaking that is also gone : but for the future, which is all before you. And, if faithful, you have the promise of help and of victory, from that mysterious and awful and all-sustaining Presence in which you will act and live.

1855.

XXI.

MORAL DISTINCTIONS NOT SUFFICIENTLY REGARDED IN SOCIAL INTERCOURSE.

"*He that walketh with wise men shall be wise; but a companion of fools shall be destroyed.*" — PROVERBS xiii. 20.

THAT "a man may be known by the company he keeps," has passed into a proverb among all nations, — thus attesting what has been the universal experience. The fact would seem to be that a man's associates either find him, or make him, like themselves. An acute but severe critic of manners, who was too often led by his disposition and circumstances to sink the philosopher in the satirist, has said, "Nothing is so contagious as example. Never was there any considerable good or ill action, that hath not produced its like. We imitate good ones through emulation; and bad ones through that malignity in our nature, which shame conceals, and example sets at liberty."

This being the case, or any thing like it, all, I think, must agree that moral distinctions are not sufficiently cared for in social intercourse. In forming our intimacies we are sometimes determined by the mere accident of being thrown together; sometimes by a view to connections and social position; sometimes by the fascination of what are called companionable qualities: seldom, I fear, by thoughtful and serious regard to the influence they are likely to have on character. We forget that other attractions, of whatsoever nature, instead of compensating for moral unfitness in a companion, only have the effect to make such unfitness the more to be dreaded.

Let me introduce what I have to say on the importance of paying more regard to moral distinctions in the choice of friends, by a few remarks on what are called, by way of distinction, *companionable qualities*, and on the early manifestation of a free, sociable, confiding turn of mind. Most parents hail the latter, I believe, as the best of prognostics; and in some respects, perhaps, it is. It certainly makes the child more interesting as a child, and more easily governed; it often passes for precocity of talent; at any rate, men are willing to construe it into evidence of the facility with which he will make his way in the world. The father is proud of such a son; the mother idolizes him. If from any cause he is brought into comparison with a reserved, awkward, and unyielding boy in the neighborhood, they are ready enough to felicitate themselves, and others are ready enough to congratulate them, on the difference. And yet I believe I keep within bounds when I say, that, of the two, there is more than an even chance that the reserved, awkward, and unyielding boy, as he grows up, will give his parents less occasion for anxiety and mortification, and become in the end the wiser and better man. The reason is, that, if a child from natural facility of disposition is easily won over to good courses, he is also, from the same cause, liable at any time to be easily seduced from these good courses into bad ones. On the contrary, where a child, from rigor or stubbornness of temper, is peculiarly hard to subdue and manage, there is this hope for a compensation : if by early training, or the experience of life, or a wise foresight of consequences, he is once set right, he is almost sure to keep so.

It is not enough considered, that, in the present constitution of society, men are not in so much danger from want of good dispositions, as from want of firmness and steadiness of purpose. Hence it is that gentle and affectionate minds, more perhaps than any others, stand in need of solid principle and fixed habits of virtue and piety, as a safeguard against the lures and fascinations of the world. A man of a cold, hard, and ungenial nature is comparatively safe so far as the temptations of society go: partly because of this very impracticableness of his nature; and partly because his companionship is not likely to be desired or sought even by the bad: he will be left to himself. The corrupters of innocence in social intercourse single out for their prey men of companionable qualities. Through his companionable qualities the victim is approached; and by his companionable qualities he is betrayed.

Let me not be misunderstood. Companionable qualities are not objected to *as such.* When they spring from genuine goodness of heart, and are the ornament of an upright life, they are as respectable as they are amiable; and it would be well if Christians and all good men cultivated them more than they do. If we would make virtue and religion to be loved, we must make *ourselves* to be loved *for* our virtue and religion; which would be done if we were faithful to carry the gentleness and charity of the gospel into our manners as well as into our morals. Nevertheless, we insist that companionable qualities, when they have no better source than a sociable disposition, or, worse still, an easy temper and loose principles, are full of danger to their possessor, and full of danger to the community; especially where, from any cause, but little regard is paid to moral distinctions in social intercourse. We also say, that in such a state of society the danger will be most imminent to those whom we should naturally be most anxious to save, — I mean, persons of a loving and yielding turn of mind.

And this brings me back again to the position taken in the beginning of this discourse. The reason why companionable qualities are attended with so much danger is, that society itself is attended with so much danger; and the reason why society itself is attended with so much danger is, that social intercourse is not more under the control of moral principles, moral rules, and moral sanctions.

My argument does not make it necessary to exaggerate the evils and dangers of modern society. I am willing to suppose that there have been times when society was much less pure than it is now; and again, that there are places where it is much less pure than it is here: but it does not follow that there are no evils or dangers now and here. On the contrary, it is easy to see that there may be stages in the progressive improvement of society, where the improvement itself will have the effect, not to lessen, but to increase the danger, *so far as good men are concerned.* In a community where vice abounds, where the public manners are notoriously and grossly corrupt, good men are put on their guard. Good men will not be injured by such society, for they will have nothing to do with it. A broad line of demarcation is drawn between what is expected from good men, and what is expected from bad men ; so that the example of the latter has no effect on the former except to admonish and to warn. But let the work of refinement and reform go on in general society until vice itself is constrained to wear a decent exterior, until an air of decorum and respectability is thrown over all public meetings and amusements, and one consequence will be that the distinction between Christians and the world will not be so clearly seen, or so carefully observed, as before. The standard of the world, from the very fact that it is brought nearer to the standard of the gospel, will be more frequently confounded with it; Christians will feel at liberty to do whatever the world does, and the danger is, that they will come at length to do it from the same principles.

Besides, are we sure that we have not formed too favorable an opinion of the moral condition of general society, — of that general society in the midst of which we are now living, and to the influence of which we are daily and hourly exposed? We should remember that, in pronouncing on the character of public opinion and public sentiment, we are very likely to be affected and determined ourselves, not a little, by the fact that we share in that very public opinion and public sentiment which we are called upon to judge. I have no doubt that virtue, in general, is esteemed even by the world, or that, *other things being equal*, a man of integrity will be preferred on account of his integrity. But this is not enough. It shows that the multitude see, and are willing to acknowledge, the dignity and worth of an upright course; but it does not prove them to have that *abhorrence for sin*, which it is the purpose and the tendency of the gospel to plant in all minds. If they had this settled and rooted abhorrence for sin, which marks the Christian, and without which a man cannot be a Christian, they would not only prefer virtue to vice, "other things being equal," but they would do so whether other things were equal or not; they would knowingly keep no terms with vice, however recommended or glossed over by interest or worldly favor, or refined and elegant manners.

Now I ask whether general society, even as it exists amongst us, will bear this test? Is it not incontestable that very unscrupulous and very dangerous men, if they happen to be men of talents, or men of fashion, or men of peculiarly engaging manners, find but little difficulty in insinuating themselves into what is called good society; nay, are often among those who are most courted and caressed? Some vices, I know, are understood to put one under the social ban; but it is because they offend, not merely against morality and religion, but against taste, against good-breeding, against certain conventions of the world. To be convinced of this it is only necessary to observe that the same, or even a much larger amount of acknowledged criminality, manifested under other forms, is not found to be attended with the same result. The mischiefs of this state of things are felt by all; but especially by those who are growing up in what are generally accounted the most favored walks of life. On entering into society they see men of known profligacy mingling in the best circles, and with the best people, if not indeed on terms of entire sympathy and confidence, at least on those of the utmost possible outward respect and courtesy. They see all this, and they see it every day; and it is by such flagrant inconsistencies in those they look up to for guidance, more perhaps than by any other one cause, that their own principles and their own faith are undermined. And besides, being thus encouraged and countenanced in associating with dissipated and profligate men in what is called good society, they will be apt to construe it into liberty to associate with them *anywhere*. At any rate the intimacy is begun. As society is constituted at present, corrupting intimacies are not infrequently begun amidst all the decencies of life, and, it may be, in the presence and under the countenance and sanction of parents and virtuous friends, which are afterwards renewed and consummated, and this too by an easy, natural, and almost necessary gradation, amidst scenes of excess,—perhaps in the haunts of ignominy and crime.

If one should propose a reform in this respect, I am aware of the difficulties and objections that would stand in his way.

Some would affirm it to be impracticable in the nature of things. They would reason thus: — "The circle in which a man visits and moves is made *for* him, and not *by* him; at any rate, it is not, and cannot be, determined by moral considerations alone. Something depends on education; something on family connections or mere vicinity; something on similarity in tastes and pursuits; something also on equality or approximation in wealth and standing. A poor man, or a man having a bare competency, if he is as virtuous and industrious, is just as *respectable* as a rich man; but it is plain that he cannot afford to pitch his style of living, or his style of hospitality, on the same scale of expense. It is better for both, therefore, that they should visit in different circles." Perhaps it is; but what then? I am not recommending an amalgamation of the different classes in society. I suppose that such an amalgamation would neither be practicable nor desirable in the existing state of things. All I contend for is, that in every class, open and gross immorality of any kind should exclude a man from reputable company. Will any one say that *this* is impracticable? Let a man, through untoward events, but not by any fault or neglect of his own, be reduced in his circumstances, — let a man become generally odious, not in consequence of any immorality, but because, perhaps, he has embraced the unpopular side in politics or religion, — let a man omit some trifling formality which is construed into a vulgarity, or a personal affront, — and people do not appear to find much difficulty in dropping the acquaintance. If, then, it is so easy a thing to drop a man's acquaintance for other reasons, and for no reason, — from mere prejudice, from mere caprice, — will it still be pretended that it cannot be done at the command of duty and religion?

Again, it may be objected that, if you banish a man from general society for his immoralities, you will drive him to despair, and so destroy the only remaining hope of his reformation. What! are you going *to keep society corrupt* in the vain expectation that a corrupt state of society will help to reform its corrupt members? Besides, I grant that we should have compassion on the guilty; but I also hold that we should have compassion on the innocent, too. Would you, therefore, allow a bad man to continue in good society, when the chances are a thousand to one that he will make others as bad as himself, and not more than one to a thousand that he himself will be reclaimed? Moreover, this reasoning is fallacious throughout. By expelling a dissipated and profligate man from good society, instead of destroying all hope of his recovery, you do in fact resort to the only remaining means of reforming one over whom a fear of God, and a sense of character, and the upbraidings of conscience have lost their power. What cares he for principle, or God, or an hereafter? Nothing, therefore, is so likely to encourage and embolden him to go on in his guilty course, as the belief that he will be allowed to do so without the forfeiture of the only thing he does care for, his reputable standing in the world. On the other hand, nothing is so likely to arrest him in these courses, and bring him to serious reflection, as the stern and determined threat of absolute exclusion from good society, if he persists.

Another objection will also be made which has

stronger claims on our sympathy and respect. We shall be told that the innocent as well as the guilty will suffer, — the guilty man's friends and connections, who will probably feel the indignity more than he does himself. God forbid that we should needlessly add to the pain of those who are thus connected! But we must remember that the highest form of friendship does not consist in blindly falling in with the feelings of those whom we would serve, but in consulting what will be for their real and permanent good. If, therefore, the course here recommended has been shown to be not only indispensable to public morals, but more likely than any other to reclaim the offender, it is clearly not more a dictate of justice to the community, than of Christian charity to the parties more immediately concerned. Consider, also, how much is asked, when a good man is called upon to open his doors to persons without virtue and without principle. Unless the social circle is presided over by a spirit which will rebuke and frown away immorality, whatever fashionable names and disguises it may wear, — unless your sons and daughters can meet together without being in danger of having their faith disturbed by the jeers of the infidel, or their purity sullied by the breath of the libertine, neither they nor you are safe in the most innocent enjoyments and recreations. Parents at least should take a deep interest in this subject, if they do not wish to see the virtue, which they have reared under the best domestic discipline, blighted and corrupted before their eyes by the temptations to which their children are almost necessarily exposed in general society,—a society which they cannot escape except by going out of the world, and which they cannot partake of without endangering the loss of what is of more value than a thousand worlds.

I have failed altogether in my purpose in this discourse if I have not done something to increase your distrust of mere companionable qualities, when not under the control of moral and religious principle; and also of the moral character and moral influence of general society, as at present constituted. Still you may ask, "If I associate with persons worse than myself, how can it be made out to be more probable that they will drag me down to their level, than that I shall lift them up to mine?" The answer to this question, I hardly need say, depends, in no small measure, on the reason or motive which induces the association. If you mix with the world, not for purposes of pleasure or self-advantage,—if you resort to society, not for society as an end, but as a means to a higher end, *the improvement of society itself*,—you do but take up the heavenly mission which Christ began. For not being able to make this distinction, through the hollowness and corruption of their own hearts, the Pharisees thought it to be a just ground of accusation against our Lord, that he was willing to be accounted the friend of publicans and sinners. Let the same mind be in you that was also in Christ Jesus, and we cannot doubt that the spirit which inspires you will preserve you wherever you may go. It is of such persons that our Lord has said: "Behold, I give unto you power to tread on serpents and scorpions, and over all the power of the enemy; and nothing shall by any means harm you." Very far am I, therefore, from denying that we may do good in society, as well as incur danger and evil. Even in common friendships frequent occasions will present themselves for mutual service, for mutual counsel and admonition. Let me impress upon you this duty. Perhaps there is not one among you all, who has not at this moment companions on whom he can confer an infinite blessing. If there is a weak place in their characters, if to your knowledge they are contemplating a guilty purpose, if they are on the brink of entering into dangerous connections, by a timely, affectionate, and earnest remonstrance you may save them from ruin. Remember, we shall all be held responsible, not only for the evil which we do ourselves, but for the evil which we might prevent others from doing: it is not enough that we stand; we must endeavor to hold up our friends.

Very different from this, however, is the ordinary commerce of society; and hence its danger. If we mix with the world for the pleasure it affords, we shall be likely to be among the first to be reconciled to the freedom and laxity it allows. The world is not brought up to us, but we sink down to the world; the drop becomes of the consistence and color of the ocean into which it falls; the ocean itself remains unchanged. In the words of an old writer, "Though the well-disposed will remain some good space without corruption, yet *time*, I know not how, worketh a wound in him. Which weakness of ours considered, and easiness of nature, apt to be deceived, looked into, they do best provide for themselves that separate themselves as far as they can from the bad, and draw as nigh to the good, as by any possibility they can attain to." "He that walketh with wise men shall be wise; but a companion of fools shall be destroyed."

1849–1858.

XXII.

ST. THOMAS, OR THE DOUBTING DISCIPLE.

"*But Thomas, one of the Twelve, called Didymus, was not with them when Jesus came. The other disciples said unto him, We have seen the Lord. But he said unto them, Except I shall see in his hands the print of the nails, and put my finger into the print of the nails, and thrust my hand into his side, I will not believe.*" — JOHN XX. 24, 25.

IT is a singular fact that the company of the Apostles, though but twelve in number, comprised almost every possible variety of mind and temper. There were the contemplative and affectionate John, the vehement Peter, the guileless and confiding Nathaniel, the judicious James, the selfish and plotting Judas, the sceptical Thomas. And I cannot bring myself to believe that this was accidental, or that it was without a particular design in the overruling providence of God. Certain it is, that, for us who must believe in the leading facts of Christianity on historical testimony, the circumstance here referred to has given a peculiar weight to that testimony. It shows that the evidence for these facts to eye-witnesses was of such a nature as to produce conviction, not merely in one sort of minds, but in all sorts of minds, and among the rest, in minds constitutionally distrustful and incredulous.

Under this point of view, let our attention now be called to the conduct and character of Thomas, who, though "one of the Twelve," had a mind so slow to accept the supernatural, that he could say when told of our Lord's resurrection, "Except I shall see in his hands the print of the nails, and put my finger into the print of the nails, and thrust my hand into his side, I will not believe."

Let us begin by glancing at what had been previously said of this Apostle by the sacred writers, considered as defining his position and illustrating his character.

He is introduced to us in the first instance, when Jesus was on the eve of suddenly returning to Judea, that he might raise Lazarus from the dead. Jesus had just left that country, retiring with the Twelve into Peræa on the other side of Jordan, which was beyond the jurisdiction of the High Priest and his Council at Jerusalem; and this he had done partly at least that he might escape out of their hands, for they were now bent on his destruction. On his announcing unexpectedly his determination to go back, his disciples remonstrated with one voice, for the impression of the blind fury with which the ruling party among the Jews were actuated against him was still fresh in their minds. They protested, therefore, against the temerity of putting himself so soon into their power again; but when they found it was to no avail, Thomas turned round, and said to his fellow-disciples, "Let us also go that we may die with him."

Here certainly there was no want of affection, fidelity, or self-devotion; but the action of these fine qualities was mingled with gloomy forebodings which had their spring in a nature prone to doubt and despondency. In moral principle and generous feeling, Thomas does not seem to have fallen below the other Apostles; his infirmity consisted in a constitutional tendency to distrust, which tempted him to look at the dark side of things. He did not doubt the reality or the obligation of virtue; what he doubted was the promises made to it, at least as regards this life. He was not a sceptic in respect to principles, but only in respect to promises. Accordingly, conscience and kind affection never forsook him, though hope did. In the particular case under consideration, he had no intention of deserting his Master, come what would. He felt, he knew, that Master to be worthy of any sacrifices on his part he could be called upon to make, even though they should involve the sacrifice of his life. He was ready to die *with* him or *for* him. Finding it impossible, therefore, to dissuade our Lord from the rash enterprise, as his Apostles regarded it, on which he was bent, Thomas' was the foremost to say, "Then let us follow him; let us stand by him to the last; let no one entertain the thought of abandoning him now." These certainly were utterances of love and duty, and not the less so because half in despair.

The same spirit is also evinced by this apostle on his next appearance in the evangelical narrative. The Supper of the Passover, the last which our Lord took with his disciples, was over; the Traitor had just left them in order to keep his appointment with a party whom the High Priest had sent to arrest Jesus; and Jesus himself, though darkly and as it were by degrees, as they were able to bear it, had announced his approaching departure. Meanwhile, the whole company had become exceedingly sorrowful and depressed by the turn which the conversation had taken, and the gloomy but indistinct apprehensions it had awakened in their minds; and it was with a view to alleviate, as far as might be, this despondency, that Jesus began to speak of the benefits to accrue to them and others from his going away. "In my Father's house are *many* mansions: if it were not so, I would have told you. I go to prepare a place *for you.* And if I go and prepare a place for you, I will come again and receive you to myself; that where I am, there ye may be also. And whither I go ye know, and the way ye know." And so, it would seem, they might; but a veil was on their hearts, through the Jewish prejudice respecting the earthly kingdom of the Messiah, which hindered them from understanding these words to refer to his death, to his passing into another world. Thomas especially, — who was, as we have seen, naturally slow, cautious, and distrustful, depending much on the evidence of the senses, and finding but small encouragement in vague prospects of good, and who, in this particular instance, like Peter before him, appears to have understood Jesus as alluding to some temporary place of concealment to which he was about to retire from his pursuers, — breaks out into an expression of something like impatience: "Lord, we know not where you are going; how then can we know the way?"

Here again, however, there is no want of affection or fidelity. On the contrary, it is this very affection and fidelity which is at the bottom of his uneasiness and dissatisfaction. It is not his indifference, but his love for Jesus, which makes him impatient of the obscurity in which the latter had wrapped his thoughts and his plans. He is solicitous to know and see with his own eyes the retreat concluded on, and the way to it, that he and the rest of the disciples might judge of its security; and this, too, not so much on his own account as on that of his revered Master. Whatever else he suspects, he never, you will observe, suspects Jesus himself; he never distrusts him; he never betrays, in the slightest degree, a want of confidence in the entire truthfulness and rectitude of our Lord: which is the more remarkable, as that, from the sceptical turn of his mind, was almost the only thing in which he was disposed to trust.

The third and only other occasion, on which Thomas comes forth prominently into notice in the gospels, is in connection with the evidences of our Lord's resurrection.

Notwithstanding all our Lord had said and done to prepare the Twelve for his violent and ignominious death, it is evident that this event took them by surprise, disconcerted all their cherished hopes, and led them to give up all for lost. It was not that they could remember any thing in his life, any thing which had transpired in their long and familiar intercourse with him, that should abate their confidence in his truth and sincerity, or in the reality of his many wonderful qualities and mighty works; but the single fact that he had been arrested, and given over to die an ignominious death, was utterly irreconcilable with their preconceived notions of THE MESSIAH. For this reason, and for this reason alone, they thought it could not be "He who was to restore Israel," and therefore that they must "look for another." Accordingly, having come to the conclusion that now nothing more was to be done for the common cause, each one's fears prompted him to consult his own safety, and the little band broke up and fled. Still, however, they lingered about in Jerusalem and the neighboring villages; and after the Crucifixion, and especially after the third day had come, a common interest, a common danger, a common affection, — coöperating, perhaps, with faint hopes that their Master might rise from the dead, founded on ill-understood intimations dropped by him while living, and still further quickened by vague rumors in circulation that he had appeared to the women at the sepulchre, — drew many of them together again. And, while they were together, Jesus came and stood in the midst of them, convincing them, by indubitable signs addressed to their senses, of the reality of his presence and the identity of his person.

Thomas, however, was not at this meeting, his constitutional slowness and distrust making him to be among the last to rally. And when at last he came, and was told by the others that they had seen the Lord, the same sceptical turn of mind made him refuse to give credit to what they said. He could not believe it; it was too good to be true; they had been too ready and too easy in their faith; they had not applied sufficiently severe tests; their wishes and their excited imaginations had played into the hands of the illusion; at best, it must have been a phantasm, a *mere* apparition: at any rate, *he* should so regard it, until with his own eyes he should see the prints of the nails, and with his own fingers touch the wounds in the hands and the side.

Let us not be hasty in execrating or blaming an incredulity, which, under the providence of God, has been made to answer a wise and beneficent end; which does not necessarily involve guilt, and was met, moreover, with so much kindness and forbearance by our Lord himself. Those who are for making no distinction among sceptics would do well to remember, that there are three distinct and independent sources of doubt or unbelief, each of which stamps it with a different and peculiar character.

In the first place, there is the doubt or unbelief which springs from *moral unfitness or prejudice.* By this I mean the difficulty a bad or unspiritual man finds in appreciating or accepting the revelations of the gospel, merely because he is a bad or unspiritual man. This difficulty arises partly from the essential unwelcomeness of these revelations to such a person, and partly from their not finding any response in a selfish, worldly, or corrupt heart. This is the class of whom the Scriptures speak as being "*slow of heart* to believe;" where there is no living sympathy with spiritual truth, there can be no living faith in spiritual truth. Moreover, I would not have you understand that what is here said of bad or unspiritual men applies to those only who have been guilty of high crimes and misdemeanors, or who are of vicious and depraved character in the estimation of the world. It implies, indeed, to a certain extent, a deadness or perversion of the moral sensibilities; this, however, may be owing, not to our love of evil, but to our want of the love of good, — to our want of faith and high aspiration and self-devotion. No heart is more inaccessible to religious impressions than that of your cool, prudent, self-possessed man of the world, who looks upon gross vice as a mistake, upon virtue as an amiable enthusiasm, and upon heaven as a dream.

This sort of scepticism, all will admit, argues great and serious moral defects, and is highly culpable; but there is no reason to suspect that the scepticism of Thomas resembled it, either in its origin or its results.

Another source of scepticism is to be found *in the disgusts occasioned by the errors and corruptions which have been mixed up with Christianity, and by the inconsistencies of nominal Christians.* Here again there is doubtless ground for blame; but much the largest portion of it should fall on those who cause these disgusts. Nothing is easier than to say, that Christianity ought to be judged by what it is in itself; above all, that it never should be made responsible for the misconduct of men who say that they are Christians, but are not. Nobody doubts that these are very proper discriminations; but we must not expect that all well-disposed persons will make them. Do what we may, say what we may, *actual* Christianity will pass with most persons for *real* Christianity, and the inconsistencies of nominal Christians will be charged upon the bad, or at best upon the imperfect, working of the whole system. This being the case, when men read the history of what is called THE CHURCH, and see what absurdities have been taught, and what abominations have been committed under the abused name of Christianity, who can wonder that the faith of not a few has been more or less disturbed; in other words, that their disgusts have so often refused to stop where undoubtedly they ought to stop? I am disposed to regard this as a common source of doubt; and the more so in proportion as an inquisitive and critical spirit prevails. I go further. When this doubt is unaccompanied by irreverence or moral indifference, nay, when it springs, as it sometimes does, from an instinctive repugnance to admit any thing as coming from God which derogates from His perfections, or sits like an incubus on the reason and liberties of man, I cannot help thinking that it is to a certain extent excusable. At any rate, the *most* guilty ones are those who have occasioned the scandal; not those who are misled by it. Be this, however, as it may, it is obvious that the scepticism here described is not that which troubled the apostle.

I pass, therefore, to the consideration of a third species of incredulity, having its source in organization, or in some radical differences of the mental constitution. While the multitude love the marvellous and are easily carried away by it, even to the adoption of the wildest and most absurd vagaries, it is not to be denied that individuals are occasionally to be met with in the world, all whose tendencies are to the opposite extreme, — individuals who can hardly bring themselves, on any evidence short of mathematical or ocular demonstration, to credit statements involving the extraordinary or the supernatural. Such scepticism, as all must perceive, is strictly speaking a *natural* and not a *moral* defect; — a misfortune, doubtless, and one which often exerts a baneful influence on the character, but, in itself considered, in no sense a crime. If, indeed, we yield to this natural bias further or more easily than our own reason and conscience approve; above all, if we nourish it, and pride ourselves upon it, as a sign of mental superiority, in that case we make it our own, and must answer for it as we best can. On the other hand, if we watch against the bias in question, as we would against any other natural infirmity, or constitutional temptation, — if the doubting disciple is a disciple still, sincere and humble, — in other words, if we doubt only that we may believe, and question only that we may make the foundations of our faith more sure, it is certain that a naturally sceptical turn of mind will have no other effect than to afford us a better opportunity for the display of our love of the truth.

Those who are for showing no mercy to involuntary sceptics of this description would do well to consider how differently they were treated by the Lord himself. At the first manifestation of Jesus to his assembled followers after his resurrection, Thomas, as we have said, was not present. Eight days afterwards they were together again, Thomas being with them; and Jesus stood in the midst and said, "Peace be unto you." "Then saith he to Thomas, reach hither thy finger, and behold my hands; and reach hither thy hand, and thrust it into my side; and be not faithless but believing. And Thomas answered and said unto him, My Lord and my God!"

Here was no denunciation, no upbraiding of the incredulity of the affectionate and honest, but doubting, disciple; on the contrary, an earnest solicitude to overcome that incredulity by evidence suited to his cast of mind. And the appeal resulted in complete success, as his exclamation of astonishment and recognition sufficiently shows.

Some persons are so taken up with remote doctrinal inferences from this exclamation of Thomas, as hardly to notice its more direct and immediate bearings. Perhaps it is not to be wondered at, that those who find evidence in other parts of Scripture to convince them that Christ is God, in the absolute sense of that word, should also think to see here the traces of that belief. Even they, however, must be aware how dangerous it must be to lay much stress on mere words, or turns of expression extorted by circumstances so exciting, so peculiar, so unexpected, so astounding. Suppose a friend, whose funeral we attended three days ago, should stand before us now. Who can tell precisely in what terms he would utter his sense of the fact, coupled with the bewilderment of his faculties as to how it could be? One thing is sufficiently obvious: it would be likely to be, as it was with Thomas, in the form of *a religious exclamation;* and ought perhaps to be interpreted, in both cases, as being little else than a religious exclamation, — an expression of feeling and not of thought. In the case of Thomas it signified, to be sure, that he no longer had any doubts about the question at issue; but the question at issue in his mind was *the fact of the resurrection*, and had nothing to do with any of the modern theories for or against the Divine nature of Christ. Very probably the question of the resurrection was mixed up in the mind of Thomas with that of the Messiahship, so that one suggested and involved the other. The resurrection proved Jesus to be the Messiah; but certainly it did not prove him to be God; on the contrary, it assumed that *he had been dead.* What Jew could have been made to believe, or even to entertain the conception, that Jehovah, the only Being whom he acknowledged as God in the absolute sense of that word, *had just risen from the dead?* If therefore in the exclamation, "My Lord and my God," we must understand Thomas as meaning to apply both appellatives to the risen Jesus, we must still presume that the latter is to be taken in a secondary or figurative sense, according to a common use of it in his day, which consisted in calling "them *Gods*, unto whom the word of God came."

The instructive lesson to be gathered from this apostle's renunciation of his doubts is not doctrinal, but practical. It intimates, in the first place, that if the sceptic's *love* of truth does not fail him, he is almost sure to attain at last to the truth itself; and secondly, that the only way in which he can be saved from the evil, and it may be the sin, of doubt, is by being converted from the doubt.

There are sceptics, I believe, who think to find excuse for their scepticism, though persisted in, on the ground that "one of the Twelve" was a sceptic like themselves. And so he was *for a time;* but if his scepticism had not yielded to the evidence, — in other words, if he had *continued* faithless and unbelieving, Judas Iscariot was not more certain to be ejected from his apostleship than he. Those who think themselves innocent and safe, because they *begin* as the apostle did, must take care that they also *end* as the apostle did. In one word, if they are like him in a constitutional difficulty and slowness of belief, and in honest hesitation, they must also take care to be like him in not allowing these habits to engender indifference, or to make them less open to conviction, or less disposed to accept the proof when it comes.

Will it then be said, that the proof which came to Thomas does not and cannot come to us? Will the sceptics of the nineteenth century urge: "If ocular demonstration were vouchsafed to us, it would instantly disperse our doubts. We also should be glad to believe. Let the same appeal be made to us that was made to Thomas, 'Reach hither thy finger and behold my hands; and reach hither thy hand and thrust it into my side; and be not faithless but believing,'—and we should doubtless do as he did. So that after all, taking the Scriptures as authority, we are just like the apostle; except that Providence does not interfere in our behalf, as it did in his. In our circumstances, Thomas would have persisted in his scepticism as we persist in our scepticism."

Granting for a moment that it were so,—granting also that *persistence* in scepticism, under the circumstances here supposed, is not a fault, it by no means follows that it is not *an evil*, and a great evil. Moreover, there are evils which, though not entering themselves into moral character, affect moral character nevertheless most seriously; and want of faith, even if nothing but an evil in itself considered, is certainly an evil of this description. Want of faith, religious scepticism, by whatsoever cause induced, no matter whether a sin or a mere misfortune, must have the effect to unsettle our confidence in the highest motives to duty of every kind, and in all motives to duty of the highest kind, turning our best and most distinctive aspirations, as immortal beings and the children of God, into a passing and mocking dream.

But is it true that scepticism is any more reasonable or excusable now than formerly? Of course we cannot seriously insist on being eye-witnesses of what took place twenty centuries ago. It is enough to know that there were eye-witnesses, and that *they* were convinced; nay, more, that the most sceptical man now alive had a representative there, in the person of "one of the Twelve," and *he* was convinced. What satisfied one sceptical man we may reasonably presume would have satisfied any sceptical man; and here the question obviously is, not whether you or I were actually present, but whether, if we had been present, we should probably have been satisfied.

And besides, if contemporaries had a kind of evidence which is denied to us, we also, on our part, have a kind of evidence which was denied to them. "Refrain from these men," said Gamaliel, "and let them alone: for if this counsel or this work be of men, it will come to nought; but if it be of God, ye cannot overthrow it; lest haply ye be found even to fight against God." Now, "this counsel or this work" *has stood.* Nay, more, it has not only become the accepted religion of the whole civilized world, but modern civilization is built upon it. *We* have, therefore, a proof of its Divine origin, which the most enlightened Jew of apostolic times regarded as more decisive than any to be had by contemporaries and eye-witnesses.

Nor is this all. Every truth which appeals to the sentiments as well as the understanding — as in the case of taste, morals, or religion — must depend more or less for its reception on the fact that the minds to whom it is addressed have been educated up to it. The sentiments appealed to must be already developed, at least to some degree, or those who make the appeal will "speak into the air." An unspiritual man must believe in spiritual truths, if he believes in them at all, on authority alone; but the spiritual man has a witness in himself. Hence our Lord's reply to his once doubting, but now believing disciple: "Thomas, because thou hast seen me thou hast believed: blessed are they that have not seen and yet have believed." A passage not unlike this is found in one of the Jews' books. "A proselyte," we are there told, "is more beloved of the Holy Blessed God than all the Israelites before Mount Sinai; for they saw and heard the thunderings, flames, and lightnings; but the proselyte has not seen this, yet, devoting himself to God, hath taken upon him the kingdom of heaven." The meaning is, that the best men hardly require outward evidence of any kind to convince them of spiritual realities. They find the witness in themselves, — in that spiritual tact, in that inward sense of heavenly and divine things, which constitutes the essence of a living and saving faith.

1857.

XXIII.

THE SERMON ON THE MOUNT.

"*And seeing the multitudes, he went up into a mountain; and when he was set, his disciples came unto him: and he opened his mouth and taught them.*" — MATTHEW v. 1, 2.

AT the age of thirty, our Lord entered on his public ministry, and was baptized by John. Then followed his Temptation in the Wilderness, — a mysterious experience, which perhaps is best explained by supposing it to have been the temptation attendant on a new consciousness of power. It was suggested to him that he could take this power and turn it to selfish purposes, supplying his physical wants, and acquiring distinction, wealth, and fame. But the temptation had no effect upon him; it did not even so much as sully the purity of his thoughts; though "in all points tempted like as we are, yet without sin." After that, he proceeded to collect around him a chosen and small band of disciples, to be near his person continually, listening to his conversation, asking him questions, and beholding his mighty deeds;

that they, at some future day, might be in a condition to take up the same great work when he should be called to lay it down.

He was now in Galilee, in the neighborhood of Capernaum. Multitudes had begun to flock to him from all parts of the country, some attracted by the fame of his wisdom and his miracles, others by a natural curiosity to see with their own eyes and hear with their own ears a man about whom there were so many questions and so much mystery. Up to this time, he seems to have done but little towards declaring himself, — nothing certainly which amounted to what is commonly understood by defining one's position. He felt that to delay doing this any longer would be hardly consistent with openness and fairness of conduct; his followers, before they went any further, ought to know what they had to expect from him, and what he expected from them in return. Full of this idea, he repaired to an elevated spot in the vicinity, from which to address his disciples and the multitude; and, when these had come and arranged themselves around him, he opened his mouth and taught them, pronouncing the longest, and in my judgment, beyond question, the most important and significant, of all his discourses, — the Sermon on the Mount.

I now propose to call your attention to this discourse under a single point of view, that of its being the original and first proclamation of the distinctive peculiarities of Christianity, — a formal statement by our Lord himself of what would be required in the citizens of the new kingdom he had come to set up, — the platform, so to speak, the programme of the new movement.

Restricting myself to this large and general view of the subject, it will not be necessary to take up minor criticisms; but there is one which deserves a passing notice, as it goes to the extent of questioning whether any such proclamation was ever made; whether, in short, the Sermon on the Mount was ever delivered, — that is to say, as we find it in Matthew. Every thoughtful reader of the New Testament must have observed that there is a report in Luke of apparently the same discourse, though in a mutilated form, and with considerable additions and variations; and furthermore, that there are disjointed fragments of this discourse occurring from time to time in both Luke and Mark, apparently as if suggested by passing events. To reconcile and explain these facts, two theories have been advanced. One is, that the discourse was really delivered as given by Matthew, what we find of it in the other Evangelists being of the nature of imperfect sketches, or mere repetitions. The other is, that Matthew, in order that the force and consistency of our Lord's teachings might be more felt, has brought together what he said on various occasions, and given it as one continuous and connected discourse. The first mentioned of these theories is to me the most probable and satisfactory; either, however, may be adopted without essentially affecting my argument. In one case, we have our Lord laying down in the beginning what his followers must be in order to enter into the kingdom of heaven; in the other, we have in one place a collection and summary of all our Lord's teachings on the subject, inculcating, however, the self-same doctrine.

There is also another objection to the use I am going to make of the Sermon on the Mount, which it will be proper to consider for a moment in the outset. It is said, that, to ascertain what constitutes the essence of Christianity, we must resort, not to the *first* statements of it, but to the *last*, on the ground that every system is a gradual development from small and imperfectly understood beginnings. Now, in replying to this, I would not be thought to exclude the great law of development, even from Christianity. Undoubtedly it has its place there, but not, as I suppose all will agree, without some distinctions and qualifications. For instance, I suppose it will hardly be pretended by any believer in Christ as a Teacher come from God, that *he* did not know what constitutes a Christian in the beginning, as well as at any subsequent period. The development, therefore, did not consist so much in his teachings as he understood them, as in the capacity of his disciples to understand him. It did not have the effect to supersede the Sermon on the Mount, but only to enable his followers to enter more entirely into its profound significance. Again, by *development*, in this connection, is not meant the transforming of one idea into another essentially different, but only that the essential contents of the primitive idea are more fully unfolded and carried out. Accordingly, if the strictly moral and spiritual basis assigned to Christianity in the Sermon on the Mount is made to give place to a doctrinal or ecclesiastic basis, we affirm that this is not development; it is change, substitution, contradiction. Christianity begins by being one thing, and ends by being another. Furthermore, when our Lord said, "I have yet many things to say unto you, but ye cannot bear them now," I do not suppose he intended that the time would come when it would be necessary for men to take an entirely different view of what constitutes the central idea, the essential nature, of the Gospel.

What he meant was simply this: that there were connections, applications, and extensions of the great doctrine of Christian holiness, which they from their Jewish prejudices, and especially from their worldly conceptions of the Messianic Kingdom, were not as yet in a condition to appreciate.

I return, therefore, to the position taken above: the Sermon on the Mount is a formal and express answer to the question, which was on the lips of every one in the vast throng of listeners. All desired to know, all had come there to learn, what this new movement meant; and what was expected from those who took part in it; what they were to gain, and what they were to do and be in order to gain it. Our Lord knew their thoughts, their wants, their longings, in one word, their particular state of mind; and the whole purpose and drift of his discourse was to meet, inform and satisfy it. Evidently it was so understood at the time by all parties, and must, therefore, be so understood now.

If, after what has been said, it should still be contended that the Sermon on the Mount was a Jewish affair, because it was originally addressed to Jews, and abounds in references to the Old Testament, the reply is obvious. The Jews are addressed, not, however, merely as Jews, but as men; moreover, the teachings of the Old Testament, or the construction put upon them, are referred to as utterly insufficient, making it necessary that there should be a *restatement* of the conditions of Divine favor and acceptance. And this restatement as here given is entirely general, general in all its requirements and in all its promises; thereby showing incontestably that it was not designed for one age only, or for one people only, but for all ages and for all mankind.

Thus much being conceded, we can be at no loss where to go, and where not to go, *in order to ascertain what constitutes a Christian.*

In the first place, we are *not* to go to the Old Testament. In saying this, I do not mean to call in question the Divine origin or the Divine authority of the Mosaic dispensation. Some persons find it hard to conceive how any thing coming from an absolutely perfect Being can be otherwise than perfect in itself, and therefore incapable of improvement. But they forget that, in God's dealings with imperfect beings like ourselves, perfection becomes a relative term. That constitution of government, that system of education, that dispensation of religion, is a perfect one, which is perfectly adapted to the condition and wants of the community. In this sense, the Law was as perfect as the Gospel, — nay, for its time and place more so, because more suitable and practicable. But it by no means follows that the Law *is* the Gospel. On the contrary, the best thing that can be said of the Law is, that it prepared the way for the Gospel, — "our schoolmaster to bring us unto Christ." We even know that provisions were retained by Moses, not because they were right, nor because he liked them, but because the people were not as yet in a condition to receive any thing better. "And Jesus answered and said unto them, For the hardness of your heart, he wrote you this precept." It is true that our Lord has said again, in that very Sermon on the Mount which we are now recommending, "Think not that I am come to destroy the Law or the Prophets; I am not come to destroy, but to fulfil." Here, however, we must understand him as meaning that he had not come to set aside or frustrate what had been the main purpose of all preceding dispensations, namely, the progressive education of the human race, but only to carry out that purpose more fully. Accordingly, he goes on to remind his hearers of what had been "said to them of old time," on topic after topic, and to set in strong contrast with it, in each case, what he requires, showing incontestably that every preceding dispensation is to be regarded as inadequate and merely provisional.

Under these circumstances, it certainly would

not seem a very reasonable course to resort to the Law in order to ascertain what the Gospel enjoins. Yet nothing is more common. Where there is one New Testament Christian, there are two, if not twenty, Old Testament Christians. Look at the importance which the Church of Rome attaches to outward ordinances and an imposing ritual. Not a syllable can be found in the New Testament requiring it, or favoring it, or sanctioning it. Much of it comes from paganism, and the rest from the Old Testament. Protestants, also, though approaching it from another direction, have fallen into the same error of mistaking the Law for the Gospel. Exalting the authority of the Bible, and of the whole Bible, against the authority of tradition and the Church, they have sometimes neglected to make the proper discriminations as to the purpose and use of the several parts of the Bible. Who can read the history of the Scotch Covenanters, or of our Puritan ancestors, without being struck with the fact that their characters, though admirable in many respects, were yet seriously hurt by being modelled to so great an extent, inwardly as well as outwardly, after the heroes of the Old Testament? One of the Apostolic Fathers has said: "It is inconsistent to speak of Jesus Christ, and at the same time to follow Judaism. For Christianity hath not believed in Judaism, but Judaism in Christianity, that those of every tongue, having believed in God, might be united together." [1]

Again, in order to learn what is essential to the Christian character, we are not to go, as it seems to me, certainly not in the first instance, to the Epistles of Paul. Here the objection is not that the standard is an imperfect one, as in the case of Judaism, but that, from the nature and form of the compositions, it is imperfectly stated or hard to be understood. They are letters written to small communities, struggling under peculiar difficulties and trials, and in danger from peculiar local traditions and prejudices, or from the officious interference of this or that false teacher. Now we say that such writings must, by necessity, be more or less local and temporary both in substance and form. It was not the Apostle's aim to give a full and connected view of what constitutes a Christian, but to impart special instruction, as the case seemed to require; that is to say, to guard the particular community he was addressing against certain errors in opinion or practice, to which he had reason to believe that particular community was especially liable.

I do not deny that we have in these Epistles the application of *Christian principles* to a great variety

[1] *Ignatius ad Magnes,* § 2.

of conditions and circumstances; and hence their interest and value. But in order to take these principles and apply them to ourselves, we have first to disengage them from all that is special and peculiar in their form and dress as originally applied by the Apostle; and this is often no easy task. Because we have before us Paul's Epistle to the Romans, or that to the Galatians, it would be presumption in us to assume that we are therefore in a condition to say what sort of an Epistle he would write to the Churches in Boston or Cambridge, if he were now to return to life. From this and other causes, the difficulty of understanding the Apostle was felt and acknowledged even by his contemporaries. Peter, expressly referring to his Epistles, says, "In which are some things hard to be understood, which they that are unlearned and unstable wrest, as they do also the other Scriptures, unto their own destruction." Whence it appears that honesty of purpose and common-sense are not the sole requisites of a safe interpreter of these writings; that the obvious sense is not always the true sense; that the "unlearned," however piously disposed, merely from not knowing how the obvious sense is to be qualified by the occasion and circumstances, may wrest the passage to his own destruction. At the best, all we can hope to do in such cases is to seize and disengage the Christian principle which the Apostle intended to apply in a very different state of things from the present, and apply it anew. Certainly, therefore, it would seem to be better and safer to take that very principle, as given in its simplest and most intelligible form in the Sermon on the Mount.

But there are other discourses of our Lord, and above all his life, his own actions and sufferings, to indicate what we ought to be and do in order to become his faithful and consistent followers. And this is true. Far from me the thought to question or undervalue these means of spiritual light and help. Nevertheless, I repeat, it is only in the Sermon on the Mount that the Great Teacher undertakes to give a full and connected statement of what is required of all. His discourses and conversations on other occasions were necessarily brief or fragmentary; or they had special reference to some exigency of his immediate disciples; or they looked rather to the growth of the religion, than to the life of individuals. And what shall I say of our Lord's personal life, as set forth by the Evangelists? As a manifestation of the Divine in the human, as an independent proof that he came from God, more effective on some minds than any other, as a sublime and inspiring impersonation of a perfect moral beauty and holiness, never entirely lost sight of by the Church, however imperfectly understood, its value and importance never have been and never can be overstated. But when you and I proceed to apply this great life to our small concerns, to our ordinary and daily duties, we see at once that we are not expected to do the same things, but only to act from the same principles and dispositions. What these principles and dispositions are, those who can enter entirely into the spirit and significance of our Lord's outward life can gather from that, because they can see the principles and dispositions which underlie it; others must gather them, at least in the first instance, from his teachings. What we need to know most of all is, not our Lord's outward life as given in history, but his inward life, the sources, the springs of his goodness; and these are nowhere set forth so plainly and distinctly as in the Sermon on the Mount, and especially in the Beatitudes, with which it opens.

Obviously, therefore, we must go to this discourse, first of all and above all, if we would know what constitutes a Christian in the highest and best sense of that word. At the same time, in thus defining what I conceive to be the special purpose and use of the Sermon on the Mount, I do not mean to make it to be every thing, and the rest of the Gospel nothing. There are other portions of the New Testament, equally important and necessary, and perhaps more so, though for other purposes and uses; and to these we must go for the history of Christianity, and for many of its evidences, and motives, and sanctions. Take away the rest of the Gospel, and it is hardly to be supposed that much regard would be paid to the Sermon on the Mount. Still it is none the less true, that this Sermon contains the original and authentic statement, from the lips of our Lord himself, of what is peculiar and distinctive in the Christian character, — the Christian ideal of goodness; not merely how good men differ from bad men, but how the good Christian differs from the good pagan, or the good Jew, or the good deist. Here, more distinctly and authoritatively than anywhere else, is set forth that peculiar type or style of holiness by which the real Christian is known.

The practical consequences to be deduced from this position are of great moment.

Experience has shown that the attempt to found a right to the Christian name on doctrinal unity is an idle dream. I do not mean that one theology is as good as another; for this would be to forget that we have intellectual as well as moral wants. As science and civilization advance, and education becomes more and more general, it is of the utmost importance that the doctrines of Christianity should appear to be in harmony with men's ideas on other subjects; otherwise a general defection from the popular faith, either open or secret, may be expected. But this I say, let a man think as he will as regards mere doctrine; if it does not hinder him from acting out in his daily life the ideas contained in the Sermon on the Mount, it will not hinder him from being a Christian in the highest and best sense of that term.

A similar remark is applicable to ecclesiastical distinctions and ordinances. To pretend that there can be no salvation out of this or that church is the extreme of arrogance and presumption. Of course there must be some order of worship, and it is natural that men who think alike should worship together. Nay, more; as men are differently constituted, and have different receptivities, one church may be best for one person, and another for another. "One man," says the Apostle, "esteemeth one day above another: another esteemeth every day alike. Let every man be fully persuaded in his own mind." Observe, however, the condition: every one must be "fully persuaded in his own mind;" in other words, he must really believe what he professes to believe. And the reason is obvious. No professions, no rites, no observances are likely to be of much avail with one who does not really regard them as of Divine appointment; and, besides, it is really to corrupt our whole moral life at its heart's core, if, in our most solemn intercourse with God, we substitute, for an enlightened and honest belief, a shallow and fashionable *make-belief.* Be this, however, as it may, what I would now impress upon you is, that no church, no outward and visible church, can be of any service to you or me as Christians, except in so far as it helps us to *live* the Sermon on the Mount; that is, to act out, in all our relations to ourselves, to society, and to God, the ideas contained therein.

Yes, to be Christians indeed, we must bring our whole lives, inwardly and outwardly, into conformity with "the pattern shown us in the Mount." And here it is to no purpose to say that this is more than any man can do. No man can do it *perfectly;* but the only legitimate inference from this is, not that he cannot be a Christian in this way, but that he cannot be a *perfect* Christian in this way or in any other. It does not follow that a man cannot be a Christian, because he cannot be a perfect Christian, any more than it follows that a man cannot be a friend or patriot, because he cannot be a perfect friend or patriot. A man can be a Christian according to his measure and degree; but he can be so on the sole condition of living up to the Sermon on the Mount according to his measure and degree. And this is not all. If we sincerely and earnestly *strive* to live up to this divine rule *in all respects*, it will show that we have at least a *perfect* faith, meaning thereby a perfect *spirit* of faithfulness, and this *faith* may be counted for righteousness. That is to say, in the next world we may be rewarded according to what we sincerely and earnestly strove to be and do, — the *will* as it came from the heart, and was only baffled by the essential infirmities of our nature, being taken for the *deed*.

Our Lord has not left it for others to tell us whether we are Christians or not; he has told us himself. Can you suppose, therefore, that, in the long discourse in which he has done this, he is to be looked upon as speaking into the air, as laying down a standard and criterion which is above our reach, or which we cannot apply? Remember the words with which it closes: "Therefore whosoever heareth these sayings of mine, and doeth them, I will liken him unto a wise man who built his house on a rock; and the rain descended, and the floods came, and the winds blew, and beat upon that house; and it fell not, for it was founded on a rock. And every one that heareth these sayings of mine, and doeth them not, shall be likened unto a foolish man who built his house upon the sand; and the rain descended, and the floods came, and the winds blew, and beat upon that house; and it fell, and great was the fall of it!" 1860.

XXIV.

THE POWER OF CHRIST'S RESURRECTION.

"*That I may know him, and the power of his resurrection.*"—PHILIPPIANS iii. 10.

THE corner-stone of Christianity, considered as an historical religion, is Christ's resurrection. A circumstantial narrative of the fact is given by each of the four Evangelists. It is also again and again referred to, reaffirmed, and dwelt upon by the Apostles, as a cardinal point in the new faith. "Jesus, and the resurrection," to "know him and the power of his resurrection," is the sum and substance of their doctrine.

I am not going to renew an examination of the witnesses to the great historical event here alluded to. I am not going to take up the question of a future life, as if it were still an open question with Christians, for it is not; nor yet to go behind Christianity, with a view to establish the antecedent veraciousness and probability of such a life. All these subjects are well enough in their place; but they do not reach, as it seems to me, the main difficulty; or rather, perhaps I ought to say, they do not meet or supply the main deficiency. The main deficiency is not that of a speculative, but of a practical, faith. In a Christian community like ours, most persons are ready enough to assent, at least in words, to the doctrine of Christ's resurrection, and of the general resurrection; but how few know and feel its "power" as they might and ought!

Some have even gone so far as to maintain that, if the doctrine of a future life were to be struck out of being, it would produce no sensible change in the conduct of mankind. If this statement were confined to a merely speculative faith in the doctrine, and to its direct effect on human conduct, it would not be far from the truth. The reason is that men's actions are not determined and governed, at least not necessarily and immediately, by their speculations; but by example, by habit, by constitutional propensity. It is so in every thing. Because a man's opinions are right, it does not follow that his dispositions are right, or that his conduct will be right. Moreover, it is a mistake to suppose that, in order to convert a speculative faith into a practical faith, nothing else is required but more evidence; that the difference between them is one of degree only. They differ essentially. The former denotes a state of the understanding, the latter a state of the affections and the will; one we *think*, the other we *live*.

What we want is, not merely to see the truth of the doctrine of immortality, but to know and feel its "power." What we want is, habitually to recognize the reality of the spiritual world and a future life, in the same sense and in the same way in which we habitually recognize the reality of the sensible world and the present life.

Let no one say that this supposes either an impossible or a mystical state of mind. An impossible state of mind! We know it to have been actually attained by multitudes of men and women in different ages and countries,—not merely by Christians, but even by Jews and pagans and Mahometans. I do not mean that such persons think of nothing else but another life; this would be to neglect their nearest and most imperative relations and duties. But when there is occasion for it, the thought of another life comes in; and then, not as of something that may be, but as of something that really is. In times of great public anxiety and distress, or of domestic sorrow, or of private disappointment and suffering, their hope is not in man, but in God. Death itself cannot scare or unsettle this hope. How many confessors have stood up for the truth against the world, without a touch of fear! How many martyrs have been burnt at the stake with songs of triumph on their lips! Knowing that God and eternity were on their side, they did not care who or what was on the other side. To such men, the visible heavens in which the stars shine are not more real, than the invisible heavens in which God reigns.

Equally unfounded is the notion that the state of mind here recommended is mystical or inexplicable, or in any sense extravagant or unreasonable. If we are Christians, or even deists, we must be presumed to accept, in some form or other, the doctrine of a life to come. Look at the monuments, read the inscriptions, in any of your cemeteries: all speak of a life to come. It is the generally received faith. Not one in a thousand buries a child, or a parent, or a dear and venerated friend, with the sad and forlorn impression that he is no more for ever. Some may never have thought much on the subject; others may have great difficulties about it; with some, faith in immortality may be little more than a tradition; with others, little more than a feeling: yet, shadowy and imperfect as the hope is, the offer of all the "kingdoms of the world, and the glory of them," would not tempt them to let it go. Under such circumstances, the wonder, the great practical mystery, is not, I insist, that "the power" of this faith should be felt by so many, but that it should be felt by so few. What more does it suppose or require, but that we should act out our professions, live as we believe, do as we say? And is this mysticism? Is it not the very soul of practical consistency and good sense?

The radical error on this subject consists, as it seems to me, in not recognizing the part which rightfully belongs to *the will* in matters of *practical* conviction. We must make a distinction between speculative questions, where the end is opinion, and practical questions, where the end is action. In the latter case, to be for ever deliberating is to forget that it is a practical question. Of course, the will has nothing to do in determining the preponderance of evidence, as evidence; but it has a great deal to do in determining when, on the strength of this preponderance, we shall begin to act. Here, more perhaps than anywhere else, an irresolute will and a corresponding feebleness of character betray themselves, — not in one thing only, but in every thing. The young man who consumes the best part of his life in making up his mind as to what he ought to do, and even then makes it up hesitatingly and with reserves, is not likely to do much. What makes the great statesman, the great military commander, the great man of business, but this very thing, — that he knows how long to deliberate, and when to strike?

And so in religion. I do not mean that there is no occasion here for inquiry and judgment, that there is no distinction between a blind and superstitious worship or service, and an intelligent and rational worship or service. But this I say: there is no proper worship or service of any sort, until it takes a practical form. The turning point in every man's religious experience is, not when he says "I believe," but when he says "I will."

A man is not a Christian in proportion to the amount of truth he puts into his *creed*, but in proportion to the amount of truth he puts into his *life*. Accordingly, the great question respecting the doctrine of immortality is, not whether we believe it, but whether we *live* it. Are we prepared to say, "Discussion has done its work. The evidence for a future state is sufficient for all practical purposes. I will no longer look upon it as a matter in debate, but as a settled point. It shall take its place in all my views and plans of life as *a reality*, throwing its light on all other realities, and requiring that they should be adjusted to it, and judged by it"? Are you prepared to do this? Are you prepared to say, "I will"? If so, "old things are passed away; behold, all things are become new." You are in a condition, not merely to recognize the truth and importance of an immortal hope, but also to feel its "power."

With this sense, — I do not say with this profession or this belief, but with this *sense* of immortality on our minds, what will follow?

In the first place, it will help to reconcile us to the inequalities and incongruities of this world. Considered but as the opening scene of an endless career, it is easy to conceive that all will come out right at last. "What I do, thou knowest not now, but thou shalt know hereafter." A life of fewer troubles and difficulties and temptations might be less fitted to accomplish the end for which this life was given; it certainly would be less fitted to call out and educate and strengthen personal character. Even the greatest perplexity of all, — difference of moral and religious privilege, — yields to this explanation. How common it is for the men who struggled against the greatest disadvantages in the outset, gaining little by little, to succeed best in the end! The reason is, that these very disadvantages, though a hindrance to *progress* in the beginning, are the best school for developing a man's latent energies; that is to say, his *power to make further progress.* Thus a compensation is provided, — less progress, perhaps, up to a given time, but more power for the time to come; and when we consider that the time is infinite, we see it to be compensation which can never fail the deserving.

Again; a proper sense of immortality will not only reconcile us to life, whatever it may be, but also to death, whenever it may come.

If a man thinks at all on the subject, his mind must be in hopeless perplexity until he has formed a clear, or at least a practical, conception of the leading purpose and end for which he is placed in this world by Divine Providence. If we are to live again, the life that now is must have some connection with that which is to come; our present state has some bearing on our future state: otherwise, our present existence is a mere excrescence, unconnected with the rest of our being, absolutely without meaning or object, — not even a first step, as it is all to go for nothing, and we are to begin anew. But what is this connection? What is this bearing? These questions, of such vital moment to a seeker after truth and happiness, are sufficiently answered, as it seems to me, by saying that the Creator has placed us in this world, under the existing constitution of things, with a view to such an excitement and development of our moral and spiritual nature as will qualify us for action and enjoyment in another world, under a different constitution of things.

Thus is it with our education on earth. *This* is

not begun and completed in *one place.* And why? Because it is not found to be practicable to teach every thing in one school; but, beginning with the lowest or primary school, we make a certain degree of proficiency there; and then, quitting that school, we go up to a higher, and so on to the highest. Let us not speak disparagingly, much less contemptuously, even of the lowest school, or of the lowest form in the lowest school; for all must *begin* there. One school is as indispensable as another to the final result, and should be looked back upon with respect and gratitude. Nevertheless, it would be preposterous, as all must perceive, for any one to say that he will never quit the lowest school, that he will complete his education there. He cannot do it; he can only *begin* his education there. And so with the moral and spiritual training of the immortal soul. It has not been found practicable for our nature to attain its full and perfect development in one place, under one constitution of things, under one set of influences. Hence we are placed here in order to receive our first discipline, to put forth our first efforts, to learn our first lessons, and so to make a beginning. Still, all we can do here, at the best, is merely to make a beginning.

Many, I fear, look upon death as if it would put a period to our progress; but in point of fact it is intended to prevent a period being put to our progress. This life is one step in our being, and but one step; we die that we may take another step. We go as far as we can go in this world; we die that we may go farther, that we may go on to perfection. You would not wonder to hear a child say, "I would not be a child always." And why not? Because you think it natural and reasonable for the child to wish that, as he is prepared for it, he may be admitted to a wider sphere of duty, activity, and enjoyment. But is it not equally natural and reasonable for a man to wish that, as he is prepared for it, he also may be admitted to a still higher sphere of duty, activity, and enjoyment? If the child would not stop with being a child, but hopes to become something more and better, why should not man be unwilling to stop with being a mortal man, but hope to become something more and better? I repeat it, we do not die that we may *stop;* we die, that we may *go on.*

Moreover, a living and practical faith in immortality will help to reconcile us to death, *come when it may;* — that is, to an early death, or to waiting for it in extreme old age.

We can understand that men must die, for so it is decreed in their very organization, — as the leaves fall in autumn; but the leaves do not fall in spring. It has ever been accounted one of the darkest and most painful mysteries in Divine Providence, that so many, in the flush of health and spirits, full of promise, with their work but just begun, and knit by a thousand ties to loving hearts, should be suddenly cut off, while the old and infirm and worn out still linger on, often against their will. Perhaps the best answer to this difficulty is found in our incompetency to fathom the Divine counsels. But though we cannot understand particular cases, it is not difficult to see that the *general law* under which they take place is wise and good.

Consider, for a moment, what would follow if childhood, and youth, and early manhood were exempt from mortality; if, for example, nobody died until he was sixty. Is it not as certain as it is that man is man, that the early part of life would be given, by the great majority, to thoughtlessness and present indulgence, or to extreme worldliness; and that all earnest self-culture, and all serious preparation for eternity, would be postponed to near the close of the period on which they could certainly calculate? Who has yet to learn that most persons are extremely indisposed to act, and that many seem wholly incapable of acting, earnestly and decidedly for a remote object? God, therefore, by making us liable to death from the moment we begin to breathe, and by making us feel that death is continually impending over us, has wisely and mercifully so arranged it as to make our mortality an *ever-present* motive or restraint. Hence the secret of the amazing power exerted over mankind by the thought of death; which does more, as I firmly believe, to keep alive a spirit of religion in the world, and, through that, a spirit of virtue and order, than all other causes put together. There are doubtless higher principles than this, and men who can enter into the spirit of these higher principles; nevertheless, take away from the bulk of mankind the motives and restraints to be found in the mysterious overhanging of death, and I do not believe that society could be held together. And the power of this thought, let me remind you, is not found in the *final* certainty of death, but in the certainty that it may come *at any moment.*

And besides, why say of those who die early, that they die prematurely, their destiny interrupted and broken off? We never shall think justly, rationally, consistently of death, until we come to look upon it, not theoretically alone, but practically, as being neither more nor less than a change of abode for the immortal spirit. Putting away all the illusions of the senses and the imagination on this subject, and giving ourselves up to the impressions and convictions of our better nature, illuminated and confirmed as they are by the Word and the Spirit of God, we must come to regard death in no other light than as a transition from one mode of existence to another. To be Christians indeed, we must habitually feel and act under a deep and abiding assurance that what we call death is not the extinction of a single particle of real life; but only the separation from life of all that is mortal, that nothing but life may remain. What we call death takes place, and "mortality is swallowed up of life." The dead, then, are *not* dead. Our friends, who are absent from the body, are present with the Lord. They are not *here*, but they are *there;* they *live*, — fully to carry out, under more favorable circumstances, every purpose for which they were created.

Is it not a presentiment of this which makes the death-bed of the young, as a general rule, so much more bright and hopeful than that of the old? Death itself would wear a harder and more repulsive look to us all, if we did not so frequently see it reflected back upon us from the placid and beautiful faces of those whom the world has never touched with its sorrows or its cares.

And what shall I say of old age? Very far is it from being barren of uses and satisfactions. In the primitive ages, when wisdom was found in personal experience, and not in traditions or in books, the old were looked up to for counsel or authority more than now. Even now, however, there is a beautiful and touching reverence everywhere paid to men remarkable for their virtues and their years. But there is one great drawback: so far as this world is concerned, old men must live in their recollections, and not in their hopes. Cicero has been complimented for the ingenious turn he has given to this objection. "An old man," he says, "has nothing indeed to hope for; yet he is in so much the happier state than a young man, since he has already attained what the other only hopes for." But this will hardly satisfy. That we have lived to some purpose should reconcile us to *having* lived, but it has nothing to do with our continuing to live. I can think of nothing more dreary than to be waiting for death, without having that death lighted up and transfigured by an unshaken trust in another life.

There is no ignoring, there is no concealing the inconveniences, the infirmities, which steal over us as we descend into the vale of years. What is to give peace, contentment, and dignity to the evening of our days? It is a great thing, for an old man to retain his faculties and his natural cheerfulness to the last. It is a great thing, to keep up his interest in good objects, and in his favorite studies and pursuits. It is a great thing, to be surrounded by kind friends, and all the endearments and appliances of a happy home. But greater than all, "to know Christ, and the power of his resurrection," — as a hope full of immortality. With this hope, he still has something to live for, and something to die for. This world and all it contains are fading away; but his eyes are fixed on "a better country, that is, a heavenly," — "a city which hath foundations, whose builder and maker is God."

1861.

XXV.

OUR DUTY IN RESPECT TO OTHER MEN'S CONSCIENCES.

"*Conscience, I say,—not thine own, but of the other.*"—1 CORINTHIANS, x. 29.

IF there were but one conscience in the world, and that were mine, my course would be plain and straightforward, so far, at least, as conscience is concerned. I should only have to settle it in my own mind what is right, and that would be right; —right for me, and right for everybody. Other men, not having any consciences of their own, if they wished to act conscientiously, would have to regulate their conduct by my opinion of right. They would have to look at me, and do as they see me do. Men's consciences have sometimes been called their watches; each one consults his own: but in the circumstances here supposed, my conscience would be more than that; it would be the Town Clock.

But in point of fact it is far otherwise. There are as many consciences as there are individuals;

and what makes it worse is, that these consciences, to all appearance, are not agreed. They do not always lead the same way; they often lead different, and sometimes opposite, ways, even in matters of public interest and duty. Your conscience says, *this* ought to be done; my conscience says, *that* ought to be done; and, in such cases, what *shall* be done? Shall your conscience give way to mine? Or mine to yours? Or shall both give way, some compromise being adopted? Or shall neither give way *voluntarily*, — the question, What is right? being left to turn on the question, Which is the stronger?

Naturalists tell us of animals which cannot be turned from their course; so that, when two chance to meet, each begins to raise himself on his legs as high as possible, and the one which can raise himself the highest, travels directly over the other's head. Something like this not unfrequently takes place among men, when they come into collision with one another on the ground of contested right. The two parties meet, but instead of making room for each other on terms of mutual concession and respect, they follow the example of the animals referred to above. Taking their stand on what they call conscience, they immediately begin to stretch themselves up as high as possible; and that party which can make itself the superior in prestige or influence, or popular clamor, travels directly over the other's head.

As might be presumed from what is known of the overbearing and despotic propensities of human nature, this evil has always existed to a greater or less degree; and many things at the present day, though in themselves good, tend to increase it. I allude here especially to the progress and diffusion of knowledge and civil and religious liberty. In proportion as men become enlightened and free, each man's individual judgment stands for more, and, at the same time, mere tradition, mere authority, and, I may add, mere law, stand for less. Under these circumstances, a man of an arbitrary and despotic turn of mind is more likely than ever to set up his own conscience, or that of his party or clique, as the standard of right, other men's consciences to the contrary notwithstanding.

Hence the growing importance, in a practical point of view, of looking into this whole subject a little more carefully. What is due to the plea of conscience, — "conscience, I say, not thine own, but of the other"? What is our duty as Christians in respect to other men's consciences, especially when from any cause they happen to be at variance, and perhaps in conflict, with our own and the public conscience?

We are first to ascertain whether the plea of

conscience is well-founded. There is more room for this question than is commonly supposed. All is not conscience that passes for it in this world. And here I do not refer wholly, or mainly, to deliberate hypocrisy, to false appearances, to men pretending to be what they are not. Undoubtedly there is not a little even of this; undoubtedly there is not a little of hollow pretence in modern society, and we naturally look for it among those who pretend to the most. When a man lays claim to a great deal of conscience in one matter, and yet shows only a common degree of conscience in other matters, we have a right to suspect him.

Be that, however, as it may, what I would chiefly insist upon here is, that men are continually mistaking what constitutes conscience. Let it be that a man is both sincere and consistent, it does not necessarily follow that he is conscientious in any proper sense of that word. Nay, more, he may be devoted to a particular measure, or system, or party, and be ready to make great sacrifices for it, and even to die for it, and yet not for conscience' sake. It may be, undoubtedly it often is, pride of opinion, or mere persistency or obstinacy of character. There are multitudes with whom a stiff adherence to ground once taken has very little to do with morality; it has a great deal more to do with temper. We have had more than enough of this determination, on the part of headstrong men, to act out their purposes under the name of conscience, though the heavens fall. It is a mistake to suppose that such a disposition argues, of itself, extraordinary conscientiousness; much oftener it originates in extraordinary self-confidence and presumption, and a determination to have one's own way. Extraordinary conscientiousness always supposes an extreme anxiety *to be* right, as well as *to do* right; and wherever this anxiety exists, it must certainly induce some degree of caution, hesitancy, self-distrust. The zealot, therefore, who rushes on, manifesting none of this caution, none of this hesitancy and self-distrust, may be a man of courage and daring; he may count his life as a very small thing compared with the objects he has in view; he may strike hard and strike home: but it is a palpable mistake to single him out as illustrating the power of conscience. In nine cases out of ten, it is the power of *will.*

Let us now take another step. Assuming that the plea of conscience is well-founded, assuming a man really to act from a *sense* of right, what value or authority does this circumstance alone give to his *opinion* of right?

Some persons, I believe, are not a little puzzled in making it out, how two disputants can be equally conscientious, though on opposite sides of the question as to what ought to be done in a particular case. But it is because they do not begin by clearing up their conception of conscience itself. Conscience, properly so called, belongs to our emotional, and not to our intellectual, nature. It is a *sensibility* and not a *judgment*; it is a feeling that we ought to do right, leaving us, however, to make up our opinion as to *what* is right in particular cases, as we make up our opinion on other subjects, and with the same liability to difference, change, and mistake. Accordingly, though we come to widely different conclusions as to what ought to be done in particular cases, it does not follow that we differ at all in our love of right, or in our sense of moral obligation; that is to say, in conscience, properly so called. In other words, it is not conscience against conscience, but merely opinion against opinion; and, what is more, one fallible opinion against another fallible opinion.

Keeping in mind the distinction here pointed out, it is easy to see the only ground on which any man can claim respect for his opinion of right in difficult matters. It is not that he is more conscientious, but that he is more intelligent, and more intelligent in respect to the particular question at issue. In a great majority of cases, the right is so obvious and patent as to raise no question, the only thing which keeps men from doing it being a want of conscience. The continual recurrence of such instances has probably led to the mistake, that conscience alone is all-sufficient, informing us what to do, as well as commanding us to do it. But the moment we are in serious doubt as to what ought to be done, the conviction is forced upon us that no degree of mere conscientiousness will supply the place of study, experience, and a sound mind. Hence it often happens that we entertain a sincere respect for a man's *sense* of right, but no sort of respect for his *opinion* of right. If it is a question of statesmanship, he must know statesmanship; if it is a question of law, he must know law; if it is a question of commercial or social or moral reform, he must be versed in all the difficulties and intricacies and entanglements of these subjects: else, no matter how conscientious he may be, his opinion of right is not worth a straw.

Here, however, another question arises. What is to be done with a man who conscientiously holds "opinions of right" deemed not only worthless, but injurious, and perhaps fatally so? Some persons of a speculative vein, not at all inclined to be persecutors themselves, insist nevertheless that the *logic* of persecution is irrefragable. If the Church really believes that an obnoxious heresy is fatal to morals and religion, how can the toleration of it be reconciled with notions of public duty, or even with compassion for the infected individuals? Under the name of sanitary or quarantine regulations, we enact stringent laws, and inflict heavy penalties, in order to prevent the spread of a contagion which threatens to kill the body. On the same principle, and from a similar though much higher motive, ought we not to do at least as much to prevent the spread of a contagion which threatens to kill the soul?

I answer, that for any man, or any body of men, large or small, laic or cleric, to lay down their opinions, however honestly entertained, as an ultimate standard of truth, is to forget that they are fallible beings. It is practically to assume that they are *infallible*, when they *know* they are not. In other words, it begins by assuming as *true* what they *know* to be *false;* and if so, then every form of despotism in matters of faith, every form of spiritual domination, must be acknowledged to have its root in a manifest contradiction and lie. Perhaps some will argue, that what I *think* to be true *is* the truth *for me*, at least for the time being. And this in a certain sense, and with certain limitations, must be conceded. Mark, however, the words, — the truth *for me.* Because it is the truth *for me*, it does not follow that it is the truth *for my neighbor;* — certainly not, if he happens to think differently. On the contrary, if there is any force in the argument here insisted on, — that is to say, if what I think to be true is the truth *for me*, then it would seem to follow, that what my neighbor thinks to be true is in the same sense, and to the same extent, the truth *for him;* so that we find here a ground, not for punishing or restraining dissent, but for universal toleration.

The Church of Rome, aware of this objection, thinks to save her consistency by professing to build nothing on opinion against opinion, nor even on accord of mere human opinion, untrustworthy at the best, especially as regards "the things of God." She claims absolute infallibility in matters of faith; but it is on the ground of a Divine inspiration perpetually renewed. And this would be very well, except for one circumstance. The inspiration thus confidently asserted, by which I mean *the fact* of the inspiration, must be *proved;* and here there is nothing but opinion against opinion, and, what is more, nothing but one human and fallible opinion against another human and fallible opinion: for, of course, it will not do to plead the inspiration, while the very question at issue is whether there really is any inspiration or not. Obviously, therefore, the boasted consistency of Romanism resolves itself, for the most part, into a trick of logical sleight-of-hand. It consists in so shuffling out of sight the question of the fact of the inspiration, that what is manifestly the previous and main question, indeed the question of questions, is made to seem as if it were no question at all, in short, as if it were something which everybody is to begin by taking for granted.

I come, therefore, to the conclusion that the fundamental doctrine of consistent Protestantism, entire freedom of thought, remains untouched. So much at least is due to conscience ; "conscience, I say, not thine own, but of the other." We may feel little or no respect for another man's opinions of right, but we must nevertheless respect his right to the opinions, at any rate until he begins *to act them out.*

I have said, "until he begins to act them out," — which brings up another question of greater difficulty and perplexity. What shall be done with a man, who, in acting out his honest convictions of duty, comes into conflict with *law?*

Exciting and embarrassing as this subject is under some of its aspects, there are two or three things respecting it, which are sufficiently plain. In the first place, law, *to be law*, must be taken as an expression, not of arbitrary will, but of the public opinion of right, of the public conscience as at present instructed. When, therefore, we consider and pay a proper respect and deference to law, it is not to forsake conscience and follow another guide. We still follow conscience, and not the less conscience because it is the collective conscience of the community. But am I not called upon to give up my own conscience in favor of this so-called public conscience? No such thing. I am not even so much as called upon to give up my own opinion of right, when it differs from that expressed in the law. All that I am called upon to do is to refrain from acting it out; and this too, as a general rule, and in ordinary times, no farther than my own conscience, in view of my duty as a good citizen, prompts and requires.

Again, the law restrains the fanatic from acting out new, dangerous, incendiary doctrines, or punishes him for it, not with a view to invade his rights, but to hinder him from invading the rights of others. So long as his conduct injures nobody but himself, it is seldom, if ever, that the law interferes; but as soon as it begins to injure others, it is preposterous to suppose that they will bear it, or that society will suffer it. Society, government, the State, is, and must be, of the nature of a compromise; each one giving up a part of his natural liberty of action, that he may retain and be protected in the rest. And this is not a mere human contrivance, but the will and decree of God; for God has evidently made us to live in society, and society cannot exist without it. Now we say, that to be continually playing fast and loose in this matter, to give it up to-day and take it back to-morrow, is not conscience; it is not even rational liberty; it is a breach of contract; it is sheer injustice and wrong. Room is still left for the true martyr. All honor to the true martyr; but the true martyr is one who suffers *himself* for his opinions, — not one who makes other men suffer.

And besides, nobody will pretend that conscientiousness is the whole of goodness; we are to take into view a man's tastes and dispositions in other respects. The radical error and vice of every form of fanaticism consists in practically disregarding this obvious fact; in presuming that mere conscientiousness, mere fidelity to one's opinions, will make up for the lack of any other and every other needed grace. St. Paul was of a different mind. In looking back on the exterminating zeal with which, while a mere stripling, he had hunted down the Christians, he saw at once that there was nothing in the circumstance of his being self-deceived, nothing in the plea of the honesty of his convictions, to justify or excuse his self-confidence, his arrogance, his precipitancy, his cruelty. He knew that these qualities of character are always bad, however connected; that they are as bad in conscientious men as in unconscientious men, and ought to be restrained.

Undoubtedly, under every human government there are bad laws; undoubtedly, there is a higher law; but it is a mournful, not to say a shameful, thing, if the so-called "higher law" represents the ignorance and the passions of the community, and not its intelligence and sober judgment. So long as the world stands in need of agitators and reformers, there will be occasion from time to time for bold and daring spirits, who are for compromising nothing, who are for carrying out their new theories, come what may. When such men appear, there is a touch of heroism about them, which fascinates like military glory, and causes them to be lauded much above their deserts. Be this, however, as it may, thus much is plain: they are *exceptional* men alike in their office and their virtues, and, when out of place, become a social pest.

One word, in conclusion, on what is due to the scruples of those who are offended and hurt by our freedom, — the scruples, as the Scriptures express it, of the "weak" brethren.

Of course, the spirit of concession in such cases must have its limits; otherwise the "weak" brethren would virtually rule. And again, it must not be claimed on the ground of absolute right, but on that of Christian tenderness and solicitude for the good, and especially for the moral good, of others.

Thus qualified and explained, it seems to me that a constant anxiety lest our own example, however justifiable in itself, may have the effect to lead astray the inexperienced and weak, is the natural growth of the Christian consciousness, and indeed the spontaneous act of every truly generous mind. In the words of the apostle, "All things are lawful for me, but all things are not expedient: all things are lawful for me, but all things edify not."

I know it is an old objection, "Why is my liberty judged of another man's conscience?" Why am I called upon to give up rights and privileges, or even lawful and reasonable indulgences, merely to humor the scruples of the weak-minded? But this is not stating the case fairly. We have many rights which, however, we have a right to waive; nay, more, rights which under certain circumstances we feel that we *ought* to waive, and *do* waive. Neither is it any infringement of our liberty. Grant that I am at full liberty to partake of this or that indulgence on the ground of its innocence and reasonableness; it must also be conceded, on the other hand, that I am at liberty not to partake of it. I am at liberty to partake of it or not, as I please; and if from any reason or motive I please not to partake of it, this is just as much a vindication and exercise of my liberty as if I were to indulge myself without restraint. And why talk about being called upon to do this merely to humor the scruples of the weak-minded? We are not called upon to do it merely to humor the scruples of anybody. We are called upon to do it, that we may not unnecessarily offend or disturb another man's faith, or hurt his conscience, or make him weak, or lead him into temptation, thus putting an occasion to fall in a brother's way. Now I ask any one, and every one who professes to act on Christian principles, or indeed to have the feelings of a man, whether this is not reason and motive enough for practising a little self-restraint?

After all, however, there is a higher duty we owe to the consciences of the weak and ignorant, than that of consulting their scruples; I mean the duty of enlightening and strengthening their consciences, and making them truly Christian. Starting with the mistaken notion that conscience is a light as well as a motive, many persons slide into the error of supposing that conscience alone is a sufficient guide; that every one knows what is required of him, whether he practises it or not. It is far otherwise. Very probably the bulk of mankind know what is required of them in order to stand well with their neighbors, or to maintain credit in business, or to hold up their heads in what is called good society. But they do not know what is required of them in order to enter into the Kingdom of Heaven; they do not know the degree to which inward purity and the higher virtues are insisted on in the New Testament; they do not even so much as know what constitutes the peculiar type and style of Christian righteousness, by which it is distinguished from the righteousness of the pagan or the Jew. It is precisely here, therefore, as I conceive, that Christian instruction is most needed; — not that men may have consciences, for they will have consciences of some sort or other at any rate; but that they may have *Christian* consciences. The great and essential peculiarity of the Gospel is found, as it seems to me, not in its doctrine of God, nor in its doctrine of ordinances, but in its doctrine of holiness. "For if ye love them which love you, what reward have ye? Do not even the publicans the same? And if ye salute your brethren only, what do ye more than others? Do not even the publicans so? Be ye therefore perfect, even as your Father which is in heaven is perfect."

1860.

XXVI.

PERFECTION THE CHRISTIAN'S AIM.

"*Therefore, leaving the principles of the doctrine of Christ, let us go on unto perfection.*" — HEBREWS vi. 1.

HOWEVER unlikely or impossible it is that we shall ever meet with a perfect man on this earth, still, if we were to meet with one, we should see, that, instead of being a monster, he would be of all men the most entirely natural, the most truly human. It is no objection to this, that when we see one yielding to a burst of inordinate passion, or carried away by excessive love of fame, or money, or pleasure, we are apt to say, "See there human nature, — poor human nature!" And so we do, in a certain sense of that word, and perhaps in the most common sense; for the propensity in question is a human propensity, and in its existing and disproportionate state of development it is natural that a man should give way to it. It is a development of our nature which makes the miser or the voluptuary, but not, I contend, a *natural* development of our nature ; and this is a distinction which a discriminating thinker will be careful to observe. For there is a *natural* development of our nature, and an *unnatural* development of our nature. The miser and the voluptuary become what they are in consequence of a development of human nature ; but then it is in consequence of an unnatural, one-sided, distorted development of human nature. If human nature were developed naturally, that is to say, according to its just and intended order and proportions, there would be no misers or voluptuaries. The misers and the voluptuaries, — they are the monsters.

But if a perfect man would be so natural in all his ways, if human perfection would be nothing but a full and perfect development of human nature in its just and natural order and proportions, how happens it, some may ask, that we never meet with some of these paragons, — one, at least, in a nation, one in an age? Let me answer this question by bringing into view an analogous and familiar fact. Go into a forest, — nay, go from forest to forest, — and you cannot find a single perfect *tree;* perfect, I mean, in every branch, in every leaf. Yet such a tree would be only true to its nature, — that is, perfectly natural. Most clearly, if such a tree could be found, it would not be a monster.

Perhaps I shall be told that the impossibility of actually finding such a tree is owing to external influences, — to the soil, the frost, the insects, the mildew. And so it is. But so, too, it is with man. His nature also, while in its course of development, comes under countless influences from without of a most diverse character and tendency, some of which begin to operate before he is born, some of which are wrought into his physical organization, and some of which essentially modify his education and the whole structure of his moral and social being. Now under such diverse and conflicting influences we do not say that he will become wholly bad or wholly good; but we do say that the character he forms will be a mixed character; it will not be a perfect character. The race growing up under such circumstances will not be divisible into the perfectly good and the perfectly bad; but every individual will be partly good and partly bad. *Every* man's character will be, and must be, and is, *mixed.*

Accordingly Mr. Wesley has defined human perfection as being "such a degree of the love of God and the love of man, such a degree of the love of justice, truth, holiness, and purity, as will remove from the heart every contrary disposition towards God or man; and that should be our state of mind in every situation, in every circumstance of life."

Even he, however, admits that this perfection, at its greatest height, does not include absolute freedom from error or mistake, nor exclude the possibility of continual progress in knowledge and holiness. We also find, that, as he grew older and wiser, and saw more of the abuses to which the doctrine of perfection is liable, he was more and more disposed to modify it and soften it down; until, in writing to one of his female disciples, who seems to have applied for advice under a desponding sense of her imperfection, he could say, "Indeed, my judgment is, that (in this case particularly) to overdo is to undo; and that to set perfection too high is the most effectual way of driving it out of the world."

Still, it is not to be denied that the advocates even of a nominal and qualified perfectionism, like this, have done not a little to suggest and foster hurtful and dangerous errors. In the first place, they have led men to be content with inward states, — with an ideal and dreamy sort of goodness; as if nothing more were required of us than that our *general* intentions and affections should be right; or as if, though our *general* intentions and affections are right, we may not sin in particular acts, or in particular manifestations of feeling. Again, they have given countenance and currency to false and extremely unsafe views of temptation, by encouraging persons, who think their hearts have been changed, to believe that now they are in no danger; that now they may expose themselves without fear to any form of seduction, — as if we did not know that the best men are liable to temptation, and liable to it the more in the same proportion as they are thrown off their guard by an overweening sense of their superiority to it. Worse than all, perfectionism is apt to degenerate into Antinomianism, perhaps the most pestilent and stupendous of all the perversions of religion; which teaches the indifference of outward conduct in the regenerate, making even injustice and sensuality to be no longer of the nature of sin, when committed by those who have once been renewed by the grace of God.

We set aside, therefore, all expectation of actually meeting with perfection among men; we confidently believe that under Christianity, as under Judaism, "there is not a just man upon earth, that doeth good and sinneth not." Still there is nothing to hinder us from maintaining, as the Scriptures seem to do, the doctrine of human *perfectibility*. Perfectibility, as here used, differs from perfection in this, — that a man may be pronounced perfectible though he never attains to perfection in fact, provided only that there is nothing in his nature itself to exclude the possibility of his perfection, and nothing in his circumstances to exclude the possibility of his continually going on towards perfection.

While, therefore, we give up human perfection, we stand fast for *human perfectibility*. There are no arbitrary or determinate bounds set to any man's progress in this life, whatever may be his condition and circumstances. You cannot say, "He can go so far, and there he must stop. He can go so far, and there he will meet a bar which will make further progress impossible." There is no such bar. The way is open to every one ; or, if not entirely open, there is nothing in the nature of the obstructions which makes them absolutely insuperable. I do not say that, in every instance, a man can leap over these obstructions at an easy or a single bound. Sometimes he will be able to surmount them only by patience and toil ; and sometimes he will have to cut his way through them with courage and force. All I affirm is, that there is nothing in the nature of these obstructions, or of any other obstructions, which must needs bring his self-improvement to a stand for a day or an hour, so long as his faculties retain their natural vigor. Even while struggling with the difficulty in question, and before he has succeeded in mastering it, if he struggles manfully and in a true spirit, he is continually growing wiser and better and stronger in himself through the new demand thus made on his energies, and the new exercise to which his faculties are thus put. I repeat it, then: no limit is fixed or can be fixed to any man's progress, so long as his faculties retain their natural vigor, except by his own consent. I do not say, simply, that man is a progressive being, but also that he is a being capable of unlimited progress; so that, of course, there is nothing too high for him to aim at, and nothing too good or too great to become the object of his aspirations.

This is all which I understand the Scriptures to mean in the text, and in other passages where they enjoin it upon us to be perfect, to go on unto perfection, and to become perfect men in Christ Jesus. They do not hold up this perfection as something of which any Christian can as yet be personally conscious, or on which he can look back as already attained; but as the goal in the distance after which all can and should continually aspire. "Not as though I had already attained," said an apostle, "or *were already perfect;* but I follow after, if that I may apprehend that for which also I am apprehended of Christ Jesus. Brethren, I count not myself *to have apprehended;* but this one thing I do, — forgetting those things which are behind, and reaching forth unto those things which are before, I press toward the mark for the prize of the high calling of God in Christ Jesus."

So far, then, and only so far, can the Christian doctrine of human perfectibility be fairly urged. Man is not only made capable of progress, but, with the aids which the Gospel supplies, of *unlimited* progress. The consequence is, that he cannot only conceive of an ideal perfection, and see that perfection realized in Jesus Christ, but make it the object of his own aspirations, — not in his dreams alone, but in actual life, as there really is nothing in the way of his *continually advancing towards it* but the weakness or the perverseness of his own will. It is man himself who sets limits to his own wisdom and virtue ; and this he does by resting content with the degree of wisdom and virtue he has already attained, or by not choosing to make the efforts or the sacrifices necessary to further progress. It is a false and mean shifting of the blame from himself on something else, to say that these limits were ordained by his nature, or his circumstances, or his Creator. It never is so. I do not suppose that all men, with their different capacities and opportunities, are capable of an equally *rapid* progress ; but I do suppose that they are equally capable of making *some* progress, and this, too, without limit, intermission, or end. There are no exceptions to this law. It is the universal condition of humanity. I know that we are not all spirit. We have a body as well as a soul, — a body with its grovelling appetites and tastes, and earthly tendencies, to weigh us down and keep us from realizing in this life many of our brightest visions. But even while we continue connected with this body, and in some sense the slaves of it, we do not work like slaves tethered to a pillar or a rock, which will let us go so far and no farther. We work rather like slaves with a clog, — we can go as far as we please, only we must carry our clog with us; but with this cheering consciousness from day to day, that, the greater our progress in wisdom and virtue, the less the clog is felt, until it is hardly perceptible as an obstacle, or even as a burden, in our onward course.

And here let it be distinctly understood, that, when we speak of human perfectibility, we do not bring it in as a weak rhetorical flourish, or as a fine-sounding word which will help to point a moral or turn a period. We mean all that we assert; we bring into notice a sober fact, which has much to do with the direction and government of every man's daily conduct. We can go on continually towards perfection, though we never arrive at it; we can make it to be our goal in the distance, after which we are continually to aspire, and which in reality we can and ought continually to approximate. If we stop in the way, it is *of our own accord*, and not because we are obliged to stop. We can go on, *if we please*. Some, doubtless, can go on faster than others; but all can go on. This is the great truth which lies at the bottom of every well-grounded and immortal hope; which we are not at liberty to wink out of sight, or overlay and bury up under miserable commonplaces borrowed from superficial views of life and human nature, or the shortsighted cunning of this world. Bring me the man who has become so wise that he cannot become any wiser. You cannot do it. Bring me the man who has become so good that he cannot become any better. You cannot do it. You cannot fill a man's mind with knowledge until it cannot hold any more, as you can fill a vessel with water until it cannot hold any more. On the contrary, every new acquisition of truth only serves to enlarge his mind for the comprehension of more truth, so that the more he knows the more is he in a condition to learn. And the same is likewise true of his progress in virtue. Because he mastered one bad habit yesterday, that has not destroyed but only increased his power to master another bad habit to-day; because he put forth one new virtue yesterday, that has not destroyed but only increased his power to put forth another to-day: and so on, without any assignable limits. The Bible fixes no limits, our nature fixes none; neither reason nor imagination can fix any. But this ability to go on involves the *obligation* to go on. If he stops, no matter in what stage of his progress, he goes backward; for in stopping he ceases to improve, — and this is not merely not to obey, it is to disobey. He must go on; and thus it is, and only thus, that the path of the righteous, at first dimly and uncertainly seen, grows brighter and brighter to the perfect day.

Let me add, that I express the doctrine too tamely when I say that a man is *capable* of unlimited progress. There burns within him an instinctive desire of growth, of ceaseless progress. This principle begins to manifest itself long before that of a cool and calculating selfishness. You see it in the boy, who is not satisfied unless he can spin his top, or fly his kite, better and better; and he would feel this desire, and find pleasure in its gratification, even if he dwelt alone on a desolate island, apart from all thoughts of interest or rivalship. Or if you call it rivalship, then I should say that every man is made, in the very constitution of his nature, to be the rival of his *past* self. We see it also in the artist, whose eye has caught glimpses of an unearthly beauty, which he strives to bring out and embody on the canvas or in marble. And at last, perhaps, he succeeds; but now his eye has caught glimpses of a beauty still more transcendent, and he is not satisfied until he can realize that. And thus it is that his ideal of excellence in art for ever flies before him; but not in vain, as it only flies to beckon him on from excellence to excellence, and from glory to glory. The same principle takes effect also in our whole moral and spiritual life; for we are so made, that, if our minds are in a healthy state, we are never entirely satisfied with what we are. We are always seeking to rival and outdo our former selves; but no harm is likely to come of emulation or of competition, so long as a man is his own rival: or of ambition, if it does but consist in this inextinguishable thirst for excellence itself.

There is however one danger to be apprehended from a too exclusive occupation of the mind on ideal visions of excellence and perfection, which I ought to notice distinctly before I conclude. Persons of this description, it has been said, "are deeply impressed with the idea that they are required to be *perfect before God;* but their idea of perfection being altogether of an abstract and spiritual character, the zealous fulfilment of ordinary duties, and a conscientious attention to common transactions, seem to have no affinity to their object; and hence they direct all their longings to a state of spiritual and vague feeling, of which they know not either the form or limits, and the desire of which has no tendency but to unfit them for all effectual and successful discharge of the duties of life. It is perhaps the besetting error of those who are commonly denominated serious and pious men; and it is also not unfrequently the last refuge of those, who, having run, in preceding portions of their lives, a career of thoughtlessness and folly, at last betake themselves to this *vain sighing after perfection*, — instead of devoting themselves, as true wisdom would direct them, to a zealous and persevering reformation of their whole plan of life, and to an effectual discharge of every duty pointed out to them, as active and social, as religious and moral beings."

There is much good sense and force in this caution; but it only shows that the instinctive desire of perfection, which is wrought into our very constitution, may be misconceived, perverted, and abused. The *idea of perfection* is held up before us, not to be the object of vain longings and sighings, but to cheer and sustain us in the many weary steps we must take in its pursuit. We are still to reflect that we must actually traverse, with our own feet, the almost measureless distance that separates us from the far-off goal; and also, that, if a man is to go round the globe, he cannot take any longer strides than if he were going to the next village. Besides, perfection after all is our *ultimate* object; not our *next* and *immediate* object. Our next and immediate object, both as men and as Christians, is always the faithful discharge of the common and obvious and present duties which press upon us in that particular sphere of activity, be it high or low, in which Divine Providence has placed us.

Only a small and comparatively inconsiderable part of this unlimited progress in knowledge and holiness is to be wrought out here, even by the most diligent and best disposed. But we can *begin* it here; perhaps I ought to say, we *must* begin it here; for there may be something in the character of the *first* attainments of spiritual growth, in consequence of which, if we throw away our opportunity of making them here, it may never be offered to us again. Heaven itself, for aught we know to the contrary, may be a place in which it is impossible for a man to *begin* a life of faith and prayer. However this may be, is it not a glorious thought that we can begin the career of angels and archangels in these dwellings of dust? How much more glorious the thought, that, when these dwellings of dust are dissolved, we shall "be clothed upon with our house which is from heaven!" But who shall dare to anticipate, even in imagination, the stupendous disclosures that are to burst upon the disembodied spirit? Of one thing, however, we may be sure; a never-ending, ever-brightening career of knowledge, improvement, and happiness will still spread itself out before the followers of Christ, — the same which they began here. And, along the innumerable ranks of the heavenly host, a voice will still be heard proclaiming the law, "Let us go on unto perfection!"

1834.

Cambridge: Press of John Wilson & Son.

www.ingramcontent.com/pod-product-compliance
Lightning Source LLC
LaVergne TN
LVHW020934110826
845150LV00004B/861

* 9 7 8 1 4 2 5 5 5 2 1 8 3 *